THE
GLIDER GANG

BOOKS BY MILTON DANK
The French Against the French
The Glider Gang

THE GLIDER GANG

An Eyewitness History of World War II Glider Combat

MILTON DANK

J. B. LIPPINCOTT COMPANY
Philadelphia and New York

ILLUSTRATION CREDITS

U.S. Air Force Photographs: Pages 87, 88 (middle), 145 (bottom), 146, 147 (top, bottom), 148 (top, middle), 149, 200 (bottom), 201 (bottom), 227 (bottom), 228.
U.S. Army Photographs: Pages 88 (top, bottom), 145 (top), 199 (top, middle), 201 (top), 202 (top).
Dr. Charles Hubner: Page 147 (middle).
Major H. N. Andrews: Page 229 (top left).
All photographs not otherwise credited were taken by the author.
The two cartoons on page 259 were drawn by Dale Oliver.

U.S. Library of Congress Cataloging in Publication Data

Dank, Milton, birth date
   The glider gang.

   Bibliography: p.
   Includes index.
   SUMMARY: Describes the glider missions in European airborne operations during World War II and the exploits of the pilots who participated in them.
   1. World War, 1939–1945—Aerial operations.
2. Gliders (Aeronautics) [1. World War, 1939–1945—Aerial operations. 2. Gliders (Aeronautics)] I. Title.
D785.D3   940.54′21   76–28201
ISBN–0–397–01161–X

To NAOMI, GLORIA, and JOAN

Contents

Acknowledgments

In the thirty-odd years since the end of the Second World War, the small band of surviving glider pilots has dwindled and dispersed. Memories have faded, allowing myths and legends to grow. Today their deeds are a little-known and poorly understood part of World War II airborne operations. Other elite volunteer groups, such as the paratroopers, the Commandos, and the Rangers, have all found their historians; only the "no-engine pilots" seem to have been forgotten.

It was to fill this gap in the history of our war, as well as to pay tribute to the gallant men with whom it was my privilege to serve, that this book was written. It could never have been done without their generous and unstinting help. In interviews, in letters and tapes, and in long telephone conversations, they relived the hours of fear and terror that constitute a glider assault under enemy fire. The commanders patiently explained the planning and the hard decisions that had to be made; the glider pilots told what all too frequently went wrong with those plans. Both willingly supplied valuable primary source material: diaries, journals, mission orders, postaction reports, maps, aerial photographs, group and squadron personnel lists, combat snapshots, and the personal details and anecdotes that make those tragic days live again. They are all to be thanked for their contributions to the story they themselves wrote in the Second German War.

Special thanks must be given to Generals Matthew B. Ridgway, James M. Gavin, Maxwell D. Taylor, and the late Anthony C. McAuliffe for describing their campaigns and their thoughts on gliders and glider pilots in interviews and by correspondence. Brigadier George J. S. Chatterton, D.S.O., and Lieutenant-Colonel Iain A. Murray, D.S.O., were equally generous in talking to the author at length about the missions of the British Glider Pilot Regiment.

Colonels Charles H. Young, Michael C. Murphy, Woodrow T. Merrill, and Hugh J. Nevins supplied a great deal of information on Troop Carrier Command and its glider forces, while Monsignor John M. Whelan, chaplain of the 439th Troop Carrier Group, wrote eloquently of the private fears of the men. Major Harold Norman "Andy" Andrews must be thanked for allowing me to use so much of his unpublished manuscript of his combat experiences as a British glider pilot.

Messrs. Brandon Barringer and A. Felix duPont, Jr., related their experiences in wartime Washington and particularly the roles played by their respective brothers Lewin Barringer and Richard duPont as advisers on the glider program. General Alfred L. Wolf not only arranged these two interviews but was most helpful in locating several senior officers of the glider pilot program.

As befitting a man of the theater, Joshua Logan painted a dramatic picture of the night before D day on a troop-carrier airfield. He also pointed out an unexpected contribution of military gliders to the postwar Broadway stage: the famous shower in which Nelly Forbush "washes that man right outa her hair" in *South Pacific* was taken directly from a similar shower made of a wrecked glider fuselage that Logan had seen in France.

For the details of the naval diversions during the landings in southern France, the author is indebted to Douglas Fairbanks, Jr., who, as a lieutenant commander, U.S. Navy, led his ship on a daring raid on the coast.

My friend and neighbor Harry Ridgway spent long hours explaining the differences between American and British glider operations. As an ex-member of the Glider Pilot Regiment, he was able to clarify such technical details as the "angle-of-dangle" indicator and how one got the tail off a Horsa glider. Also, he very generously allowed me to read his unpublished manuscript on British glider missions.

Over 170 glider pilot veterans were interviewed, answered questionnaires or queries by letter, sent in tapes, or in some other way contributed to this book. Their names can be found in the back, listed alphabetically, as a small token of my appreciation for their help.

Research on the glider war was done in this country at the National Archives and Records Service (Washington, D.C., and Suitland, Maryland); the Library of Congress, Washington, D.C.; the Office of Air Force History, Arlington, Virginia; the Albert F. Simpson Historical Research Center, Air University, Maxwell Air Force Base, Alabama; the New York Public Library; and the libraries of Princeton, Yale, and Temple Universities, and the University of Pennsylvania. One very important source is the "War Room" of the National Association of World War II Glider Pilots, where the memorabilia of its members are fondly displayed. The curator of this Dallas museum, Bill Horn, not only arranged for me to visit it but answered many of my questions on the exhibits. The association newsletter, *Silent Wings*, carried many of my queries, thus helping to locate glider pilots who participated in particular combat actions. The executive secretary, Ginny Randolph, was always helpful with roster information and with arranging interviews at the national meetings.

In England, A. J. "Holly" Hollingdale, general secretary of the Glider Pilot Regimental Association, was most generous with his time, arranging for interviews with members and supplies of *The Eagle*, the magazine put out by the GPRA. The staff of the library of the Imperial War Museum rounded up a number of official histories on airborne operations, but it was discouraging to find that the museum itself had not a single item on glider warfare on exhibit. It was at the Museum of Army Flying in Middle Wallop (Hants) that I saw the only Horsa left in England—and this wingless and tailless. My thanks to Tom Pearce, curator and wartime glider pilot, for letting me sit once more in that spacious greenhouse of a cockpit.

For many of the photographs used in this book, the author is indebted to the U.S. Air Force Central Still Photo Depository, Arlington, Virginia (Mrs. E. Fincik); the Don Pratt Museum of the 101st Airborne Division, Fort Campbell, Kentucky (Lieutenant Cody Phillips, division historian); and the 82nd Airborne Division War Memorial Museum, Fort Bragg, North Carolina (Mr. Thomas M. Fairfull, curator).

The arduous task of reading the manuscript in rough form was undertaken by Messrs. Simmon Seder, Herman Lefco, Gordon Weinberg, Arthur Kaplan, and Harry Ridgway. I would like to thank these veterans of the Second World War for courage beyond the call of friendship.

Beatrice Rosenfeld, my editor, was midwife to this work from conception to birth and managed to be fair, firm, and meticulous throughout. My thanks to Debbie Kalodner for a wonderful speedy job of typing and proofreading the final draft.

My wife and our daughters were my constant colleagues in the writing of this book. Not only did they transcribe my dictation and type several drafts, but they unselfishly gave hours from their own busy lives and careers to consult, advise, edit, and change. That this book is dedicated to them can never really repay what I owe them. There was another Milton who wrote of the "Wars of Kites and Crows, flocking and fighting in the air" and who was as deeply indebted to his wife and daughters as I am.

Lastly, let me pay tribute to the memory of my friend and fellow glider pilot, Robert P. "Rip" Hansen, who first interested me in writing and who often talked to me of the need for a book like this.

The song of the German Glider Pilots:
"The sun shines red.
Comrades, there is no going back. . . ."

The motto of the British Glider Pilot Regiment:
"Nothing is impossible."

The battle cry of the American Glider Pilots:
"Jesus Christ! More spoilers!"

Prologue

"To the glider pilots—conceived in error, suffering a long and painful period of gestation, and finally delivered at the wrong place at the wrong time."

This is the traditional toast of the surviving members of the Allied glider effort in World War II, the men who flew the canvas-and-plywood motorless craft into Normandy, southern France, and Holland, and across the Rhine. Recklessly brave and grimly determined, they had to endure not only enemy flak, but foul weather, inexperienced towplane pilots, gliders that had a nasty habit of shedding parts in flight, the Americans' lack of ground combat training, and an ignorance on the part of Allied planners of the limitations of airborne formations.

They were "conceived in error" since they were thought to be the answer to the German glider force which had just helped conquer Crete, but the German losses there had been so high that Hitler had forbidden any more large airborne assaults!

Their "long and painful period of gestation" was suffered because of the opposition of senior commanders to the idea of such an unconventional force. It was three years after Crete before the Allied squadrons were ready.

"Delivered at the wrong place at the wrong time"—a litany of mistakes almost without parallel in the war. They were dropped into the sea off Sicily, scattered at night over Normandy, and released over a thick smoke screen across the Rhine.

The American glider pilots were a mixed bag: flunked-out aviation cadets; men who were too old for flight-crew training or who could not pass the strict physical examination; ground troops who wished to get into the Air Corps; men who wanted adventure, wanted to try something new —and, above all, to fly.

The British glider pilots were from the same mold. Bored with the Army routine in an England on the defensive after Dunkirk, they volunteered by the thousands. It was the risk, the smell of danger that lured them, as it had tempted Englishmen for centuries.

Officers fled from safe desk jobs for the chance to fly and fight. Brawlers who detested discipline and lived only for combat eagerly answered the call.

This is their story.

1
Silent Blitzkrieg

The fort was a massive concrete arrowhead directly in the path of any German invasion of Belgium.

Blasted out of solid rock during the construction of the Albert Canal that formed a natural 100-yard-wide moat on its northern side, it had been built between 1932 and 1935 at great cost. Remembering 1914 and their continuing geographical vulnerability as the natural path from Germany to northern France, the Belgian government had poured millions of francs into its construction in an attempt to strengthen their frontier defenses near the German border.

The hexagonal fort had roofs and walls of reinforced concrete over five feet thick; from revolving armored cupolas, six 120-mm. cannon could reach out twelve miles to blast an invading army crossing the Maastricht "Appendix," the fifteen-mile-wide stretch of Holland that interjects itself between Germany and Belgium at this point. There were eighteen 75-mm. guns in cupolas and casements, if the enemy should be so rash as to attempt an assault across the Meuse River and the canal. One wall rose a sheer 120 feet up from the moat, and on the remaining sides concrete pillboxes, ditches, aprons of barbed wire, machine-gun emplacements, minefields, and antitank guns had been placed to discourage the attackers. Against bombers, there were many antiaircraft batteries and searchlights, as well as the latest in sound-ranging equipment. The garrison, living in air-conditioned tunnels deep below the ground, was supplied with a two-month reserve of food and ammunition. Everything possible had been done to make the fort self-sufficient and invulnerable.

From above, all that could be seen of the skillfully camouflaged emplacements was a grass-covered area over a thousand yards long on the north-south axis and eight hundred yards at its widest point, plus the dome-shaped artillery cupolas, and the trenches, which would be occupied by infantry. The fort took its name—Eben Emael—from an obscure nearby village. It was the last word in military fortification, the latest expression of an art that went back through Vauban to the Roman camps. All the experts agreed that it could not be successfully assaulted.

Late in 1939, while waiting for the man he had summoned so suddenly to Berlin, Adolf Hitler pondered the problem of the Belgian defenses. Hunched over the map in his conference room, he studied the terrain around Fort Eben Emael carefully, referring frequently to a set of aerial photographs. His knowledge of the details of the fort's construction was quite complete, for the Belgians, lacking the necessary engineering skill, had retained two German firms as consultants during the work.

Committed to an attack on France through Belgium, Hitler knew that the fort would have to be taken quickly; otherwise, there would be the same unfortunate delay that the Kaiser's armies had encountered before the fortifications of Liège. Unwilling to make the mistake of funneling his armies across the narrow German-Belgian frontier, the Führer had included Holland in his plans for the attack and had even gone so far as to send reassurances of his peaceful intentions to both the Belgian and the Dutch governments a few weeks ago. The successful six-week blitzkrieg of Poland had convinced him that his genius lay in tactics as well as in strategy, so he was certain that he had found the solution to the problem of the massive Belgian fort.

An ardent student of military history, particularly of the First World War, in which he had fought as a corporal in a Bavarian infantry regiment, Hitler knew that the Liège forts, as well as the French Fort Douaumont, had been taken only after giant 420-mm. mortars had rained armored shells on their thick concrete domes. This time the German armies could not afford the delay which such heavy artillery would inevitably cause. The fort had to be taken by a sudden decisive assault. The means of crushing the thick concrete walls of the Eben Emael gun emplacements were at hand: German scientists had developed a hollow-charge explosive which they guaranteed would do the job. But the *hohlladung* (space charge) device weighed over one hundred pounds and had to be put in place, fused, and then exploded by a team of men. How could these explosive charges be brought to the cupolas of Eben Emael?

His adjutant opened the door and announced, "Generaloberst Student."

Kurt Student, commanding general of *Fliegerdivision* Seven, the German airborne force, entered the conference room, stood at attention, and saluted.

In 1939 Student was forty-nine years old and had been in the German army for thirty-seven years. Born into a Prussian family of the minor landed gentry, he had been a cadet at the age of twelve, had been commissioned in a *Jäger* regiment, and in 1913 had transferred into the fledgling Imperial German Air Force. During the First World War he had served as a bomber pilot on the eastern front, and later as a fighter pilot in France, scoring five victories in the Champagne sector. During this period he had become good friends with Hermann Goering, who had just taken over command of von Richthofen's famous fighter squadron after the death of the renowned "Red Baron." After the war Student had remained in the truncated Wehrmacht which the Versailles Treaty had permitted Germany. At first he had spent a great deal of his time instructing German youths in glider flying, which was one way of preparing future Luftwaffe pilots for the day when Germany would rearm. On several occasions he went to Russia to serve as a technical consultant and to pave the way for training German fliers in powered aircraft on Russian airfields. This secret agreement between the German and Russian High Commands continued until Hitler came to power in 1933.

Kurt Student had been involved in all aspects of preparing for the rebirth of the Luftwaffe; it was only natural that he should play a prominent role in its technical development after Hitler cast aside the restrictive clauses of the Versailles Treaty. While in Russia, Student had observed the advances that the Soviets had made in parachute operations; he had watched an entire Russian division land by parachute from huge trimotored transports. Convinced that this was the wave of the future, he lost no time in persuading the reluctant, conservative German High Command that airborne troops would play a major role in any future war. At the same time he was concerned by the fact that the paratroopers he had seen were so lightly armed, since it was not possible to drop heavy weapons by parachute.

It was while perusing this problem that Colonel Student, the ex-glider instructor, remembered his soaring days. He presented the problem to the German Institute for Glider Research, and they quickly designed an oversized soarplane capable of carrying ten fully equipped infantrymen and landing in any clear seventy-five-yard space. By the time Student had been summoned to Berlin, ten of these experimental military gliders—called DFS-230s—had been built.

Hitler wasted no time with polite conversation. Beckoning Student to his desk, he showed him the aerial photographs of the fort, emphasizing the positions of the artillery cupolas, the machine-gun emplacements, and the numerous antiaircraft guns. It was clear, he said, that the flak defenses would make any attempt by powered planes very costly, if not impossible. Also, the sound-ranging equipment meant that any planes approaching the fort would be heard miles away, and the garrison alerted. The only solution was to put the attacking force on the grass-covered top of the fort silently so that the defenders would not be aware of their presence until they were in their midst.

What Hitler was proposing to the startled Student was to use gliders to render the most powerful fort in the world helpless!

It was Hanna Reitsch, the aviatrix and fervent admirer of the Führer, who had first given Hitler the idea. At a glider contest in 1935 she had pointed out that the motorless craft were almost noiseless while in free flight. It was this novel thought that Hitler had tucked away in the corner of his mind until a silent weapon was needed. This was the place —and the time—for gliders to be used as assault vehicles.

Bluntly, he asked if Student's glider troops could do the job.

Student continued to study the map intently to give himself time to formulate an answer. The idea was both original and daring, yet its implications were staggering. The whole German glider corps consisted of a handful of DFS-230s, each of which could carry ten fully armed infantrymen or engineers. And this force had never been tested, either in maneuvers or in battle. To throw it against a fort as well protected as Eben Emael was enough to take one's breath away. Suppose the landing failed to silence the guns? What would this do to the infantry attack across the Dutch and Belgian frontiers? It was a grave responsibility, but Student knew that Hitler, who was always intrigued by new ideas in military tactics, would insist that this one should be attempted.

Reluctantly, Student agreed that it would be possible to release gliders at high altitude far from the fort so that the towplanes would not be heard. Yes, he could put his few gliders on top of Eben Emael, but they could not carry enough explosives to make a dent in the concrete walls of the gun casements.

It was then that Hitler told him for the first time of the new hollow charges which had recently been tested success- fully on Czech fortifications. Properly placed, they were guaranteed to blow a big enough hole in the cupolas of Eben Emael to kill the gun crews and render the cannon inoperable.

Stunned by the revelation of this top-secret development, Student could pose only one condition: to keep from smashing themselves against the obstacles on top of the fort, the glider pilots would need some light by which to land. Therefore, the attack must be either at dawn or at dusk.

After some thought, Hitler agreed to a dawn assault. He knew that his generals wanted to start the invasion during the hours of darkness, but if Student's glider pilots needed light by which to land, he would hold up the armies until the gliders had touched down on Eben Emael. Thus the time schedule of the German invasion of Holland and Belgium was altered by the requirements of this small glider force for enough light to land safely on the grassy roof of the Belgian fort.

Finally, Hitler warned Student that the recruitment and training for this mission were to be carried out in the greatest secrecy. Everyone concerned was to sign a statement acknowledging that sentence of death would follow the divulgence, even accidental, of any detail of the planned assault. No date for the operation was given, for none had yet been decided upon. Student did not know how long he would have to assemble and train his assault team, but the project was given a code name: it was called "Granite."

May 10, 1940. 0300 hours.

On an airfield near Cologne, the eleven gliders were loaded in the darkness. An hour earlier Lieutenant Rudolf Witzig had opened the sealed orders, and for the first time the eighty-five members of the assault team had been told of their mission: "Force 'Granite' will go in by glider to land and take a fort in the Belgium defense system. Takeoff time is 0325." Now the men were crammed into the gliders. The final minutes ticked away.

In the gloom the towropes were attached to the nose of each glider and the tail of its tug. The thundering roar of the engines was muffled to the men in the gliders, busy checking their grenades, submachine guns, and the security of the high-explosive charges with their fuses and cords. One by one the towplanes moved onto the runway, each pulling a slab-sided high-winged glider into position. Then, with a surging crescendo of noise, the first JU-52 started its takeoff run.

"Suddenly, a jerk on the glider forced me backwards," Corporal Wilhelm Alefs later wrote. "There was a jockeying and swaying motion as the towrope tightened and swung the glider in behind the straining plane ahead . . . we all started the chant of the parachutists, 'The sun shines red. . . .'

"As we picked up speed, the roller coaster noise of the wheels, the slapping of the slipstream against the canvas fuselage, drowned out the singing. The wobble-wheeling tail noise ceased and I felt us level off on the two forward wheels. Then there was only the drumming of the wind and a low whistle. . . . We were on our way, glider and plane, to a destiny from which we could be reasonably sure only the plane would return!"

Inside each glider the paratroopers sitting astraddle the wooden bench down the center of the cabin struggled to keep their equipment from shifting by holding it with their hands and feet. It was crowded, noisy, and smelly inside the vibrating shell, and the men fought back nausea as the towplanes struggled to gain altitude. In the cockpit the glider pilot peered down through the black sky to see the signals that would mark the forty-five-mile air route from Cologne to the release point north of Aachen.

They spotted the first navigation fix right on time—a bonfire at a crossroads. Nothing else could be seen in the gloom below them, for a vigorous wartime blackout was being observed. Soon, the first untoward incident of the flight occurred. An unknown plane passed dangerously close to the JU-52 that was towing Lieutenant Witzig's glider. As the towplane swerved to avoid a collision, the rope snapped and Witzig and his team found themselves in free flight without enough altitude to glide back to the airfield. A few minutes later a second towplane waggled its wings and flashed its navigation lights as a signal for its glider to release. Since he was still too far from the fort and not at the proper altitude, the glider pilot refused to do so and grimly held on. Finally, the plane went into a steep dive, and the glider pilot was forced to pull the release lever. Thus, it was nine gliders, and not eleven, that approached the correct release point given by a searchlight on the mountains northwest of Aachen.

But even now their troubles were not over, for the laboring tugs had been unable to reach the assigned release height of 8,500 feet, and the lead pilot decided to continue on course into Dutch territory (clearly defined by the lights of the towns) for another ten minutes. It was impossible to disguise the noise of the engines. Soon the sky was filled with tracers and exploding antiaircraft bursts as the Dutch batteries around Maastricht opened up on the unidentified planes.

It was now that the gliders released from the ropes and dived away in the darkness toward the still-unseen fort.

"The surprise attack on Fort Eben Emael," Student told a British officer after the war, "was carried out by a Lilliputian detachment of seventy-eight parachute engineers commanded by Lieutenant Witzig. Of these, only six men were killed. This small detachment made a completely unexpected landing on the roof of the fort, overcame the antiaircraft personnel there, and blew up the armored cupolas and casements of all the guns with a new, highly intensive explosive—previously kept secret.

"From the roof of the fort, Witzig's detachment kept the garrison of 1,200 men in check until twenty-four hours later, when our ground troops arrived."

Student acknowledged to the British officer that the glider assault on Eben Emael had been Hitler's idea, calling it "the most original idea of this man of many brain waves."

A massive fort built to hold off armies had been taken in less than twenty-four hours by seventy-eight men at a cost of six dead and twenty wounded. How was it possible? Certainly the method of the assault had unnerved the defenders (who numbered about 850, rather than the 1,200 soldiers that Student had reported), for it had taken time to recognize that the large gray bats that came winging down on the roof of the fort were, in fact, an assaulting force. The anti-aircraft crews were prepared for dive-bombers or even parachutists, but never had it been suggested that the attack would come on silent wings. Therefore, they had stood and stared in the half-light as the gliders had swooped down and plowed into the grass-covered terrain. By the time they recognized the Nazi insignias it was too late, for their guns could not be lowered to fire at their own roof.

From the gliders, the assault teams had come out shooting. The machine-gun nests in their immediate vicinity had been quickly overwhelmed and the engineers had hurried, each to his assigned cupola. The hollow charges had been fixed, fused, and lit, the assault team retiring to a safe position. The result had been mind-numbing. A huge hole had been ripped in the reinforced concrete of the gun emplacement. Even where it did not penetrate the full five-foot thickness, the shock wave it generated spalled lethal shrapnel inside that decimated the gun crews. Those who escaped this deadly steel-and-concrete jet were stunned or knocked unconscious by the blast.

The Belgian garrison made a few feeble attempts to emerge from their underground hiding place to drive the invaders off the roof, but these attempts by men psychologically unprepared for this new form of warfare were doomed in advance. The submachine-gun fire of a few resolute attackers drove them back. Finally, the garrison contented themselves with closing and barring the huge doors that marked the entrance to the underground maze in which they now found themselves prisoners.

When the German armies arrived at Eben Emael the next day, after having been delayed when the resolute Dutch destroyed the bridges across the Meuse, they found an amazing situation. The Belgian garrison was still cowering deep in the concrete bowels of the fort, while the surface was controlled by the handful of glider men. The surrender of the fort was inevitable, and it came that afternoon, preceded by the blowing of a bugle and the waving of a white flag through a half-opened entryway. Eben Emael had fallen.

But the victory was attributed by the Allied military experts to the blitzkrieg: the sighing sound of the gliders as they landed on the roof of the fort was drowned out by the roar of tank motors and the screaming of German dive-bombers. For months the lesson of Eben Emael remained unlearned, hidden by a dense fog of misinformation. It was reported at first that the fort had been taken by parachutists, and there were rumors that some of the German engineers who had helped construct the fort had left caches of high explosives deep within it, the explosion of which had rendered the garrison helpless. In any case, little notice of the use of gliders was taken by either the British or American headquarters.

Immensely pleased with the result of his plan, Adolf Hitler decorated and promoted all the men involved in the assault. He told Student that the airborne forces would be expanded and that there would be new missions for the German paratroop and glider forces. But when the first of these missions was planned—an airborne landing in England in support of a seaborne invasion (known together as "Operation Sealion")—Student was not present; he had been shot in the head by a sniper while inspecting the German paratroops in Holland and was hovering between life and death in a hospital. In the assault on England the airborne forces were to consist of one parachute division and one airlanding division to be carried in three hundred gliders to seize a bridgehead (really an airhead) near Folkestone. However, aerial photographs soon showed that obstacles—antiglider poles and mines—were being prepared on the intended landing fields. At the end of August the idea of an airborne invasion was abandoned.

Although Hitler decided to postpone the invasion of

England indefinitely on September 17, 1940, and finally canceled it on October 12, he kept coming back to the idea. Shortly after Student left the hospital, in January, 1941, he was summoned to Berchtesgaden, where Hitler again discussed the use of airborne forces. After evaluating possible targets in the Mediterranean, the Führer returned to the idea of an invasion of England, and the way in which the expanded parachute and gliderborne forces could be used.

Student brought out a pet idea of his—an airborne landing in Ireland—but Hitler, while listening attentively, did not seem impressed by the advantages it offered. His finger wandered down the map and pointed to Gibraltar, Malta, and the Suez Canal. It was time to think of securing the southern flank of their conquest and of mounting operations against the British in North Africa.

On the day that Fort Eben Emael fell to the first glider assault in military history, Winston Churchill became prime minister of England. Even in the black days of May and June, 1940, when German tanks and planes were slicing a disastrous swath through northern France, cutting off the Anglo-French armies in Belgium and forcing their evacuation from the continent, Churchill grasped the importance of airborne attack to the future conduct of the war. On the 22nd of June, while Marshal Pétain was negotiating the French surrender, Churchill wrote one of his famous minutes to his chiefs of staff:

"We ought to have a Corps of at least five thousand parachute troops. I hear something is being done already to form such a Corps, but only I believe on a very small scale. Advantage must be taken of the summer to train these forces, who can nonetheless play their part meanwhile as shock troops in home defense. Pray let me have a note from the War Office on this subject."

The response of the Army and the Royal Air Force to this farsighted recommendation was less than enthusiastic. At a time when the RAF was frantically trying to build up its fighter and bomber strength, the need for a troop-carrier force large enough to transport five thousand parachutists or to tow the gliders carrying an airlanding brigade of that size seemed less than justified. To the Army, facing an imminent German invasion with the unarmed troops they had managed to evacuate from France, the idea of large-scale airborne operations appeared to be visionary. Although all of England was being alerted and prepared for German paratroop attack in support of a seaborne invasion, the War Office tried to bury the prime minister's recommendation under a pile of surveys, briefs, and draft papers.

Still, the suggestion could not be completely ignored. A call for volunteers for the new parachute corps brought forth 3,500 men eager for the adventure. Of these, 500 were selected for training, and the prime minister was told that it would require twelve months before the 5,000 figure he had specified could be reached. In September the Ministry of Aircraft Production ordered four hundred Hotspur gliders, a canvas and steel-strutted model designed to carry nine men, including a pilot and copilot sitting in tandem. It strongly resembled the German DFS-230s, which had been used so successfully at Eben Emael. At the same time no provision was made for a separate troop-carrier fleet, since this role would be given to the heavy bomber squadrons.

The failure to provide an independent troop-carrier lift capacity was to bear bitter fruit four years later, when British and American airborne commanders were to quarrel heatedly over the allotment of planes for their missions. Although the RAF later set up two groups (equivalent to U.S. wings) of obsolescent bombers to drop paratroopers and tow gliders, these were never available in sufficient numbers to carry a significant part of even one of the two British airborne divisions that would be available in 1944. The assignment of American planes to haul the British airborne force was to be a sore point between the Allies.

While the War Office was dragging its feet on building a British airborne force (in spite of Churchill's insistent demands), the Germans were vigorously preparing their most spectacular feat—an aerial invasion across miles of open sea which would involve a full airborne division.

The island of Crete, like a sun-blasted rock thrown by some giant hand into the blue waters of the Aegean, lies sixty miles south of the Greek mainland. Over 160 miles long, it is cut by four mountain ranges that extend almost to the coast. Except for the narrow beaches and a few small ports, it is a hostile landscape: gray rocky slopes, deep ravines, and gullies, perfect for the guerrilla fighter but difficult for a modern army. Its past lost in prehistory, it had seen many invaders and was now to see one more.

It was from this hot, dusty island that Icarus and his father, Daedalus, had escaped on wings of wax and feathers. Now a modern Daedalus was to return to Crete, carrying death in his arms.

On the island, almost 30,000 troops—British, New Zealand, Australian, Greek, and Cretan—waited without hope. Flung out of Greece by the German attack, they were exhausted and disorganized. Morale was low. They had left their heavy equipment on the mainland, and there were few tanks, little artillery, and no airplanes to help defend the island against the blow they knew was coming. To Major-General Bernard "Tiny" Freyberg, the husky six-foot commander, the prospects looked very grim indeed. At the end of April he had been warned by the War Office to expect a combined airborne and seaborne attack on Crete, in which the initial assault would be delivered by four thousand paratroopers. British headquarters in Cairo could offer him little encouragement. There would be no RAF support available, and the Navy was reluctant to operate in Cretan waters under the blows of the Luftwaffe. Crete would have to be held by the weary troops now on the island, for reinforcement from Egypt was impossible. The evacuation of the island was not even considered.

Hopeful that after the attack began he would be supported by aircraft from Egypt, Freyberg decided not to disable the three airfields on the north coast. Remembering that in Belgium and Holland the Germans had frequently crash-landed their JU-52 transport planes on beaches, roads, and fields, he decided not to block or destroy the airstrips so that they could be used later by RAF fighters and bombers. This was a fatal error—one of several made by exhausted men, mistakes which were to lose a battle that might otherwise have been won.

For Hitler, the campaign in Greece had been finished when the British and their Greek allies had been driven off the mainland. He had no interest in Crete but was engrossed in his plans for the coming attack on Russia. It was Student, anxious to display once more the power of his airborne division, who convinced him otherwise.

"He wanted to break off the Balkan campaign after reaching the south of Greece," Student later reported. "When I heard this, I flew to see Goering, and proposed a plan of capturing Crete by airborne forces alone. Goering—who was always easy to enthuse—was quick to see the possibilities of the idea, and sent me on to Hitler. I saw him on April 21. When I first explained the project, Hitler said, 'It sounds all right, but I don't think it's practicable.' But I managed to convince him in the end."

Goering's desire to redeem the Luftwaffe after the failure of its bombing attacks on England was understandable, but it was the threat to the Rumanian oil fields posed by British bombers stationed on Crete that finally influenced Hitler's decision. Also, the capture of Crete would permit Germany to dominate the eastern Mediterranean, so Student was given the go-ahead. D day for the assault was to be May 20, 1941.

The airborne force for the attack was the most formidable that had ever been assembled: the German 7th Parachute Division, plus the 5th Mountain Division (which would be landed by transport plane on the captured airfields), part of the 6th Mountain Division, an armored regiment, a motorcycle battalion, an engineer battalion, and two light antiair-craft units. The air force was even more impressive: more than a thousand planes, bombers, dive-bombers, and fighters. Seventy-five gliders were to be sent on the mission. All in all, the attack force consisted of 25,000 men.

The plan was quite simple, and more or less dictated by the unfavorable terrain. Glider-paratroop assaults would be carried out at three critical points on the north coast of Crete, with the airfields their initial objectives. As soon as these had been taken, the mountain divisions would be flown in as reinforcements. The widely separated "airheads" would then fight their way along the north coast to form one continuous battle line. The linkup would push the British over the mountains and force them to flee Crete by the southern ports.

In the crowded briefing room in the Hotel Grande Bretagne in Athens, Lieutenant-Colonel Baron Friedrich von der Heydte, who was commanding one of the German parachute battalions, was more than a little worried by the lack of precision in those plans. In Belgium and Holland they had had detailed models of the objectives to be captured, and the assault had been concentrated. Here the landings were to be scattered all along the north coast of Crete, and the German paratroopers and glider infantry were supposed to spread "like an oilspot," as Student said, until they joined. Also, they were not all going in together, since Maleme with its vital airfield would be assaulted first. Then the other two airfields on the eastern side of the island would be attacked as the planes from the first lift became available. Von der Heydte did not think that the seaborne reinforcements would arrive; the slow Greek caiques (skiffs) carrying heavy guns and vehicles had little chance of getting past the British Navy. Even under the attack of the Luftwaffe, British ships ruled that part of the Mediterranean. Nevertheless, Student was anxious to prove that his airborne forces were capable of successfully attacking a major objective and were not just small assault teams for specific isolated targets.

On the morning of May 20 the planes and gliders were loaded in the darkness. Working by the light of hand torches, ground crews tied down the mortars, ammunition, and bicycles in the cramped cabins of the DFS-230s. Towropes were stretched from the gliders to the straining trimotored JU-52s which could be dimly seen silhouetted against the first light. As the planes revved up their engines, thick dust clouds rose and blanketed the airfields. Men had to shout in each other's ears to make themselves heard.

Almost everyone was eager to go. One man who complained of illness to von der Heydte at the last moment was ordered into the plane. "You can report sick when we get to Crete," von der Heydte told him bluntly. "Our medical staff is flying with us." The reluctant paratrooper was Max Schmeling, the heavyweight boxer and onetime world champion; he had to parachute into Crete with a bad case of diarrhea.

Crowded into the noisy, vibrating planes and gliders, the assault teams sweated in their heavy camouflaged jump suits. Soon the planes had assembled at an altitude of one thousand feet and had turned south toward the Sea of Crete. It was a sunny, warm day. Beneath the slowly climbing formations the sea was calm.

Suddenly, one of the gliders started to oscillate wildly in the slipstream of a passing bomber. The pilot fought to gain control, but the strain was too much. He released from the tow and turned away, trying to make a safe landing on the island below him, but the glider had been loaded past its safe limits. The wings folded. The stricken glider plummeted downward and crashed on the island of Aegina, killing all its occupants. Among the dead was the ground commander of the assault troops, Generalleutnant Wilhelm Süssman, and most of his staff.

It was a bad omen.

Ninety minutes after takeoff, the lead glider pilot could see the craggy gray mountains of Crete rising above the sea-horizon. Behind him, in the stuffy, smelly cabin, the airborne troopers were checking their weapons, trying to catch the first glimpse of land through the yellowed plastic windows, or being terribly airsick. Even in the calm air, the gliders bounced badly in the slipstreams of the forward planes, and between spasms many a soldier vowed to transfer to the parachutists.

Soon they could see the white curl of the surf on the beaches. Dive-bombers and fighters had been softening the British defenses for hours, and pillars of dust were rising straight into the cloudless sky. Checkpoints were obscured, and it was with difficulty that the navigators were able to locate the airfield at Maleme. The towplanes turned slightly to put the gliders within range of the dry riverbed that was their landing area. One by one, like a swarm of angry hornets, they flew over the beaches and released their gliders.

So far, no one had fired on them!

To the defenders on Crete, the dive-bombers and fighter attacks seemed at first to be the usual "morning hate," but these had soon grown to a greater intensity than ever before. Giant clouds of dust and smoke billowed skyward from the churning bombardment as the men huddled in their foxholes. Then voices on the slopes cried, "Gliders! Gliders!" —and through the yellowish haze came long-winged shadowy shapes, moving slowly and silently west of the field. There were about seventy in all but, to the openmouthed troops below, there seemed to be thousands. The huge gray bats circled to landings in every direction, crash-landing on the rocky slopes and in a dry riverbed, spilling troops and equipment along their skittering path. Still deafened by the bombs, the defenders stood and stared.

The stunned silence lasted only a few seconds; then every gun in the area opened up. Rifles, machine guns, and 20-mm. cannon ripped through the slowly descending gliders as they frantically searched for a safe landing spot. Some crashed into the rocks or disintegrated among the trees; one exploded on hitting the open framework of a bridge. The

British watched several gliders shudder to a halt, seemingly undamaged, but no one leaped out. The occupants were all dead in their seats.

Only those DFS-230s that came down in the rock-filled dry riverbed, shielded from the guns, escaped the slaughter. Slithering down at forty miles an hour, their skids plowing through the dust, most of them landed safely. The ten men in each craft disappeared swiftly into the brush to capture the bridge and the antiaircraft guns that threatened the paratroop planes.

Fifteen minutes later the big kitelike transports droned in very low—some of them at four hundred feet or less—and tiny black figures leaped out. Soon the dust clouds were filled with parachutes as the Germans came swinging down, kicking their feet and firing their submachine guns. Most of them died before touching the ground. The British and Commonwealth troops killed them with rifles, machine guns, and even pistols. Completely helpless both in the air and while struggling with their harnesses on the ground, the German parachutists lost half their force to the withering fire before they were able to regroup and attack.

Despite some minor successes, the initial attack was a failure. Recovering rapidly from the surprise, the defenders clung to the high ground near the airfield and fought off all attempts of the parachutists to capture it. Without the use of the airfield, there could be no reinforcement of the surviving German troops and the assault would fail.

The battle for Crete was a murderous one, fought on the hot, dusty slopes and in the gullies and ravines. Although the German paratroop and gliderborne infantry had suffered heavily in the landings, the defenders were strangely indecisive and failed to take advantage of their initial victory. The landings at the two eastern airfields (Retimo and Herakleion), which took place in the late afternoon, were even more costly than the morning fight at Maleme. Despite their losses, the attackers slowly assembled, captured several key positions, and began their advance.

For two days the issue was undecided. By nightfall of the first day the Germans were still fighting against the stubborn New Zealanders for control of the Maleme airfield. Depleted by heavy losses, exhausted and short of ammunition, they feared a strong counterattack which would roll over them. But it never came.

The next day Student sent in his parachute reserve for the final capture of the Maleme airfield and won Crete. Soon the lumbering JU-52s were landing there under sporadic fire and were unloading reinforcements and heavy weapons. The British commander was still expecting a seaborne landing on the north coast and failed to send his troops to recapture the Maleme airfield. The British Navy intercepted the caique flotilla on the night of the 21st, sinking many and forcing the others to disperse, while subsequently losing two cruisers and four destroyers to the German dive-bombers. But this naval action had no effect on the land battle; that was lost when the German transport planes were able to use the airfield at Maleme. By the 27th, the British forces were in full retreat to the south coast, from which the survivors were evacuated to Egypt.

The Germans paid a very heavy price for Crete. Of the 22,000 men dropped on the island, over 5,000 were killed, wounded, or missing, and most of these had belonged to the crack 7th Parachute Division. One of the "casualties" was Max Schmeling, who had parachuted unhurt into Crete to become—to his surprise—a hero. When he was reported "wounded," the propaganda ministry hailed him as one of the fearless paratroopers of the new Nazi airborne forces.

Horrified by the loss of his crack parachute division just as he was preparing to invade the Soviet Union, Hitler refused to accept Student's plan for an airborne attack on Cyprus. "The days of the paratroopers are over," he said firmly. "Their initial success was due to the surprise factor, and now that surprise is gone." In spite of Student's spirited defense of the role of his airborne force, Hitler was adamant. The German parachute division was never again to be used in an airborne role, but was committed to ground action in Russia as superbly trained infantry.

This time the meaning of the battle for Crete was not lost on the British and the Americans. Just as Hitler was writing off his paratroop and glider teams, the future Allies were carefully studying the lesson to be learned from the successful airborne assault on an island hundreds of miles from the departure airfields.

The American military attaché in Egypt, Colonel Bonner Fellers, waxed poetic over the German conquest: "The drama of Crete marks an epic in warfare. The concept of the operation was highly imaginative, daringly new. Combat elements drawn from Central Europe moved with precision into funnel-shaped Greece. Here they reformed, took shape as a balanced force, were given wings. The operation had the movement, rhythm, harmony of a master's organ composition. On 20 May and succeeding days, this force soared through space; its elements broke over Crete in thundering crescendos—all stops out. For the first time in history, airborne troops, supplied and supported by air, landed in the face of an enemy, defeated him."

This 258-page report, first published in September, 1941, was to be carefully perused by the higher command levels in Washington and London. The capture of Eben Emael had been a whisper lost in the thunder of the blitzkrieg, but the successful assault on Crete had been played out in the open amphitheater of the Mediterranean. It was a strident shout into the ear of even the most conservative military planner. The results of this campaign were to be seen in the great Allied airborne invasions three years later.

Hitler had skillfully opened a Pandora's box, and inside a genie was being born that would later grip him by the throat.

2
No-Engine Pilots

"This is a sad story," Winston Churchill wrote after the fall of Crete, "and I feel myself greatly to blame for allowing myself to be overborne by the resistances which were offered. . . . The gliders have been produced on the smallest possible scale, and so we have practically now neither the parachutists nor the gliders . . . a whole year has been lost. . . ."

More impressed by the German losses in Crete than by their success, the War Office was still dragging its heels on creating an airborne force, constantly questioning the need for it while Britain was on the defensive. The Royal Air Force was reluctant to train glider pilots while its flying schools were crowded with future bomber and fighter pilots, or to assign bombers to tow gliders. The air war on Germany had to come first.

But the growling tone of the prime minister's comments alarmed the conservative military planners. Yielding under pressure, they finally ordered the formation of an airborne division and in November, 1941, gave the command to Major-General Frederick A. H. Browning, who until then had been best known as the husband of the novelist Daphne du Maurier.

"Boy" Browning was forty-four years old, tall, slim, with dark hair that he brushed straight back and a full well-trimmed mustache. Everyone remarked on his immaculate dress; his belt and buttons sparkled. Physically, he was the very model of a Guards officer, but intellectually he was to be an enigma to many of his fellow officers and later an irritating puzzle to his American colleagues.

Lieutenant Iain Murray had served with Browning in the Grenadier Guards (after five years in the RAF) and knew him well. "Browning," he said in an interview, "was a perfectionist; everything he did, he did frightfully well. Very athletic, a good runner. He had served with distinction in World War One and was very dedicated to anything he took up. When the chance came to form this new type of warfare, it was a great challenge to him. He was a very popular leader with great presence, always immaculately dressed. He wasn't a great authority on airborne skills and not a great brain, but he had sufficient knowledge of army life in general to put the glider corps together. He could get equipment for the gliders out of the War Office when a lot of other people couldn't." Murray didn't think Browning's grasp of tactics was strong, although he had commanded a division in the early part of the war and "had come through it very well."

This, then, was "Boy" Browning, whose first task was to find officers for the newly formed Glider Pilot Regiment—leaders who were both fliers and infantrymen. Iain Murray was one of them and Major George J. S. Chatterton was another.

Chatterton had served in the Royal Air Force in the 1930s as a fighter pilot and a member of a crack aerobatic team. After a near fatal midair collision, he had been transferred to the reserves. Upon the outbreak of war in 1939 his request for flying duty was refused and, rather than accept a ground job and watch other men fly, he transferred to an infantry regiment serving in France. After Dunkirk, he found infantry life boring for a man who had never reconciled himself to not flying: "One evening, bending down to the wastepaper basket for a piece of paper to light my pipe. . . . my eyes happened to catch an advertisement which read 'Volunteers for the rôle of Glider Pilot.' "

Highly qualified for the new service, Chatterton immediately applied. After being interviewed by Browning, he was named second-in-command of the First Battalion, the Glider Pilot Regiment, and ordered to report to the new training depot, Tilshead, on Salisbury Plain.

A year later Chatterton took over the First Battalion after the death of its commander in a glider accident. Lieutenant Iain Murray was given command of the Second Battalion and in one year was promoted to the rank of lieutenant-colonel—a meteoric rise even in the wartime Army.

Both men were to admirably justify Browning's faith in them.

When the call went out for glider pilot volunteers, it found a ready response among the men who had been stagnating in England since Dunkirk. Bored with the monotony of camp life, fed up with spit and polish, eager for adventure, over 100,000 men stepped forward.

Ernest Lamb had enlisted in the Army in the spring of 1939 along with "most of the members of the local rugby and cricket clubs." He had risen to the rank of sergeant in an artillery battery when the opportunity to apply for glider pilot training came. "There was a notice on the battery orders which invited people to volunteer for service in this new unit. I think that regulations forced all commanding officers to publish this and they could not stop any of their people from applying to join the Glider Pilot Regiment. Well, it was a new arm of what was going to prove a very adventurous service. It was the unknown and I suppose that the unknown always has a challenge."

Fed up with "foot slogging around Northern Ireland" and disheartened at his failure to be promoted after two years as a sergeant, Tom Pearce had been frantically volunteering for "paratroops, Special Air Service, things like that. Then they asked for glider pilots and they had a white paper which meant the commanding officers had to let you go forward if you volunteered. In most cases they tended to throw your application in the wastepaper basket."

Private H. N. "Andy" Andrews was a draftsman in the Royal Engineers whose commanding officer refused his application for glider pilot training on the grounds that Andrews's job was too important. "I was working on some drawings of a Home Guard headquarters," Andrews wrote, "and I managed to lose one sheet completely, spill a bottle of ink on another and rub some holes in a third. My application was promptly approved and forwarded!"

The love of flying made Jim Davies volunteer, and he thought that this had been the prime motivation for most of the men who joined the Glider Pilot Regiment—"men who would put up with anything for the sake of flying."

Harry Antonopoulos was a student when the war broke out and had promptly volunteered for the Royal Air Force, but because he had a Greek father and was a first-generation Englishman, he was not accepted until after the fall of France. Then he was called up and put into an antiaircraft battery. After almost a year, he said, "they must have written to all the people who had applied for the RAF and who were obviously keen on flying. By that time Greece had come into the war and shown that they were pro-Ally and therefore it didn't matter what name I had, I was acceptable. They wrote to me and asked if I would like to go into the glider pilots and I said yes. So I was one of the early ones. . . ."

Louis Hagen had problems because of his birthplace. A German Jew, he had spent six weeks in a Nazi concentration camp before fleeing to England, where he worked as a mechanic. "When the war started, I had to leave the factory because I was officially called an enemy alien like the other 100,000 refugees from Germany. The firm was not permitted to employ foreigners, especially Germans. So I volunteered for the Pioneer Corps, which was the only part of the British army where enemy aliens were enlisted. I guarded the coast of Devon with a stake because we weren't allowed to have rifles. During the Dunkirk era, they were so short of people that they used us and later one regiment after another was officially opened to enemy aliens." After a struggle with his conscience ("I'm not a militarist or an aggressive person and I don't like war. If it had not been for Hitler, I would have been a pacifist."), Hagen decided that he was going to apply for every duty available. "Every time a new regiment opened, I went to the company office and said, 'I want to volunteer.' I was in thirteen different regiments: the Pioneer Corps to the Army Ordnance Corps to the Fire Brigade to the Parachute [Regiment], the Artillery Assault Corps—every damn thing. The last one that was open to enemy aliens was the Glider Pilot Regiment, so I volunteered for that."

The first hurdle to be surmounted by the glider pilot applicants was an appearance before an RAF personnel selection board. The interviewers—who had no background in airborne operations—set the same standards they would in selecting future air crew members for bombers and fighters. They were chiefly interested in the applicant's education. There were written tests in mathematics and English. "One had to write among other things an essay," Ernest Lamb remembered. Tom Pearce, who had left school at fourteen and had picked up a smattering of geometry and algebra by studying while working on a farm, found that he had learned enough mathematics "to get me into the flying world in wartime." The selection board was interested in why he wanted to transfer from the infantry. "I told them that I wanted to do something other than march around . . . and that I didn't think I was in the right place. I wanted to do something different and to get on a bit."

While the first trainees were being weeded out (only one in twenty-five would finally get his "wings"), there was a struggle at high levels for control of the new glider force. The RAF insisted that the glider pilots be capable of flying bombers and fighters and be withdrawn from aerial operations only when airborne missions required. The Army held that glider pilots were infantrymen who only incidentally knew how to fly—and therefore should be under the Army's command. George Chatterton had his own ideas on the subject.

Chatterton, who was described by one of his glider pilots as "a super salesman who could sell you anything," persuaded Browning that the glider pilot had to be a "total soldier"— a man who could not only fly a glider for a long period of time but would be able to take a ground combat role upon landing. Chatterton knew from his own experience the desire for relaxation and even sleep that most pilots feel after a long flight, and he knew that rigorous training, strict discipline, and high morale would be required to sustain the new airborne soldier. For this purpose he obtained the services of several company sergeant-majors from the Brigade of Guards and urged them to apply the renowned Guards discipline to the new glider pilot trainees upon their arrival at the depot. The noncommissioned officers took him at his word, and Tilshead was to be an almost obscene name in the memory of the men of the Glider Pilot Regiment. "They may not have liked the Guards noncoms," Chatterton said in an interview, "but they never forgot them."

Ernie Lamb described his reception at the new depot in one word: "Hostile."

"It was a new kind of discipline," Tom Pearce remembered, "—psychological discipline. If you were on drill parade and you made a mistake, you were brought out in front of the squad, and had to face the men and shout at the top of your voice three times, 'I am a bloody idiot!' "

"You had to be fanatical to stay there," John Potts told this author, "because a speck of dust on your boots during an inspection and you were put in the guardroom. One of the chaps showed up on parade with a small cut on his face and was put on charge for being 'idle while shaving!' "

There was a great emphasis on appearance and bearing, and the hours not spent on the parade ground were spent in cleaning and blancoing of equipment (blancoing consists of whitening all leather and canvas webbing with blanco, a cake of white clay applied with a rag).

The discipline was rigid almost to the point of brutality, the idea being to discourage any man who was not completely committed to becoming a glider pilot. It was clearly understood from the beginning that anyone who became discouraged could apply for return to his original outfit, and many did. But others persevered. The Guards noncoms drove them mercilessly. "Once on parade," Lamb said, "a dog barked and every man jumped to attention!"

The flying training of the embryo glider pilot was to be the responsibility of the Royal Air Force, and the full elementary flight course for a future RAF pilot was given. In addition to instruction in flying a light plane, such as the Tiger Moth, there was training in aerobatics, cross-country navigation, and night landings, plus the ground school course in weather, aircraft engines and structures, and the Morse code. The army would teach him his combat role: he was to be a total soldier, prepared to do anything or handle any weapon, from the rifle or machine gun to mortars or light artillery.

At first there were no gliders available, and an appeal was made to civilian owners to offer their soarplanes. The response was heartening, and a strange assortment of gliders arrived at the airfield, brought in on trailers behind automobiles. Then the factories started to turn out the first motorless craft, and the ten-place Hotspur, which strongly resembled the German DFS-230, was soon available as a primary glider trainer.

Even at the elementary flying training schools, the glider pilots were not permitted to escape the strict discipline. Louis Hagen remembered that the "R.A.F. chaps who were also being trained would go home to study and not be disturbed, but we had to polish our brass and our boots, march up and down, and learn how to salute. After four years of war, it was a bit ridiculous. I was studying hard for my last examination to get my wings, and really knew that I was going to be in the regiment, when the Regimental Sergeant-Major came in again. I hated him anyway, because he was an army man, and instead of allowing us to study and really learn what was needed . . . anyway, I lost my temper, and told him to go to hell. There was a sort of army court and I was sentenced to be chucked out." Hagen was saved by his flying instructor, who pleaded that it was a waste of time, money, and a good man to eliminate him at the very end of his training. "So I was allowed to stay."

After graduation from the flying course, the glider pilot trainees returned to the depot to wait for an opening at one of the elementary glider flying schools, a wait which was frequently prolonged because of the lack of gliders and the scarcity of towplanes. When the trainee finally left Tilshead for his first glider course, he received approximately one month of training in the Hotspur glider, but all flying was done during the day. The lack of night-flying experience was to have an unfortunate effect on combat operations.

By late 1942 the Horsa glider, which had been developed as the combat glider of the British airborne force, was being turned out in large numbers. Largely built by furniture manufacturers, the high-winged monoplane had a circular fuselage of plywood glued to ribs of stronger wood. It was sixty-seven feet long with an eighty-eight-foot wingspan and a tricycle landing gear that could be jettisoned, allowing a landing to be made on a central skid. Pilot and copilot sat side by side in the nose, flying by the most elementary of instruments. On takeoff, the loaded Horsa weighed almost eight tons, half of which was useful cargo such as thirty soldiers or a jeep and ten soldiers or a six-pounder cannon and its crew. Upon landing, a quick exit could be made by unbolting the tail, after cutting the control and electrical cables, and allowing it to fall off. Since the tail had a nasty habit of sticking, a handsaw, an ax, and explosive cord were carried, should it be necessary to saw, hack, or blow the tail off to get the cargo out.

Even bigger than the Horsa was the Hamilcar (the British gave all gliders names beginning with "H": Hotspur, Horsa—even the American Waco glider, which they called the Hadrian). The Hamilcar was a monstrous wooden creation, its 110-foot wingspan and 68-foot length dwarfing even the four-engined Halifax bomber that towed it. Fully loaded, it weighed eighteen tons and could carry a light tank or two jeeps and trailers or forty passengers. The two pilots sat in tandem in an enclosed cockpit fifteen feet off the ground, conscious at all times that to turn over on landing would inevitably send the eight tons of cargo crashing down on them. It was a thought that every Hamilcar pilot took into combat with him, and that ensured a slow, soft landing—when possible.

Because of faulty design, it was found that the floor of the Hamilcar was too high off the ground to allow the tank or vehicles it carried to roll out after the landing. To remedy this, the pilots had to jump down from their high perch and let the air out of the tires and the oil out of the landing-gear struts. Then the belly of the huge glider would sink to the ground and the unloading could proceed. Doing this under fire for the first time made believers out of many a Hamilcar pilot.

After further training in either Horsas or Hamilcars, the new glider pilot was awarded his wings as a second pilot, or what the Americans called a copilot. To progress to first pilot, and to occupy the left-hand seat in a glider, required an additional course of training. As the glider operations began and demand for glider pilots increased, many of the men in the Glider Pilot Regiment never had the opportunity to take the advanced course which would qualify them to command. They could only look with envy at their more fortunate fellows who wore the larger blue wings surmounted by a lion rampant.

When, in early 1942, Winston Churchill demanded a demonstration of the new airborne forces, only one company of paratroops and nine Hotspur gliders could be scraped up. Under the eye of the furious prime minister, the weak force of parachutists jumped and missed the field completely. The glider display was an even worse disaster. Released at an altitude of ten thousand feet, far from the field, most of them overshot and ran into the crowd, one just missing Churchill. Another glider crashed into a treetop, spilling its occupants like dolls as it broke open. Chatterton observed that the prime minister looked very grim indeed.

Another demonstration to prove how safe the gliders were was even more disastrous. Two Horsas carrying fifty members of Parliament crashed on landing. In one glider which dug its nose into the ground at eighty miles an hour, Chatterton and Browning found themselves under a struggling pile of MPs, briefcases, umbrellas, and bowler hats. Other than fractured dignity, the only casualty was a lady MP who broke her ankle. A question was asked in Parliament about the efficiency of the new airborne force.

Undaunted, the Glider Pilot Regiment went off to war.

On the night of November 19, 1942, a coded radio message crackled through the air to England from a deserted snow-covered plateau in the mountains of Norway. "Sky clear with moonlight. Beautiful weather." The transmission completed, the four men of the Special Operations Executive (SOE), set up by Winston Churchill's order to carry out espionage and sabotage missions throughout Europe, settled back to wait for the arrival of the gliders.

Nine months earlier, reports had reached Allied Intelligence that the Germans had ordered the heavy-water output of the Norsk Hydro plant at Vemork in southern Norway to be tripled. Heavy water (deuterium oxide) is an essential element in atomic bomb research. Since the Germans had also prohibited the export of Czech uranium ore, another important component, it was assumed that they were preparing to build an atomic pile, the first step in obtaining an atomic bomb. In order to slow down the German research, it had been decided at a very high level to sabotage the hydrogen-electrolysis plant at Vemork, Germany's sole source of heavy water. But the factory itself was in the depths of a stone, steel, and concrete building that rose like a fortress on a cliff in the middle of heavily wooded mountains west of Oslo, and a bomber raid failed to appreciably decrease the output of heavy water. Thus, two sabotage teams in gliders were now scheduled to carry out the task from the ground.

The four highly trained SOE men had parachuted in a month earlier to determine the layout of the plant, the position of the German guards, and the weather for the night of the mission. In addition, they carried in with them the new radio navigation aid known as "Eureka," which would guide the towplanes to the landing site.

Thirty Army airborne engineers had volunteered for the hazardous mission. Divided into two groups, each commanded by a lieutenant, they were assigned to two Horsa gliders, one flown by two sergeant pilots of the Glider Pilot Regiment and one by two Australian glider pilots. Because of the vital importance of the mission and the dangers of the long tow over hostile mountainous terrain to be followed by an attack on a strongly guarded fortress factory, it had been decided to send two gliders to enable the passengers of each to carry out the sabotage independently.

According to the official history, "the forecast for the night of 19–20 November was reasonable though not ideal and with the possibility of deterioration in the weather for the remainder of the moon period it was decided to mount the operation that night. All was ready and morale was very high."

The heavily loaded Horsa gliders of "Operation Freshman" (since this was the Glider Pilot Regiment's first combat sortie) took off from an airfield in Scotland behind Halifax bombers at around 6:00 P.M. The two tug-glider combinations flew separately across the North Sea at different altitudes, since they ran into low clouds and one combination stayed below them, intending to climb upon reaching the Norwegian coast, while the other glider-tug team climbed above the clouds.

As the low-flying combination approached the Norwegian coast, a snowstorm was raging that made control of the glider difficult and identification of objects on the ground impossible. Mistaking the lights of a large town for one in the vicinity of the landing site, the tug pilot gave the order for the glider to cast off. As the Halifax turned and set off for England, it crashed into a mountain peak, killing all on board. A minute later the glider crash-landed on a rocky snow-covered slope, killing three men and seriously injuring six others. Before the survivors could escape, German troops were swarming over the scene. That night, after a brief period of questioning by the Gestapo, the fourteen British airborne troopers were shot by a firing squad in accordance with Hitler's infamous "Commando Order."

The other Halifax-Horsa team reached the landing site but was unable to identify it. Below them the four agents frantically listened to the sound of the bomber circling overhead. Although their Eureka transmitter was working, the receiver (called "Rebecca") in the bomber had failed. Finally, after circling helplessly for an hour, the tug pilot started back to England, but it was too late. Icing had loaded the wings of the bomber and the glider; they were gradually losing height in the mountainous terrain. Just before they reached the coast, the towline broke under the weight of the ice. The glider fell helplessly toward the mountains below and crash-landed, killing eight men, including the two British glider pilots, and injuring four others. All the survivors were quickly captured, and the four injured men were poisoned by a German doctor under the orders of the Gestapo, their bodies heavily weighted and thrown into the sea. The five uninjured survivors were put into a concentration camp and interrogated until January 18, 1943, when they were shot.

Thus the first combat mission of the new Glider Pilot

Regiment ended in complete failure. It was a poor harbinger for the future.

To say that the glider program was the bastard child of the United States Army Air Corps (soon to be named Army Air Forces) is an understatement. Even after Crete had made clear the value of the motorless craft in bringing in reinforcements and heavy weapons to the lightly armed paratroopers, the senior American commanders were unable to grasp the role gliders would play in the future. Gliding had not yet achieved popularity as a sport in the United States, and little was known of the techniques required to fly one or of its ability to land in small fields. Since the hierarchy of the Air Corps were all power pilots, they tended to look on gliders as toys and felt about them as a motorcyclist feels about a bicyclist. As late as 1942, the colonel in charge of glider procurement said bluntly, "The man who sold General Arnold on gliders is Hitler's best friend in the United States."

General Henry H. "Hap" Arnold, commanding the Army Air Corps, may not have been that easily impressed, but the newspapers never let him forget that the Nazis had opened a whole new facet of warfare by their use of gliders and paratroops in Crete. Arnold had a quirk to his character, most unusual in a professional soldier: he firmly believed that a civilian expert knew more on a given subject than any military man. If gliders were the wave of the future, he wanted a civilian in his office to advise him on how to recruit and train glider pilots and on what sort of gliders to buy. He remembered that in 1934 he had taken his one ride in a glider at a small airfield near Philadelphia. The pilot had been a young man named Lewin Barringer, who was well known in gliding circles and had been the first general manager of the United States Soaring Society. In the summer of 1941 General Arnold summoned the thirty-five-year-old Barringer to Washington to run the entire glider program; the job carried the rank of major.

Though an experienced pilot who had flown in many parts of the world, Barringer was unprepared for the organized chaos and hostility he encountered in Washington during the months before Pearl Harbor when the great expansion of the Air Corps began. His only power in that hierarchy-conscious organization came from his closeness to General Arnold, but he soon found that his best plans could be quickly frustrated by other echelons who were more interested in building fighters and bombers. The head of Air Corps Procurement had rashly boasted that he would produce 5,000 airplanes per month and had then frantically met his quota by turning out large numbers of light aircraft to be used as trainers and by labeling half-finished aircraft in the factories as planes ready for combat. Finding a number of these training planes hidden away at Army bases, Barringer had their engines removed and new noses built, with the front ends counterweighted to compensate for the missing engine weight. These turned out to be useful glider trainers at a time when there was little else available.

One of his biggest battles was to get officers' commissions for the new glider pilots. The senior Air Corps generals protested that only power pilots could be commissioned officers and that only commissioned officers could command an aircraft in flight. A compromise was finally reached with the creation of a new rank—flight officer—which would be the Air Corps equivalent of the army warrant officer. A cap badge and bars were designed for the new rank so that they would not be mistaken for what the glider pilots themselves would call "throttle jockeys."

The months passed in unproductive wrangling, and the glider program did not move. No one seemed to know what type of glider would be needed in combat operations, and when the Waco Aircraft Company offered a fifteen-place military glider (again strongly resembling the German DFS-230), the design was eagerly accepted by the Air Materiel Command at Wright Field, Dayton, Ohio. After all, the Waco

Company was located at Troy, Ohio, and it would be easy to work with them. The Waco CG-4A glider was quickly accepted as the combat glider of the United States Army; however, months passed before the first production contract was signed.

But men would be needed to fly these new weapons, and the call went out for volunteers for the Glider Corps.

As in England, the response was overwhelming, amazing even the jaded recruiting officers. It seemed that the Army was filled with thousands of frustrated men who for one reason or another could not get into the power-pilot training program. "I wanted to fly—anything" was the reason most often given by the volunteers. Too old for air crew training, or unable to pass the strict medical tests, they responded enthusiastically to the new program that promised not only a chance to get back into the air but the appeal of adventure. There were some who were attracted by the flight pay, which was relatively high, and the possibility of quick promotion. There were those who wanted to get out of the infantry, the coast artillery, or a dozen other ground outfits. There were those who liked the glamour of the Air Corps and the chance for a flight officer's commission. Many of the volunteers were "washed-out" cadets from the power-pilot training schools who refused to accept the idea that they were not good enough to fly and welcomed the chance to prove that the "washout" boards had been wrong. There were men who were licensed pilots in civilian life and were now trapped behind a desk. There were a few with civilian glider experience, one of whom had even built and flown his own glider. Letters were sent to holders of private pilots' licenses asking them to volunteer, and many men heard the call attractively presented on the radio.

Jack Dunn was still a civilian in Westport, Connecticut, when he applied. In a letter to the author, he wrote, "I wanted to fly. I was thirty-seven years old. There were no other options." At a much later date most of the glider pilots

would probably have agreed with Peter Franzak of Pitts-
burgh, Pennsylvania, when he ascribed his volunteering to "a
temporary loss of sanity!" There were others who would identify with Private Colin Beeson's fervent desire "to get out of
Texas!" Beeson was not the only soldier who found being stationed in the Lone Star State a particularly painful form of
"foreign service."

As the new recruits reported to the glider pilot pools before being sent out to the elementary flying schools, the struggle to get the glider program under way was still going on in
Washington. In May, 1942, General Arnold called Major Barringer to his office. He told him that preparations to open a
second front in 1943 were now starting and that his orders
were to produce ten thousand gliders in the next six months.
Barringer was horrified. Although there were blueprints for a
military glider, there was no assembly line or even jigs for the
construction of the Waco. No aircraft company in the nation
had as yet produced a single acceptable military glider of any
design.

"Sir," Barringer blurted, "that's impossible."

General Arnold bristled. " 'Impossible' is not a word used
in my office. My two sons built a glider last summer. If they
can build one glider in a summer, America can build ten
thousand in six months!"

Luckily, the plan to invade Europe in 1943 was called off
and, along with it, the demand to build ten thousand gliders
in six months.

The first stage of training for the glider pilot candidates
was assignment to an elementary flying school, most of
which were civilian-run under contract to the Army Air Corps.
Here the future glider guiders got their first taste of flight at
the controls of a Piper Cub or similar light aircraft. After being
taught the basics of aircraft control, they would take the
plane up to several thousand feet over the airfield, turn off the
engine, and glide in "dead stick" (without power). At a time

when there were only a handful of gliders and no experienced tow pilots, this was the closest simulation to glider flight that could be taught. At fields from Grand Forks, North Dakota, to Plainview, Texas, the air was soon filled with hundreds of quiet planes slipping silently downward as the students sharpened their skills in motorless flying.

At the same time an attempt was made to instill some semblance of military discipline and bearing into the future flight officers. When flying for the day was over, they would be marched back and forth across the parade ground being taught the fundamentals of military drill. At the end of the day the retreat ceremony was held. "The officer in charge," Eric "Case" Rafter remembered, "quite foolishly called for a volunteer to play the bugle and a glider pilot raised his hand. We stood at attention saluting the flag as it slowly came down, while horrible sounds emitted from the bugle. That fellow had never played a bugle before. He just made noises with it."

Every elite group such as the paratroopers, the Rangers, or the Commandos inevitably develops traditions which help to bind the men together, give them pride in their organization, and provide stamina when they go into battle. The glider pilots were no different, although their traditions horrified the military officers who commanded the training bases. Winston Churchill once said, "If you are going to kill a man, there is no harm in being polite." The glider pilots paraphrased it, "If you are going to be killed, there's no point to being polite—or disciplined—or sober." Few of them had heard of Eben Emael or Crete and no one had a clear idea of just what glider combat would be like, but they knew that it would be rough, tough, and dangerous. They set out to prepare themselves for the coming test—in their own way.

In the meantime, they had little use for the conventional military virtues and the rigidity of military life. They fostered a disdain for saluting that drove their commanders wild and a nonchalance for rules that kept company court-martials busy assessing fines and confinement to quarters. What they cherished in themselves and in their comrades was a love of flying, a skill in the air, and a devil-may-care attitude toward everything else. It was in the emerging glider pilot tradition that one of them stole a locomotive that just happened to be sitting idle nearby; he drove it twenty-five miles across the California desert, finally got it turned around, and brought it back to the starting point. There he abandoned it and fled on foot, pursued by the state police. His comrades hid him until the furor died down.

To sharpen judgment in landing in a small area, a fence of fifty-foot-high bamboo poles would be erected near one end of a field. The glider pilot trainee was supposed to bring his light plane dead stick down over the poles in a semistall, land, and roll to a stop within a hundred yards. One trainee badly misjudged the approach and, seeing that he was about to hit the poles, stuck his head out the side window and triumphantly shouted "Timber!" before plowing into the fence and scattering bamboo poles all over the field.

Since women and liquor are the natural prerequisites of the flier, the trainees felt that there was nothing wrong in going AWOL after a long day's flying to sample both.

Despite their nonchalance toward regulations, glider pilots quickly developed a professional competence and concern in the air. They were surprisingly careful in their flying, especially since there were usually others on board for whose lives they were responsible. They realized that, in addition to the ordinary risks in routine flying, there would be many more in combat, so that when they strapped themselves into the pilot's seat they were alert to all the dangers that existed. The game of "chicken," in which two aircraft approach each other head on to see which pilot first loses his nerve and turns away, was rigidly shunned; the only time it did happen the two pilots involved were killed. They were both West Pointers.

After approximately forty hours of light-plane flying, the trainees transferred to elementary glider school. For most of them it was the first time they tasted the joys of soaring. One such school was at Twentynine Palms, California, set on a large dry lake in the center of the Mojave Desert. Just off the field was a 300-foot ridge which caught the late afternoon wind and converted it to an updraft which acted as an "elevator" for the gliders. After being towed to an altitude of several thousand feet, the glider pilot could practice his maneuvers as he slowly floated down. Then, turning toward the ridge, he would find the "elevator" and climb back to three thousand feet before moving out over the desert to continue his practice.

At fields like this, the trainees constantly practiced precision landing, using civilian soarplanes and Barringer's converted light trainers. There was a white line drawn near the center of the runway, and the glider pilots were expected to land with the nose-wheel directly on the line. Those who failed to do so had to pull their gliders up to the line by hand amid the jeering of their more skillful comrades.

On January 24, 1943, Major Barringer took off from Puerto Rico in a C-47 "Dakota" en route to North Africa, where he was to coordinate glider activities in the upcoming airborne invasion of Sicily. His plane disappeared in a cold front in which severe turbulence had been reported. No trace of it was ever found.

To replace Barringer as his civilian adviser for gliders, General Arnold chose Barringer's close friend, the socially prominent Richard duPont. An internationally known glider pilot who at that time held several distance and altitude records, young duPont would set a new glider record and then lend his glider to his friend Lewin Barringer to see whether he could beat it. In spite of a Washington columnist's sneers about Arnold's appointing his friends as heads of the glider program, Richard duPont was eminently qualified to advise the commanding general on glider pilot training and glider design.

By the summer of 1943 the Waco CG-4A glider was coming off the assembly line in large numbers. Although the major contractors were mostly aircraft companies (one, however, was a refrigerator manufacturer), they had never before turned out aircraft in such large numbers. In addition, their supervision of the subcontractors who made such parts as wings, fuselages, or tails was inadequate, with poor quality control. Air Corps procurement was a scandal, as the cost of a glider ranged from $15,000 to $1.7 million (the latter price was paid to one manufacturer for the production of a single glider, which was later rejected). Because of the urgent need for gliders for the invasion of France, now scheduled for May, 1944, even the most inefficient manufacturers were permitted to keep their contracts and turn out gliders. Anyone with a woodworking or metal assembly facility could get a piece of the pie that Washington was so freely offering: furniture manufacturers, piano companies, makers of pool tables and canoes, even a coffin manufacturer, all turned out parts for the Waco glider.

Inevitably there was a tragedy. On August 1, 1943, a Waco glider made by a firm in St. Louis, Missouri, lost a wing over that city while carrying the mayor, members of the city council, and military officials. They were all killed. The inquiry disclosed that a subcontractor, who was a coffin manufacturer, had delivered an underspecification fitting that held the main spar to the wing. This had broken loose in flight, causing the wing to crumble.

Meanwhile, the first CG-4As were being delivered to the advanced tactical glider flying schools, where the future glider pilots were meeting them for the first time. It was a frightening sight. They were so big. The wings of each glider were almost eighty-four feet long, only eleven feet shorter than the C-47 that would tow it. The slab-sided fuselage stretched over forty-eight feet from the rounded Plexiglas-enclosed nose, in which the pilot and copilot sat, to the monstrous tail that stood more than twelve feet above the ground. The entire structure was covered with a gray-green painted fabric: tail, wings, and welded steel-tube fuselage. It had been designed to carry thirteen armed infantrymen, or a jeep and five men, or two men and a special 105-mm. howitzer. The useful payload was 3,750 pounds—one-half that of a Horsa and less than one-quarter that of the Hamilcar.

The nose of the Waco glider was hinged at the top to allow it to be raised for loading and unloading. The locking mechanism which kept it closed in flight was inadequate and frequently broke after a hard landing. Since all glider landings tended to be "controlled crashes," all too often a jeep or cannon would be propelled out of the front as the rear cable which secured it lifted the nose *and* the two glider pilots strapped in their seats! To have this happen under enemy fire was an extremely unnerving experience.

Flight instrumentation in the glider was minimal: an airspeed, vertical speed, and turn and bank indicator were thought sufficient for the pilot to keep his position behind the towplane and to land safely. There was also a magnetic compass, but as one glider pilot pointed out, "There was only one place we were going to navigate to by ourselves, and that was down."

A slow airspeed on the approach was vital in landing in small fields. The pilots had an understandable tendency to dive at high speeds when under fire, to try to get on the ground as quickly as possible. However, the angle of descent could be increased without excess airspeed by using the "spoilers," rectangular air brakes—one on each upper wing—which could be raised or lowered by a lever next to the pilot's and copilot's seats.

Three overhead crank pulleys set trim tabs on the rudder, elevators, and ailerons to relieve the pressure on the control wheel and make flying on tow easier. The towrope was made of one-inch diameter nylon and was attached to the glider nose and the tug tail by massive metal fittings. In flight, the 300-foot rope stretched by as much as forty-five feet like a giant rubber band. One of a glider pilot's worst fears— and it sometimes happened—was that the huge metal fitting would come loose from the towplane and fly back at the glider at high speed. Unless the rope release lever was pulled quickly, the fitting would smash through the windshield, tear off a wing, or break the main strut. Trying to dive under it would only allow it to loop over the fuselage and rip off the tail.

Although parachutes were worn by the American and British glider pilots during training, it was a point of honor not to use them in combat, since the airborne troopers—the glider infantry—did not have them. Besides, the only escape doors in a Waco glider were in the back half of the fuselage, and no one wanted to try to run the gauntlet of a dozen or more heavily armed soldiers whose only chance for survival was to keep the glider pilot at the controls.

After the delicate soarplanes they had flown in the California desert, the Waco CG-4A looked ugly and mean to the glider pilots, but it was the beginning of a great love affair. Besides—like themselves—the glider was considered expendable.

At Lubbock, Texas, the transition course to military combat gliders consisted of approximately forty hours of solo and dual flying, during the day and at night. The clumsy-looking Wacos turned out to be surprisingly easy to fly. In smooth air, if one was alert enough to stay out of the turbulent slipstream directly behind the towplane, tows of several hours' duration could be flown with little strain. But if one unfortunately allowed the glider to sink into the slipstream, the violent vortices there would cause even the most heavily loaded glider to oscillate helplessly at the end of the towrope like a tailless kite in a strong wind. Only with great difficulty could one climb back out of the slipstream or dive below it. In most cases there was so little control that the only solution was to pull the towrope release, wave good-bye to the towplane, and start searching for an appropriate landing field. Although the CG-4A did not have the high glide ratio of the soarplane and therefore the landing had to be accomplished quickly, all landings at the advanced fields were made on concrete runways or the grass strips on both sides of them. There were too few Waco gliders available to risk them in practicing landings at small unprepared fields.

With the Waco gliders coming out of the factories at an increasing rate and the training of the glider pilots well under way, some attention was now given to the next generation of military combat gliders. Hawley Bowlus, a well-known prewar manufacturer of sport gliders, had designed a flying-wing glider—the all-wood twin tail XCG-16. It could carry either fifteen soliders or a jeep behind clamshell doors in each wing. The initial test of the glider had been successful, and Richard duPont went out to participate in the first test flights of the glider in the low-tow position below the B-24's slipstream. On September 11, 1943, while the bomber and glider (in the high-tow position) were at 4,000 feet, the glider started its descent through the slipstream. A sharp jerk on the towrope shifted the sandbags which were being used as ballast to the rear of the glider. With the flying wing oscillating badly and uncontrollably, the pilot released the towrope only to find himself in a flat spin. He gave the order to jump and, although two of the men bailed out successfully, by the time duPont leaped, the glider was apparently too low for his parachute to fill. He, the pilot, the copilot, and one other soldier were killed.

To replace him as civilian assistant for gliders, General Arnold appointed duPont's brother, Major A. Felix duPont, Jr., who was then serving in the Transport Command in Washington.

After receiving their silver wings with the "G" on the badge (which they always claimed stood for "guts"), the new glider pilots were placed in holding pools at Louisville, Kentucky, and at Victorville, California, until the expansion of Troop Carrier Command created a sufficient number of new C-47 groups to which they could be assigned. When they reached their new outfit, they started to learn the technique of cooperation between glider and towplane flying in formation. They practiced night flying using only the pale blue formation lights on the towplane's wings to guide by, landing at night by the weak light of a few flare pots. They quickly abandoned the high-speed, 100-mile-an-hour "blitz" landing they had been taught at advanced glider school. It was obvious that the enemy would not be kind enough to provide 5,000-foot concrete runways for them to land on, and it was a form of suicide to bring a CG-4A into a 400-foot-long field at night at such a high rate of speed. The new technique, taught by a former stunt flier, Lieutenant Colonel Michael C. "Mike" Murphy, was to bring the loaded glider in on its final approach at about seventy miles an hour, to slip it (one wing low while holding the opposite rudder) to get over any tall trees at the downwind end of the field, to get the wheels on the ground as quickly as possible, and then, using brakes and nosing the glider up on the skids, to stop as quickly as possible. If necessary, ground-looping by putting a wing into the ground was allowed if collision with trees or other obstacles seemed unavoidable. They learned how to put the fuselage between two trees, allowing the wings to take the force of the impact and to stop the fuselage without damage to passengers or cargo. In the pinewoods of North Carolina around Fort Bragg and Camp Mackall, they practiced incessantly during the fall and winter of 1943 to get ready for the battles that were ahead. They left a lot of broken gliders in small fields and in the dreaded "Pea Patch"—a stump-filled wooded field at Fort Bragg—but when the New Year dawned, they were ready to go.

As quickly as the new troop-carrier groups were declared ready for combat, they were posted abroad. Most of them went to Europe, the air echelon flying there in new C-47s by way of South America and Africa. The glider pilots boarded ships on the East Coast, taking the long thirteen-day trip to England in convoys.

As one of them walked up the gangplank of the *Queen Mary*, he suddenly remembered that he had never fired a gun. His friend told him not to worry about it: "We'll get on-the-job training."

3
Sicilian Vespers

It was impossible—even mad!

Colonel George Chatterton, commanding the British glider pilots in North Africa, listened with mounting horror and disbelief as Major-General G. F. Hopkinson outlined the plan. Ever since he had taken over the 1st Airborne Division after Browning moved to General Dwight D. Eisenhower's staff, "Hoppy" Hopkinson had been anxious to get the division committed to the assault on Sicily. Without Browning's knowledge, he had "sold" General Bernard L. Montgomery on a night glider assault to capture a vital bridge near Syracuse. Later, parachutists and more gliders would be sent in to seize crossings at Catania and Augusta. Excited and pleased at the prospect of action, the feisty little major-general brushed aside Chatterton's protests that his men had not flown for over three months and had had little experience in night flying. "We will soon put that right," Hopkinson said. "The U.S. Air Force are going to supply tugs and gliders."

Stunned at this revelation, Chatterton began to protest anew. His men had had little enough training on British Horsas, but none at all on American Wacos. To send them in at night in unfamiliar gliders . . .

When Hopkinson replied, it was in a stern, uncompromising voice. "Now look here, Colonel Chatterton, I'm going to leave you for half an hour, and in that time you can study the photographs. If at the end of that time you still feel that this is too difficult for you, you can consider yourself relieved of your command." He stalked angrily from the room.

The aerial photographs of the proposed landing zones were sickening: uneven rock-filled fields sloping sharply on the side of a mountain. There were steep cliffs on the likely approaches; the fields were surrounded by high stone walls and spotted with olive groves. A more unsuitable spot for a mass glider landing would have been hard to find, and to attempt it at night with men who had not been in a glider for three months, flying strange American Wacos, was suicidal.

Chatterton was faced with a brutal choice. The operation would take place with or without him. Hopkinson was determined to get the airborne division into action lest they never be used at all, and Montgomery would use them because they were available. If Chatterton were to be relieved of his command, there would be no one with his experience to take over. He had to stand by his men at any cost.

When Hopkinson returned, nothing more was said about the difficulties of the mission. "He was like a little boy," Chatterton noted. "He was so pleased."

Three months before the airborne invasion of Sicily, Chatterton frantically went to work to prepare his men. The first problem was gliders—there were none available at their camp on the Mascara plains. When a shipment of Wacos arrived at Oran, he sent fifty glider pilots there to uncrate and assemble them. With only a manual and one American corporal to instruct them, the British glider pilots put together thirty gliders which were picked up by American C-47s and flown off to the troop-carrier airfields.

It was decided to bring out a number of Horsa gliders from England to North Africa—a long-distance tow of 1,200 miles, something which had never been attempted before. In addition to the strain of the ten-hour flight, the Halifax-

Horsa combinations had to fly through bad weather and evade enemy fighters. On several occasions when they were intercepted by German planes, the glider pilot made the brave decision to cut off tow and take his chances in the sea to allow the tug plane to escape.

Sergeant Harry Antonopoulos had the misfortune to ditch twice. The first time, a towrope snapped and the Horsa went down in the waters off the coast of Spain. A corvette spotted the three-man crew the next day and took them back to England. A week later Antonopoulos was back at the controls of a Horsa, accompanied by a copilot and a relief pilot, when the Halifax tug was attacked by two German Focke-Wolf bombers over the Bay of Biscay.

"We took evasive action," Antonopoulos told the author, "following the tug through some very steep turns. Finally, the towplane pilot spoke over the intercom and said, 'It's no good. Would you please pull off?' I pulled the rope release lever and the Halifax quickly climbed into the clouds and disappeared. One Focke-Wolf was just below me, and I dove at him. I don't know what was in my mind, but I thought, 'I'll get this bastard.' It must have worried him because he stopped firing, and at the last second we both turned away.

"There was no problem about landing—I was the greatest ditcher of all time and had written the definitive report on how to do it. We went out the top hatch, inflated the dinghy, and got in. We tied the dinghy to the nose of the glider, which would be much easier to spot from the air, but the waves kept lifting the glider bodily and smacking it down again . . . the dinghy was drifting under one wing and I could see us being hammered into the water, so we cut the rope and drifted away."

For days they huddled in the dinghy, watching the horizon, listening for planes, and seeing nothing. Large waves swamped the rubber raft repeatedly and they were soaked to the skin. Much of their food was spoiled by salt water, and their stomachs refused to hold what little they could swallow. There was continual retching as they bobbed up and down in the heavy swell. The nights were cold and they shivered.

"Until the second day," Antonopoulos continued, "we weren't too worried. We had our rations, a flare pistol, and some rum in a hip flask that my mother had given me, but as the days passed and nothing came along, we started getting a bit despondent. Once a Halifax with a Horsa on tow flew over but failed to see our flares. We saw ships several times, but they did not see us. At first we were too proud—I don't know what you might call it—we weren't going to give ourselves up to a German ship.

"On the fourth day we were turned over by a huge wave, and we lost our food, the flare pistol—almost everything. That changed the whole complexion of things; from then on, we were really desperate. We had no means of attracting attention or feeding ourselves, and we started getting thin and weak. Paddie Conway got sunstroke and started telling us the story of his life. He kept offering to go over the side and leave us all the rations (which we had lost anyway), but we talked him out of it."

The time seemed endless and their position more and more hopeless. Their bodies were covered with painful saltwater rashes; their tongues were thick and it was difficult to swallow the Ovaltine tablets because of the lack of saliva to dissolve them. The dinghy was slowly losing air, and it took most of their remaining strength to keep it filled with a bellows three or four times a day. They were often delirious. "In the daytime," Antonopoulos said, "I could not focus my eyes too well and did not realize it for there was nothing to focus on except the horizon. At night, I would look up and see six moons in a row."

On the eleventh day, they awoke to find themselves in a thick fog. "Suddenly we heard the sound of an engine, a sort of chug-chug-chug sound. Out of the mist came this little fishing trawler . . . we had whistles and I started blowing mine. We hadn't much strength and, although I thought I was blowing very hard, I wasn't. There was a fellow leaning on the rail of the boat, and I remember the look of surprise on his face when he spotted us. Soon they were alongside and pulling us aboard. They were Spaniards and all I could do was to remember some long-forgotten Latin and say 'aqua.' One of the men corrected me, saying 'agua,' but they gave us water."

When Antonopoulos arrived back in England, sympathetic comrades encouraged him: "Keep trying, Harry. You'll make North Africa yet!"

While the Horsa pilots were struggling across the Atlantic, Colonel Chatterton was working desperately to prepare his men for the mission. Not only the Waco gliders but the towplanes and their pilots were being encountered for the first time. He could handle the troop-carrier people, but to train his men in flying the unfamiliar gliders, he decided to use some of the American glider pilots then in North Africa.

The American glider pilots seemed to have been in Tunisia almost by accident. They had sailed from Newport News, Virginia, in late December, 1942—destination unknown. After a stop in Rio de Janeiro, they had rounded Africa and headed for Australia. When they got within a day's sail of Sydney, they suddenly turned northwest toward India. Although the rumor mill had them destined for Burma, the ship sailed into the harbor at Aden and then on to Port Suez. Here they debarked after forty-three days on the ship and took a rickety train north to Ismailia. "We had one glider pilot on board," Flight Officer Wesley Hare told the author, "who never got out of his bunk during the whole trip. Joe C. was his name, and he was the smallest man in the outfit. He had this terrible fear of the water; he just couldn't look at it. We used to bring him food, and once we sent a doctor down to check him. Nothing could drag him out of that bed."

Three months later they had moved to Tunisia and

were instructing the British in flying Waco gliders. "One day," Flight Officer Bob Wilson remembered, "there was a notice on the squadron bulletin board asking for five volunteers for detached service with the British. Nothing was said about flying into Sicily, just 'detached service' . . . my name was fourth on the list.

"When we reached the British camp, we were greeted by a Colonel Chatterton, who was in command of that glider operation. He gathered us together and thanked us for volunteering for the invasion of Sicily. That's about as close to being scared to death as I have ever felt.

"We were issued red berets and Sten guns, which we had never fired before. One day, on our way to the firing range, we encountered a caravan of cars, so we got off the road and jumped under the wing of a glider to stay out of the sun. It turned out to be General Montgomery coming to review the airborne troops. The general got out of the car and we could see him talking to Colonel Chatterton and the two of them looking in our direction. The colonel must have told Monty that we were part of the Yanks who had volunteered to fly into Sicily, because suddenly the general fired a salute at us. That really made me feel good."

Originally the plans for the Sicily invasion had called for an assault by the British Eighth Army on the southeast shore, to be followed two days later by an American landing on the western beaches. Both of these were to involve paratroop drops to hit the beach defenses from the rear, and the American assault had been put off two days since there were not enough planes to carry the British and American paratroopers in one lift. Dissatisfied with these plans, General Montgomery had made drastic changes at the last minute. He convinced Eisenhower that the two beachheads were too far apart and that it would be better if the Americans would land in the central sector near Gela at the same time as the British came ashore. Since the paratroopers were too lightly

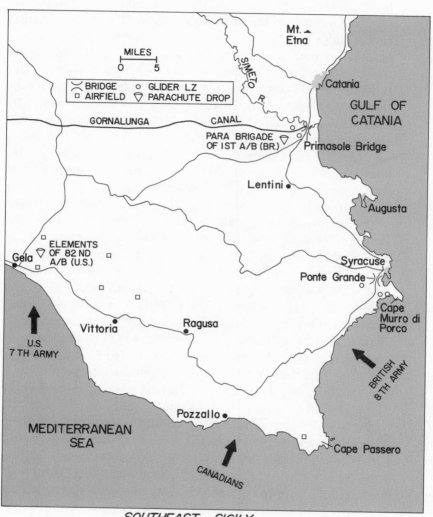

MILES
0   5

BRIDGE   ○ GLIDER LZ
AIRFIELD   ▽ PARACHUTE DROP

SIMETO R.

Mt. Etna

Catania

GULF OF
CATANIA

GORNALUNGA   CANAL

PARA BRIGADE
OF IST A/B (BR.)   ▽ ○   Primasole Bridge

Lentini ●

Augusta

ELEMENTS
OF 82 ND
A/B (U.S.)

Gela ●

Syracuse

Ponte Grande →

Cape
Murro di
Porco

U.S.
7 TH ARMY

Vittoria ●   Ragusa ●

BRITISH
8 TH ARMY

Pozzallo ●

MEDITERRANEAN
SEA

Cape Passero

CANADIANS

SOUTHEAST SICILY

armed to overcome any strong beach defenses such as pill-boxes, their proper role was to drop farther inland to cut off any German or Italian counterattack. It was also decided that a glider assault (and this was probably Hopkinson's suggestion) would take place on the vital coastal ridge just south of Syracuse. The addition of the glider mission at the last minute was unfortunate, since the only American troop-carrier wing trained in towing gliders had already modified their planes to carry the British paratroopers. Time was too short to permit a switch.

Overall coordination of the airborne plans was in the hands of General Browning, whose headquarters unfortunately were several hundred miles away from the troop-carrier airfields, making such coordination difficult. Also, Browning and other British officers tended to take a rather patronizing attitude toward their American allies, whom they considered inexperienced in airborne operations.

"They had no great respect for our soldierly qualities, and even less for our knowledge of modern warfare on the grand scale," said Major-General Matthew B. Ridgway, commanding officer of the United States 82nd Airborne Division. This disdainful attitude of the British, which engendered resentment in their American counterparts, led to a number of disputes. "Practically all the troop-carrier aircraft were United States," Ridgway later wrote, "and we didn't have enough C-47 aircraft to fill the minimum combat needs of both United States and British airborne forces who were to jump into Sicily. Every plane allotted the British therefore meant less combat strength my men could take into battle. A running argument developed with General Browning as to how these planes were to be allotted between my division and the British 1st Airborne Division. I also began to feel that General Browning from his post at Supreme Headquarters [where he was General Eisenhower's airborne commander] was in a position to exert an undue influence both on the allocation of aircraft to American airborne troops and on their actual tactical deployment."

Ridgway had other reasons for concern. In North Africa the paratroop operations of the 82nd Airborne had been on the scale of a battalion, but in Sicily it would be the first airborne operation on a divisional level. In addition, for the first time it would be taking place in the air above a fleet that might be under enemy attack and over beaches being assaulted by landing troops. Worried about the possibility of friendly fire on the troop-carrier planes as they came over at night, he expressed his anxiety in letters to Generals Dwight Eisenhower and George Patton. The naval commanders offered to guarantee that no ship would open fire if the aircraft approached no closer than five miles and would fly at an altitude of six thousand feet or more. But at that height the planes would be picked up by enemy radar, so it was decided that the troop-carrier columns would fly at low altitude no closer than five miles from any of the naval convoys. The ground-force commanders accepted the responsibility of informing their men not to fire on any aircraft unless it was definitely identified as hostile. The orders were sent out warning the ground troops and the Navy of the coming airborne mission and the routes that the planes would take, but Ridgway was still worried: "Whether green troops in the dark of night and the excitement of their first battle would remember the safe-conduct, no one could tell." Also, there were a large number of merchant ships in the invasion force, and their crews tended to be very jittery about low-flying planes at night. It was known that, after dark, unauthorized firing by any vessel would inevitably mean that all ships in the vicinity would open fire.

In spite of detailed planning and widespread warnings, the stage was set for one of the most tragic incidents of the war.

Two days before the glider attack on the bridge at Syracuse, which had been given the code name of "Ladbroke," the wind began to rise and blow gale force. Since the troop-carrier pilots had refused to come any closer to the Sicilian coast than three thousand yards for fear that losses to flak would endanger later lifts, Colonel Chatterton was worried about the effect the strong wind would have on the glider landings. If the release altitude was too low, the gliders would never make the shore and would come down in the sea. If it was too high, some of them would overshoot the assigned fields and land too far inland among the olive groves and cliffs. Finally he decided to raise the release altitude to 1,900 feet. As for the possibility that the strong, gusty winds would break the towropes, one could only pray it would not happen.

A few hours before takeoff, one of Chatterton's officers asked him to inspect the intercom wires which were wound around the towrope and secured at both ends to provide telephone communication between the glider and the towplane. As Chatterton examined the wire on one towrope, he noticed black insulating tape wrapped around it near one of the fittings. He unwound the tape and found that the wire had been cut. A careful check revealed that several other intercoms had been tampered with. According to Chatterton, an Italian-American mechanic had tried to prevent an attack on his country of origin. The intercom connections were reattached. (The saboteur did not realize that the lack of radio communication with the towplane would not have prevented the glider from reaching its objective; indeed, in training flights the intercoms had proved to be notoriously unreliable.)

On the night of July 9, 1943, the wind was gusting to forty-five miles per hour in North Africa. At the six airfields that would launch the glider assault, heavy swirls of gray dust covered the dirt runways and spattered against the sides of the planes and gliders. On these fields 144 planes, one-fourth of them British, stood ready to tow 136 Wacos and 8 Horsas through the dark, turbulent night to Sicily. All the glider pilots were British, but twenty-eight American glider

pilots who had helped train them in the Waco gliders volunteered to fly the mission as copilots. Knowing that the British
had less than five hours' total flying time in the American
glider and that only one hour of this had been at night, they
had chosen to take their place in the right-hand seat to lend
the mission the benefit of their experience. Also, there was
a certain eagerness, a certain valor of ignorance, as no one
knew what lay ahead.

Each glider was assigned to a specific mission and a
designated landing field. Six of the Horsas were to land near
the bridge called the Ponte Grande, in a *coup de main* attack.
The Wacos and the other two Horsas would carry General
Hopkinson and the British Air Landing Brigade, along with
seven jeeps and six six-pounder guns to reinforce the attack
in the area south of Syracuse.

Flight Officer Bob Wilson watched a trailer being loaded
into his glider, then peeked under the lashed-down cover.
"It really gave me a shock: it was material for marking graves
—canvas bags, tags, and wooden crosses. Somebody already
knew that we would not all be coming back."

Sergeant H. N. "Andy" Andrews worried about the excess load he would be carrying in his glider. Instead of thirteen
passengers, there were fifteen, including two colonels and a
chaplain. Conscious of the meager forty-five minutes he had
spent at the controls of a Waco at night, he was happy to
meet his American copilot, Flight Officer Morris B. Kyle of
West Virginia, who had had hundreds of hours in Waco
gliders and powered aircraft. Andrews could not remember
whether he had fully loaded his Sten gun magazines—something which was done at the last minute to keep from over-
loading the weak springs—but now it was too late. It was
time to take off.

"The tugs revved up," Andrews wrote to the author,
"and were immediately lost in clouds of dust. The first part
of the takeoff was into a sandstorm with zero visibility. We
were dragged through this dirty yellow wall, mesmerized by

the short length of towrope that we could see. It seemed ages before the overloaded glider gained enough speed to stagger up above the dust cloud and line up with the tug."

They were off at last; there was a sense of relief that the waiting was finally over. As the formation made one large sweep over the airfield to allow the later elements to close, "Andy" Andrews caught a glimpse of some Roman ruins painted pink by the setting sun.

As the pilots settled down to the four-hour flight, the long line of towplanes and gliders was already being shortened by the inevitable mishaps. One plane had made a forced landing when the jeep in its glider broke loose from its mooring and threatened to shake the glider apart. Five of the British transport planes were forced to turn back because their overloaded gliders were acting strangely.

Their first checkpoint was Malta. They flew so low that the spray from the Mediterranean washed over the planes and gliders, the American planes at an altitude below 250 feet and the slightly faster British tugs above them but still below 500 feet. In the gusty air as the gale whipped the sea below them, it was difficult for the gliders to hold their positions. At one point a horrified Chatterton found himself flying alongside his towplane.

The sun had set and it was very dark when they sighted the flashing beacon on the eastern tip of Malta, their turning point. By this time the formation had degenerated, some planes being blown far off course, many straggling, and others overrunning formations ahead of them owing to the different airspeeds. On the island, the Allied commander, General Eisenhower, had gone up into the hills to watch them fly over: "In the wind and storm it was difficult for them to keep direction. Our plotting board in the air operations room showed that many planes and tows were blown far off course, but generally the columns kept on target and when the one we were watching had passed overhead, we returned to headquarters to await reports. . . . The first messages in the morning were a mixture of good and bad. A number of the gliders participating in the airborne attack on the British front had been cast loose too far from their targets and the high wind had dropped some into the sea. We feared a heavy loss of life. . . ."

From Malta it was seventy miles to landfall at Cape Passero on the southeast tip of Sicily. In this run two more gliders were lost: a Waco was accidentally released from its tug and a Horsa had broken its towrope in the turbulent air. Both disappeared into the stormy sea below.

As they turned left and crept up the eastern coast of Sicily, searchlights appeared and antiaircraft fire began all along the beaches up to Syracuse. The fire was inaccurate but unnerving to the inexperienced troop-carrier pilots. The shoreline and release points were obscured by huge clouds of dust, whipped up by the forty-mile-an-hour wind. Unable to see the shore and thus judge their distance, the pilots became confused. Some turned west to get around the dust cloud and tried to see the land silhouetted under the low quarter moon. Others climbed to give the gliders more altitude to compensate for the gusting wind. Quickly the formations broke up, with some planes and gliders even turning back through the oncoming columns. As usual the intercoms were unreliable, at least one-third of them having failed during the trip, so that the towpilots were unable to give a verbal signal to cast off. Releases were made at haphazard points, and soon the air was filled with gliders at all altitudes and moving in all directions, desperately seeking some landmark by which to orient themselves. As the gliders were released, the towplanes dropped their ropes and turned south toward home.

Bob Wilson told the author that he had been so fascinated by the red tracers and flak that he was startled when his British first pilot asked him if this was the proper spot to cut off. " 'Go ahead,' I said, 'you have to make the decision. This is your show.' He hit the release lever and turned immediately toward the island. Then, for the first time, I saw how far out we were. It was a terrible sight because I just knew we would never make it."

Since he had had many more hours in a Waco than the first pilot, Wilson violated one of the unwritten rules of the air and talked the British glider pilot into a landing in the sea. Just before they hit the water, he said, "Pull that nose up and stall this thing out. Drag the tail and we won't hit hard—at least not in the forward direction."

"He did a fine job, but as soon as we splatted down, we were under water. The glider sank until only the wing was afloat. . . . When we crawled up on the wing, there were two men missing. . . . I swam back down through an open door to look for them, but they were gone."

From the light of parachute flares and the searchlights that were sweeping the water, Wilson estimated that they were about two miles from the beach. There were eight of them clinging to the wing and being frequently washed off by the heavy swells. "After we swam back, climbed aboard, and counted noses for the umpteenth time," Wilson said to the author, "I told them to kick holes in the wing fabric to anchor their feet. We got soaking wet when the waves hit us, but at least we did not have to swim back."

After eight hours in the water, they were picked up by a British cruiser, transferred to a transport, and taken to Algiers.

The confusion caused by the high wind, the dust and smoke, the antiaircraft fire, and the inexperience and poor navigation of the tug pilots was fatal to the mission. At least sixty-nine Waco gliders came down in the wind-whipped sea, and over two hundred men—glider pilots and passengers—drowned. Seven Wacos and three Horsas vanished without a trace, including one copiloted by Flight Officer Joe C., who was so deathly afraid of the water.

Colonel George Chatterton ditched into the sea and was pulled from the submerged cabin onto the wing. Annoyed by persistent machine-gun fire from the beach (the Italian gunners fortunately aimed too high), he and his passengers swam ashore. As they pulled themselves onto the rocky beach, a plane hit the water nearby and exploded. The whole sea caught fire and all the exhausted Chatterton could think of was the lighted brandy on a Christmas pudding.

Trying to keep his voice as calm as possible, Sergeant "Andy" Andrews told his passengers, "I don't think we are going to make it. You had better take your equipment off and blow up your life jackets, but don't undo your safety belts yet."

"I had no sooner said this, when Colonel Henniker (whose nickname was 'Honker') barked out in his best orderly room voice, 'Don't be a damned fool. We have to get on land. We can't get wet!' "

Being a good soldier, Andrews reconsidered the situation. There seemed to be only one hope. He had spotted a searchlight located on a promontory that he might be able to reach if he stretched his glide. The place was undoubtedly occupied by enemy troops, but it was either land on an Italian strongpoint or come down in the sea and face the colonel's wrath. Deciding quickly, Andrews banked the glider toward the searchlight.

"Luckily," Andrews wrote the author, "the searchlight crew were so interested in picking out my chums, most of whom had come down in the sea, that the light was depressed and they never spotted us. We landed among them with hardly a bump—Morris Kyle [his copilot] kept repeating 'Take it slow—keep the airspeed down'—and the whisper of the slipstream gave them little warning.

"For a moment, there was a deathly silence, then two shots rang out. No one was hit, but we moved as if the shots were the start of a hundred-yard dash. The firing was from the direction of the sea, so most of us bolted out the other door. Unfortunately, the chaplain, Father Hourigan, and one of the signallers left by the door nearest the enemy and were captured. The next day, when the invasion fleet appeared off the coast, a panicky Italian soldier threw a grenade into the room where they were confined. The signaller jumped under a bed and was saved, but Father Hourigan was killed."

After a futile counterattack to rescue the two missing men, which succeeded only in setting the glider on fire when one of the colonels lobbed a phosphorous grenade short, the party reluctantly abandoned the attempt. "Everyone felt bad about it, but we all knew that the bridge was the main objective and it appeared to be a good way off."

Only 54 of the 144 gliders which had set out on the mission landed in Sicily—four of them in their designated landing zones. Of the six Horsas that were to attack the Ponte Grande, two landed in the immediate vicinity of their target. One, piloted by the popular Captain J. N. C. Denholm, came in downwind, hit the bank of the canal at high speed, and blew up, killing all on board. Inspecting the wreckage the next day, Chatterton found that "the crew and passengers had been blown forward as if down a funnel but of the pilot there was no sign. . . . I stood looking at this macabre and tragic pile of bodies. . . ."

Crashed and burned gliders were everywhere. One of them was stuck in the top of a tree, with a jeep and a dead driver still inside. Another had been carrying a six-pounder antitank gun which had burst loose on impact, crushing the pilot. Still another was smashed against the face of a cliff; the pilot and copilot were strapped in their seats dead, but the passengers had survived.

In the midst of this chaotic scene, there was one tragicomic incident: one of the Horsas which landed about a mile from the bridge had been flown from England and had traveled more than 2,000 miles over the Atlantic, the desert and mountains of North Africa, and finally the wind-ripped course to Sicily. Having finally glided through the darkness to a landing in an orchard with a minimum of damage, they found that they were unable to remove the glider's tail to unload the jeep and ammunition. Unwilling to undertake the long, noisy task of sawing off the tail, they employed the emergency technique of wrapping a strip of Primacord explosive around the tail and setting it off. It worked magnificently. Not only did it blow off the tail but it blew up the glider—jeep, ammunition, and all. The horrified crew and their passengers could only stand and watch their precious cargo burn in the Sicilian night.

One Horsa glider, piloted by Staff Sergeant D. P. "Galp" Galpin, landed close to the bridge, having been guided down by a helpful Italian searchlight which followed it right down to ground level, lighting up the bridge and the adjacent fields. Without wasting time worrying about the five missing Horsas, the platoon leader assembled his men and attacked the pillboxes protecting the 400-foot-long concrete bridge. They split into two parties, one of which swam the river and the canal to take the enemy on his flank and the other making a frontal attack. The Italian defenders, shocked by the surprise assault, quickly surrendered.

During that nervous night the little group of thirty men held the bridge and waited to be relieved by the airlanding brigade. Early in the morning they were reinforced by the crews and passengers of two other gliders that had landed some miles away and by others from Wacos that had come down to the north.

One of the reinforcements was Flight Officer Samuel Fine of Flushing, New York. His Waco, carrying twelve men and an ammunition cart, had crash-landed in a small tree-filled field. "Immediately upon landing," he wrote the author, "the enemy opened fire with machineguns and rifles shooting into the glider as we came to a full stop. A machinegun burst caught me on the right shoulder, just grazing the skin. As one of the airborne troopers emerged, he was shot in the back. . . ."

Prompt return fire by a Bren gun discouraged the hidden

enemy, allowing the glider men to unload as much equipment and ammunition as they could carry and to start for the bridge. Momentarily stalled by a pillbox across their path, they decided that "all the glider pilots and about forty of the airborne troopers would circle the pillbox and head for the bridge," Fine recalls. "Flight Officer Russell D. Parks and I were the only Americans in the group. . . .

"As we approached the bridge, we could see the red berets of the airborne forces who had taken the bridge after a fast and furious struggle. They had cut the wires that the enemy had installed to blow it up. It was 0700 hours, July the 10th." Some of their group, including Parks, had stayed behind to attack a machine gun in a tower that had barred their approach to the bridge. Fine did not see Parks again until they met in Syracuse the next day.

By midmorning the enemy garrison had motored down from Syracuse to attack the weakly defended bridge. The Italian commander, dressed in a gold-braid-encrusted uniform, drove haughtily up to the barrier and demanded that it be raised. A second later every gun in the vicinity was fired into his car; the survivors were hustled into a nearby blockhouse. "Our first sight of the counterattack," Sam Fine wrote, "was the sight of enemy troops creeping down on us from the northwest. We held them for some time and then they began shelling us with three-inch mortar shells. Almost every shell hit the bridge with remarkable accuracy. . . . Finally, we had to abandon the bridge and take positions along the embankments of the river and the canal." In addition to the mortars, a small field gun had been brought up to harass the defenders. One of its first shells hit the blockhouse, killing all the Italian prisoners.

The unequal struggle could have only one conclusion. By the middle of the afternoon the north bank of the canal had been overrun. Some of the airborne tried to swim to the south bank, but few made it. The others, without ammunition or grenades, surrendered. Then the thirteen men holding out gallantly in a small dry ditch on the south bank of the canal fired their last shots and gave up.

With one-third of their ranks killed and one-third wounded, the last group of "Red Berets" and glider pilots held out on the bank of the river. "We were covered from all sides," Fine recalled, "with no hope of escape. With the few rounds of ammunition we had left, we foiled an attempt by the enemy to blast us out with hand grenades. All I had was two bullets for my .45 caliber automatic. I had already used up all the ammunition for the Italian rifle taken from one of the prisoners, so I tossed it into the river. . . . At 3:15 P.M., we surrendered. . . ."

Stripped of their pens, pencils, watches, and trinkets, the survivors were marched cross-country toward Syracuse. Sam Fine remembers how relieved the Italians were: "They had had more than enough from this brave band of fighters."

Their captivity was short-lived. Less than an hour later, they ran into a British captain and a Sten gunner who fired on the Italian guards and captured and disarmed them.

Thus, a handful of the five hundred men who had been assigned to the mission had captured the Ponte Grande, held it in the face of overwhelming odds, lost it for an hour, and then recaptured it for good.

Sergeant "Andy" Andrews and his party arrived at the bridge too late to help defend it. They had been delayed by enemy fire en route and had gallantly attacked and captured a large Italian gun emplacement. They showed up late in the afternoon with many prisoners and a donkey cart containing Colonel "Honker" Henniker and a glider pilot, both of whom had been badly hurt in the fight. The wounded were cared for and the others sent to a defensive position on the far side of the bridge. "The march across the bridge," Andrew recalls, "started with everyone's morale very high, but the talk and chatter died to a pregnant silence as the bodies of friend and foe were seen. Some were in grotesque positions like posed waxworks. Their last earthly actions were frozen in nightmarish attitudes that the memory cannot forget."

As they passed the main crossroads, the airborne soldiers smartened their pace when they spotted General Hopkinson standing there, looking, according to Andrews, "rather like a policeman. He appeared small and tired. As he returned our salute, I could not help interpreting the look in his eyes with his own unspoken words, 'Thank God, that's over. Not many left, are there?' " Hopkinson had also landed in the sea and had been dragged out, spitting water and cursing the American tow pilots. (The following September, General Hopkinson was killed at an advanced outpost in Italy by a machine-gun burst in the head.)

Even as the bridge was being finally secured, in North Africa an armada of planes was taking off to reinforce the American beachhead in Sicily. Four battalions of the 82nd Airborne Division (about 2,000 men) were scheduled to drop near Gela just before midnight. The formation of 144 Dakotas (C-47s) had taken off at 7:00 P.M. from Tunisia.

Twenty-four hours after the high winds had so badly dispersed the glider landings, the storm had dissipated and the sky was calm with a bright quarter moon. Since the whole flight would be over friendly territory, the plane crews and the paratroopers felt themselves safe. This, they thought, would be a "milk run."

General Ridgway was not so certain. He had demanded assurances from the Navy that no antiaircraft fire would be permitted during the time the transport planes would be making their run for the target. At first the Navy (knowing that they had little control over nervous gunners, particularly on the merchant ships) refused; but when Ridgway proposed to cancel the mission, they changed their minds. If the planes avoided the ships bunched off the south coast and made their final run through a narrow corridor over land, antiaircraft fire would be withheld. Still concerned that his men would be fired on by friendly troops, Ridgway got General Patton to issue an order to all his commanders warning them of the paratroop drop in the Gela area. But even this would not be enough.

The air convoy made its turn at Malta and proceeded toward Sicily. In the cabins the paratroopers smoked quietly or slept or peered out of the cabin windows like tourists. There was some isolated antiaircraft fire from single ships along the way, but no damage was done. Nevertheless, some of them thought that this was a bad omen; obviously, the Navy was very trigger-happy that night.

In the ships off the coast of Sicily and on the beaches where the Allied soldiers were fighting fiercely against a stubborn enemy, everyone was jittery. All day there had been air raids by Italian and German planes. Transports had been hit and several destroyers straddled by near misses. In the afternoon, the ammunition ship *Robert Rowan* had taken a direct hit and had exploded in a mountainous gray cloud riddled with red flames. Sinking in the shallow waters, its bow still exposed, the *Rowan* had been left burning, a vivid beacon for the enemy bombers.

Just before 10:00 P.M. the enemy had returned in the worst air raid of the day. In the darkness, flying through the tracers and flak bursts, they had pounded the ships in the harbor and the troops huddled on the beaches. Every gun on every ship and on all the beaches had fired frantically in the darkness at the dimly seen Nazi bombers. Only a few minutes after the enemy had left, the troop-carrier planes crossed the coast and blundered into the area.

Strangely enough, the lead flight got through the narrow two-mile corridor safely, flying at the assigned altitude of one thousand feet. It dropped its paratroopers accurately on the airfield near Gela, but the rest of the formation was unwittingly flying into a slaughterhouse.

Suddenly, somewhere, one machine gun opened fire.

"Nobody knows who fired first," General Ridgway said in an interview with the author, "and probably we never will know. It came either from a ship in the harbor or from the U.S. First Division area. After that everybody opened up. They later said that the Navy had not been notified of the route that the planes would fly, but that's not true because I saw to that myself. Evidently the word had not reached the gun crews of all the ships. Remember, these were not all Navy ships; there were many transports manned by merchant seamen. Probably the best answer is that nervous and excited gunners who had been under heavy attack forgot that friendly planes were to be in the area at that hour and continued firing in the belief that our C-47s were enemy bombers making another attack."

Under the shattering fire, the troop-carrier planes scattered, courageously tried to reform, and then scattered again. They frantically flashed their recognition lights, but these were either ignored by the antiaircraft crews or not seen amid the light of the tracers and the explosion of shells. Eight pilots gave up the attempt to reach the drop zone and turned back. The others dropped the paratroopers as best they could, most of them miles from the airfield that was their objective. Tragically, some of the men drifted into the sea and drowned; others were killed by ground fire as they floated down. Six planes loaded with paratroopers were shot down before their passengers could jump.

Rather than risk running the gauntlet along the narrow land corridor again, many pilots turned directly for the coast and out over the sea. They flew low over the water, taking evasive action, but were easy targets for the naval gunners, who proceeded to blast them out of the sky. Some planes were under fire until they were thirty miles from the Sicilian coast. Of the 144 Dakotas that had taken off from Tunisia, 23 were shot down and 37 others were badly damaged, many beyond repair.

"The legend of a navy which shot from the hip without

distinguishing friend from foe spread widely and lingered long among the troop-carrier units," wrote a U.S. Air Force historian.

The Allied paratroop and glider landings in Sicily were a profound shock to Adolf Hitler. He had denied General Student's request for an airborne attack on Malta, saying, "The day of parachute troops is over," and the British failure to use airborne units in their raids on Dieppe and Saint-Nazaire had convinced him that he had been correct. The paratrooper and glider attack in Sicily impressed him so much, however, that he ordered a rapid expansion of the German airborne forces. But as Student later said gloomily to a British officer, "That change of mind came too late, because by then you had command of the air and airborne troops could not be effectively used in face of a superior air force."

Student was all for immediately counterattacking the Allied landings in Sicily with his two airborne divisions, but Hitler ordered instead that the 1st Parachute Division be sent as ground troops to reinforce the scanty German forces which were fighting there. The division was flown in immediately and dropped behind the German lines south of Catania.

Three hours later British paratroopers followed by gliders dropped on top of them!

The operation was code-named "Fustian"—an unfortunate choice since it means something bombastic or banal. The Primasole Bridge, seven miles south of Catania, was to be seized by the British 1st Parachute Brigade, flown in by American Dakotas. Two hours after the paratroopers had secured the landing fields near the bridge, eight Wacos and eleven Horsa gliders would bring in antitank guns. No one knew that the area selected was now in the hands of Student's tough paratroopers.

The flight had been routine, the weather being calm and

a bright half-moon making navigation easier than it had been on previous missions. The turn at Malta was clearly signaled by a searchlight and, although the air train was fired on by individual ships on the flight to Sicily, no damage was done.

A five-mile-wide danger zone had been designated around the eastern Sicilian coast, and the troop-carrier pilots had been warned to stay well clear of the naval convoys huddled near the beaches. Every precaution had been taken to prevent a recurrence of the disastrous "friendly" fire that had destroyed the paratroop mission. Despite all the warnings, Fustian was not to escape a hostile reception by trigger-happy naval gunners.

Once again the fleet had been subjected to Axis air raids that, though more annoying than damaging, had made the Navy crews very nervous. In addition, there had been an alert against an attack by enemy torpedo bombers and, when the transports flew over, the cargo racks under the wings of the Dakotas were mistaken for torpedoes. The crew of one ship opened fire and, since antiaircraft fire at night is contagious, the rest of the fleet started shooting.

Two transport planes were shot down, one in flames. Nine others were forced to turn back to North Africa either because of damage to the planes or because of the wounded on board; six others gave up the struggle and turned back. Those who pushed on through the "friendly" antiaircraft bursts were now faced with a barrage of hostile fire. All along the coast the enemy sent up a curtain of exploding flak shells and machine-gun tracers. Since the C-47s were unarmed and lacked any armor or even self-sealing fuel tanks, the result was devastating. Nine planes fell in the space of a few minutes. Others wandered blindly up and down the east coast of Sicily looking for a way through the flak barrage. Finally, their gas running low, their checkpoints obscured by smoke and flame, ten of the planes headed back for Tunisia with their passengers still on board. The rest flew

Interior of a Waco CG-4A glider. The seats were removed when a jeep or a cannon was carried. Earlier models had a single control wheel that could be swung from pilot to copilot.

Cockpit of a Waco CG-4A glider. Note the minimal instrumentation. Parachutes were worn on training flights but not on a combat mission.

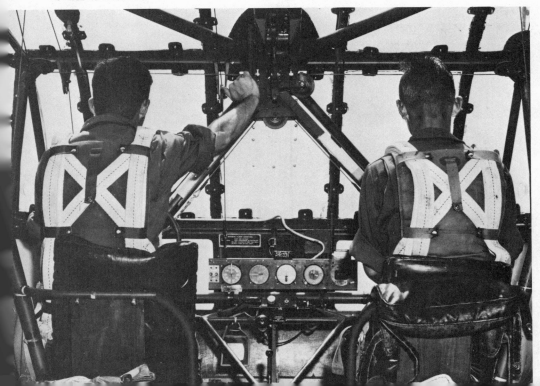

The wreck of a Waco glider after a broken towrope smashed the right elevator and stabilizer during flight.

A Waco glider washed up on a beach in Sicily.

Major General Matthew B. Ridgway (center) and members of his staff in Sicily.

close to the ground and on to the target. They flew so low that they hit trees and haystacks, taking violent evasive action to escape the machine-gun and rifle fire.

Very few of the planes found the unmarked drop zones. The others were scattered as far away as the slopes of Mount Etna, which towered twenty miles north of the assigned fields. Of the 1,900 men of the 1st Parachute Brigade, only 200 were in a position to attack the Primasole Bridge.

At one o'clock in the morning, in the midst of a furious battle, the gliders arrived and began to land under intense enemy fire. One of the paratroopers making his way to the bridge told how he had been "disturbed by the ghostly sound of rushing wind as a glider swooped in over our heads to crash-land on the road near the bridge. Then came another which seemed to be making straight for us when it just failed to clear the top of the riverbank and, with a fearful crash and rending of material, broke its back, the rear half subsiding into the river, taking with it a welter of men and equipment. We rushed across and found two pilots badly smashed and cut-about lying on the grass where they had been thrown through the Perspex windows of the cockpit. The glider had been carrying an antitank gun and crew, and some of the survivors crawled out of the wreckage, their faces a deathly white under the black makeup which they had applied. I thanked God that I went to battle by parachute and not by glider."

Only four Horsas landed close enough to the bridge to make any contribution to the battle. With the three six-pounder guns that they carried, the two hundred paratroopers assaulted the Axis defenders of the bridge, who had been reinforced by Student's paratroopers. Although the British initially secured both ends of the bridge, the north end was lost the next day to strong German forces advancing from Catania. Under serious artillery attack, the British dug in at the south end but were finally forced away from the bridge. In the foothills nearby they formed a defensive perimeter and stood firm, aided by the heavy guns of a cruiser off the coast. Just at dusk British tanks appeared in the distance and the Axis troops disappeared from the bridge.

The fighting had been very confused and the casualties on both sides were heavy. The mixup in the forces fighting in the dark had been so bad that one British glider pilot reported that he had been advancing across a field at night beside someone he thought was a comrade when the shadowy figure suddenly asked him, *"Haben sie meine Schmeisser gesehen?"* ("Have you seen my submachine gun?") Another glider pilot, who had landed many miles from the bridge, was captured by German paratroopers while trying to reach the landing area and suffered the indignity of being shelled by Allied artillery and strafed by American fighter planes. His copilot was killed in this strafing attack, another victim of "friendly" fire.

Thus ended "Operation Fustian," the last of the ill-fated airborne missions in Sicily.

Sicily was almost the end of Allied airborne divisions. So disillusioned were the senior officers with the poor performance and excessive casualties that they proposed to restrict the use of airborne forces to units no larger than a battalion. The chorus of denunciation and criticism grew louder and louder. General Browning was particularly sharp in his criticism of American troop-carrier units: "In spite of the clear weather, suitable moon, the existence of Malta as the checkpoint only seventy miles from Sicily, and the latter's very obvious and easily recognizable coastline, the navigation by the troop-carrier air crews was bad." He made no mention of the fact that the navigation routes were needlessly complicated, that the crews had not been trained in close night-formation flying, and that their formations had been disrupted by "friendly" antiaircraft fire.

Even General Eisenhower had lost faith: "I do not believe in the airborne division . . . even if one had all the air transport he could possibly use, the fact is that at any given time in any given spot only a reasonable number of air transport can be operated because of technical difficulties. To employ at any time and place a whole division would require dropping over such an extended area that I seriously doubt a division commander could regain control and operate the scattered forces as one unit." He was firmly seconded by Lieutenant General Leslie J. McNair, commanding general of the Army Ground Forces, who wrote: "After the airborne operations in Africa and Sicily, my staff and I had become convinced of the impracticability of handling large airborne units. I was prepared to recommend to the War Department that airborne divisions be abandoned. . . ."

But General Ridgway and his subordinates still had faith in large-scale airborne operations. They studied the Sicilian operation very carefully and laid down some guidelines for the future. It was clear that gliders could not be released over water at night. Landing fields had to be marked either by lights or radio navigation aids to permit the transports and tugs to find them. Troop Carrier Command had to improve its training in close formation flying, particularly at night, and especially its navigation. Routes to the landing zones had to be made simpler, and concentrations of antiaircraft artillery, friendly or hostile, had to be avoided. There could be no reliance placed on ground identification of friendly planes overhead. General Ridgway kept his faith in airborne assault on the division scale and pleaded their case at Allied Headquarters.

It was finally agreed that Sicily had not been a fair test of the division concept of airborne operations and that the lessons learned there could properly be applied in the future.

And the future was to be in the hedgerow fields of Normandy.

4

Girding for Battle

As the troop ship was slowly eased to the dock in Liverpool, the American glider pilots crowded the rails for their first sight of embattled England. It was 1943, the fourth winter of the war; the bomb damage in the city and the charred remains of warehouses could be clearly seen. On the wharf a British Army band played fighting airs to which they responded with cheers, whistles, and a shower of coins. Not all of them felt that they were arriving in a foreign country, for some had spent hundreds of classroom hours under the tutelage of spinster teachers who were secretly in love with Byron or Shelley, and had studied the language, the literature, and the history of this island nation. Many of them sensed that it was part of their own heritage that they had come to help defend.

They marched down the gangplank to the tune of "Colonel Bogey," groaning under the weight of their equipment: duffel and flight bags jammed with their combat and flying gear, helmets, rifles or carbines, knapsacks, and gas masks slung over the heavy military topcoat. Caesar's legionnaires had traveled lighter—and complained less. "As usual there was a foul-up somewhere," one glider pilot recalls, "and we sat on the docks for two hours. A British Army canteen called NAAFI gave us mugs of steaming hot coffee. I never fully realized what was meant by the 'horrors of war' until

I tasted that coffee." Finally they were marched down to a railroad siding where they boarded trains for their new stations. As the trains sped through the night, some of the men turned out the lights in their compartments and lowered the blackout windows to watch the little stations that whizzed by, many with quaint names like Cuckney, Far Duckmanton, and Cuerdley Cross.

Everything was new and exciting, and there was little sleep and a lot of animated conversation. They examined their English coins and paper money, and a number of arguments arose about their "real" value in dollars and cents. After looking thoughtfully at a handful of farthings, florins, ha'pennies, and thr'pennies, one glider pilot offered the solemn opinion, "Any people who can think up and master a currency like this can never be conquered."

The glider pilots arrived at their airfields to find the air echelons which had made the long and dangerous flight by way of South America and Africa waiting for them. For both it was the beginning of a period of delighted recognition and cultural shock. As one man said to his friends in a Nissen hut, "Do you know what I saw today? Sherwood Forest!" The shock came also from the unfamiliar: honeybuckets (portable toilets), emptied every night by "honey maids"; warm beer; washing in stone troughs in unheated washrooms; and worst of all, orange marmalade, which was served at every meal and which they learned to detest. The American fliers, shivering in their wool-lined helmets, jackets, pants, boots, and gloves, were shamed by the sight of red-cheeked English boys running around in short pants and open-necked shirts.

The buildup of the airborne forces for the invasion of France continued at an increasing rate through the winter and into the spring of 1944. More and more troop-carrier groups arrived from the United States and from Italy until the original bases around Nottingham were no longer adequate. New fields west and southwest of London were acquired; now the training of crews and assembly of a large number of gliders began.

Although the British had turned over more than 300 Horsas to the Americans, the American glider pilots were never happy with the large plywood craft. Although it could carry double the payload of a Waco, they thought it too fragile, too tiring to fly, and too difficult to land in a small field. At times the compressed-air supply which operated the flaps and wheel brakes leaked, and without air it took a very long landing run to slow down a Horsa. Such ideal fields would not be present in France. On the other hand, the British were not happy with the Waco gliders they had been given. After their experience in Sicily, in which so many of them had come down in the sea, they tended to look upon the Waco CG-4A as a jinx.

This attitude was apparently held by the British sergeant major of the Glider Pilot Regiment who observed the assemblage of Waco gliders by an American crew, including the author. Each glider came packed in five huge wooden crates—one containing both its wings, one the fuselage, one the tail, etc. After the first glider had been assembled and was standing there in the bright sunlight, squat and ugly, the sergeant major, his pacing stick firmly under his arm, walked stiffly around it, peering in the Plexiglas windows and tapping the canvas sides. When he had finished his inspection, he offered the bitter suggestion, "Burn the bloody gliders and fly the bloody crates!"

By the spring of 1944 England was a vast aircraft carrier. As they floated along behind their tugs, constantly practicing formation flying or giving orientation rides to new airborne units, the glider pilots felt that they were never out of sight of an airfield. No sooner had the runways of one disappeared before another came in sight. The tempo of the rehearsals increased steadily. First squadrons, then groups, then wings took to the air, grimly practicing for D day. Meanwhile, at command headquarters in Ascot and London the plans for the airborne assault on Normandy ("Operation Neptune") were being prepared—not without some dissension and outright hostility between the American and British airborne planners.

General James M. Gavin, who had led the elements of the 82nd Airborne Division in their jump near Gela on the first night, told the author of the "considerable tension between Ridgway and Browning in Sicily. Browning was Eisenhower's senior airborne adviser, and it seemed to us that he wanted to take over our troop-carrier and airborne troops himself. . . . In November, nineteen forty-three, I flew to London to take over as Eisenhower's airborne adviser, and I ran into Browning at a meeting. He criticized Ridgway to me for not parachuting into Sicily. I didn't like that, and I said that Ridgway did what he had to do—two-thirds of the division had still not been sent in and Ridgway was responsible for the whole division."

The American suspicions of a British "power grab" increased during the planning stages of the Normandy mission. "Shortly after our meeting," Gavin recalls, "Browning went to General Lewis Brereton [Ninth Air Force commander] and proposed that the British and American Troop Carrier Commands be organized into one—that is, with one commander. Brereton said that would be fine, but the commander must be an American. Browning did not pursue the idea any further."

The overall invasion plan (called "Overlord") had been in a state of flux for months. First, the original debarkation area had been extended to include Utah Beach on the east side of the Cotentin Peninsula. To cover the exits from Utah (five causeways across a flooded area), it was planned to drop two American airborne divisions, the 82nd and the 101st. The drop area for the 82nd had originally been on the western side of the peninsula, but when a German division suddenly moved into this region, it had been shifted to the east to adjoin the 101st's area. The British 6th Airborne Division would land southeast of Caen to protect the left flank of their seaborne assault from a possible German counterattack from the north. British paratroopers and glider men would land during the night to carry out *coup de main* assaults on certain critical bridges and the German batteries that commanded their beaches.

The lessons of Sicily were gone over again and again. To avoid the complicated routing that had caused so much trouble there, it was decided to send the American planes and the first glider mission into Normandy by the back door, across the west coast; later glider missions would come in from the east over Utah Beach. Remembering the losses suffered from "friendly" antiaircraft fire, troop-carrier commanders insisted on an absolute prohibition of naval fire during the time their planes would be approaching and leaving Normandy. Still feeling guilty over the Sicily fiasco, the admirals agreed to this, although they feared what might happen if German bombers were to appear while the troop-carrier planes and gliders were overhead.

There was a great deal of nervousness about using gliders at night, particularly after a long trip across water, but losses to flak during daylight hours were considered prohibitive. The Americans decided that on the first day, glider missions would be flown just before dawn and just after dusk. With good weather and a full moon, the landings in the small hedgerow fields of Normandy should be possible. To prevent the widespread dispersal of paratroopers and gliders that had occurred in Sicily, the use of "pathfinders" was contemplated. These would be teams of paratroopers flown in by specially trained aircrews to drop into the landing zones with a series of navigation aids. Colored lights, distinctive panels, radio, and radar were all to be used to guide the C-47s to the correct spot. The chief hope was on the radio aid consisting of a "Eureka" transmitter (which would be carried in by the pathfinders) and a "Rebecca" receiver in the lead planes. In case enemy opposition was encountered, two pathfinder teams would be sent into each of the drop and landing zones.

The plan to use the airborne forces tactically to cover the seaborne landings displeased General George C. Marshall, the American Chief of Staff. He wrote to General Eisenhower in February, 1944, urging him to consider a plan to drop an airborne division to seize the airfields in the Evreux-Dreux area southwest of Paris and sixty miles from the nearest invasion beach. After the paratroopers and glider infantry had captured the airfields, a standard infantry division could be flown in and the airhead would "directly threaten the crossings of the Seine as well as the city of Paris. It should serve as a rallying point for considerable elements of the French underground."

"The trouble with this plan," Marshall wrote provocatively, "is that we have never done anything like this before and frankly that reaction makes me tired." He asked Eisenhower to study the plan "before your Staff tears it to ribbons."

After Eisenhower had studied it and had conferred with other senior commanders, he found that he could agree with the idea of a "mass vertical envelopment" but had to disagree with the timing. The airhead would have to be relieved quickly by the forces breaking out of the beaches or else the lightly armed immobile airborne divisions would be overwhelmed. He told Marshall that the first priority must be given to securing a foothold in France and that required the tactical use of the Allied airborne divisions to protect the seaborne landings. There would be plenty of opportunity later, after a foothold had been established on the continent, to use a mass vertical envelopment ahead of the advancing Allied armies. If the Allies failed to establish their beachhead in Normandy, the airhead in the Evreux-Dreux area would be doomed. The same would be true if the airhead could not be relieved quickly by the invading forces (the Anglo-American armies breaking out of the Normandy beachhead did not reach the Evreux-Dreux area until ninety days after D day).

Although Eisenhower firmly rejected Marshall's plan, the idea of a "mass vertical envelopment" had been proposed for the first time and the seeds of the disaster at Arnhem in the following September had been planted.

In the middle of March, wild rumors swept the troop-carrier fields about a supposedly disastrous glider mission on the other side of the world. Although the reported casualties among the glider pilots—including Jackie Coogan, the film actor—were grossly exaggerated, the effect of the Burma fiasco was to shake the morale of the men who thought they were preparing to face a more formidable enemy than the Japanese and the jungle.

The plan had been to aid Major General Orde Wingate's long-range penetration of Japanese-held Burma by seizing two landing zones ("Broadway" and "Piccadilly") and constructing two airstrips on them. Then two brigades of Indian troops would be flown in and a third would march in from the north.

On the night of March 5–6, twenty-seven C-47s, each towing two Waco gliders, were ready at airfields in India. Just before takeoff, recent aerial photographs arrived showing "Piccadilly" littered with tree trunks and other obstacles. At this last minute the plans were changed and all the gliders were ordered to land at "Broadway." The 250-mile flight was a nightmare: engines overheated as the tugs struggled to climb over the towering Chin Hills, pulling two heavily overloaded gliders. Towropes left too long in the damp grass and exposed to the sun snapped, dropping their gliders into a hostile jungle from which many of the pilots and passengers never emerged.

Of the fifty-four gliders that started the mission, only thirty-seven arrived at "Broadway," and their ordeal was just beginning. Hidden in the tall grass of the clearing, unseen by the aerial photographs, were dozens of large tree trunks—perfect antiglider obstacles. In addition, the field was criss-crossed by deep ruts where tree trunks had been pulled across it.

When the carnage was over and the last glider had skipped across the ruts out of control and smashed into the wreckage of another, there were only three flyable gliders left. Yet, in spite of a long casualty list, the bulldozers survived and the airstrip was built.

The rumor of Coogan's death was succeeded by the tale of his capture by the Japanese (he actually landed his glider safely at a third field some miles away and was never a prisoner). Those who had met the feisty ex–child actor when he was an instructor at Twentynine Palms wondered at his reception by Hollywood-crazy Japanese soldiers. The general opinion was that no harm would come to a man who had been married to Betty Grable.

While the troop-carrier tug and the glider pilots trained for the coming invasion, the planners quarreled over such details as the feasibility of using gliders at night, the allocation of transport planes, and the need for more night formation training. Spring in England is not a good period for flying. Days of rain and low clouds restricted the training, but every clear day found the C-47s and gliders in the air as Troop Carrier Command ordered more and more practice.

"We were stationed in Devonshire, south of Taunton," a glider pilot said. "In the mornings there were usually fog and low ceilings, but this would improve about eleven o'clock. Then we would take off and fly a triangular course, practicing formations. We had to be back at the field no later than four in the afternoon because at four thirty, like clockwork, it would rain. It was amazing how regular these showers were. As we were coming back to the field, we could see the rain clouds building up over the Black Down Hills, and we were out of the planes on our way back to the tents when the showers began."

On days when flying was impossible, the glider pilots

reviewed loading procedures or supervised the installation of intercoms, landing lights, parachute arresters (which were installed on less than half the gliders), and the Griswold glider nose (a triangular frame of heavy metal intended to facilitate knocking down antiglider poles). In spite of fervent pleas to Washington, there were still no armor and no self-sealing tanks for the C-47s. In fact, the constant urgent requests so annoyed the fighter and bomber advocates that the head of the glider program, Major A. Felix duPont, Jr., was banished to Australia and his post abolished.

On April 18 there was a rehearsal of glider landings at dawn. Forty-eight gliders were released over small unprepared fields that resembled those in Normandy (an area then known only to a very few high-level planners at Supreme Headquarters). The results were very discouraging. Although there was only one major accident, which killed the glider crew and passengers, over half the gliders were wrecked or their cargoes disabled.

Air Chief Marshal Sir Trafford Leigh-Mallory, the Air Commander-in-Chief, had been pessimistic about the chances of a successful use of gliders for some time. He now wrote a letter to General Eisenhower stating his firm belief that the planned glider operations would not succeed. In light of the glider fiasco in Sicily, there was nothing to refute his gloomy forecast except the feeling of optimism by the troop-carrier and airborne commanders. General Lewis Brereton asserted that "while I think a high percentage of losses may be incurred, I am convinced that the glider operation will be effective." His confidence was based on the advanced state of training attained by the troop-carrier teams, who had flown over 30,000 hours in a series of night and day airborne exercises in the month of April alone. Nevertheless, the doubts would not go away and, although there was optimism about the paratroop drop, there was nothing but "fatalistic resignation" about the planned glider operations.

Slowly the weeks passed. As one American pilot recalled those days, "that damp, piercing cold didn't help our morale";

the tensions built up. Everywhere there were signs of the coming invasion: troops, ammunition dumps, vehicles, tanks,
planes, cannon—the island seemed to groan under their
weight. Twice that spring, the preinvasion security routine
was tested. Travel, telephone, and postal service between
England and Ireland were cut off; access to the airfields was
restricted. Outgoing mail was placed in special bags to be sent
out after the invasion began. Paratroopers moved into special
security quarters on the departure airfields and were guarded
behind barbed wire. But these turned out to be false starts or
the prelude to another rehearsal. The glider pilots had been
trained to a fine cutting edge and were becoming nervous under the growing tension that preceded the mission. "Waiting
was always the worst part," one recalls. "We tried not to talk
about it and concentrated on getting our gear in order, but
every hut had a map of France on the wall with lines drawn
showing where we thought we were going to go in. Most of us
chose the Pas-de-Calais because that was the shortest Channel
crossing. One college boy picked the coast near Caen, saying
that this was where William the Conquerer had left to win
England and he thought that this was very significant."

They crowded the pubs in the nearby towns and tried
to cover their nervousness with heavy drinking and loud talk.
British hospitality was generous and open. Many of the new
soldiers were invited into English homes until Eisenhower had
to remind his troops that the British were on short rations
and that bringing one's own food during these visits would be
an appreciated gesture. Not all the British appreciated the
inundation by callow, boasting Yanks. As one bitter complaint had it, they were "overpaid, overdressed, oversexed,
and over here." Also, Sicily had not been forgotten and there
were some pub brawls between the British airborne and the
American troop-carrier crews who were accused of dropping
gliders in the sea out of fear of flak.

The English girls, whose men had been serving overseas
for so many years, had few complaints about the attentive
Americans. Once the hurdles of the language had been over-

come and the Yanks realized that "come around and knock me up sometime" was an invitation to rap on the girl's door and not to impregnate her, the social and sex lives of both groups flourished. There was some hostility from the British soldiers over the ease with which the Yanks corralled the most desirable women, but, in the main, American admiration for the fortitude of the British people standing alone against Hitler, and British tolerance of foreign customs and habits, led to mutual understanding and respect.

By the end of May the American airfields were crowded with over 1,200 troop-carrier planes, more than 1,100 Waco CG-4As, and 300 Horsas. Final plans had been drawn up for the employment of the American airborne forces: paratroopers would go in on the night of D-minus-one and would be reinforced at dawn the following day by fifty-glider serials to each of the divisions. There would then be a dusk glider landing on D day to bolster the 82nd Airborne, with a smaller number of gliders going to the 101st. Major glider landings would also be made at dawn and dusk on D-plus-one, with subsequent glider missions to be determined by the tactical situation. For the dawn landing on D day, the gliders would be brought in over the west coast, safely, it was hoped, protected by the dim light; all other glider serials would be towed in over Utah Beach on the east coast.

The movement of a German infantry division and the parachute regiment commanded by the fiery von der Heydte into the Cotentin Peninsula (in the exact area in which the 82nd Airborne was originally to drop) caused the greatest misgivings. Already pessimistic about the American airborne plans, Leigh-Mallory appealed in person to General Eisenhower to cancel them. Because of new enemy flak positions and the antiglider poles which had suddenly blossomed in Normandy, he predicted that 50 percent of the paratroopers and 70 percent of the gliders would be shot down before they reached their drop and landing zones. "I couldn't believe it," Gavin said to the author. "He was recommending that the American airborne not parachute and glide into Europe. He didn't say the British; he said the Americans. This would make all the troop-carrier lift available to the British, and we would be left sitting back in England. . . . Even today it makes me seethe in anger."

For Eisenhower it was one of the most agonizing decisions he had to make. If his air commander was correct, he was needlessly sacrificing two fine airborne divisions and his glider force. But if the American airborne assault was called off, the landings on Utah Beach would be in great danger, thereby jeopardizing the entire seaborne invasion. He sweated over the decision alone and finally decided that the airborne must go in. After all, what Leigh-Mallory was predicting was only an estimate which could be wrong, but the failure of the airborne to cover the exits from Utah Beach made the success of the seaborne landing there highly improbable. A repulse at Utah would have inevitable consequences for the possibility of winning the other beaches. The paratroopers and glider men would have to take their chances.

At the same time that Eisenhower was arriving at this decision, Supreme Headquarters was shaken by what appeared to be a terrible disclosure of the airborne invasion plans. In a London bookstore a staff officer had idly picked up a book called *Paratroops* by Captain F. O. Miksche, a Czech officer serving with the Free French. Glancing through it, the staff officer was stunned to see a map of the Cotentin Peninsula showing airborne drop and landing zones almost identical to those in the invasion plan. Miksche had taken a professional soldier's interest in the German airborne operations in Holland, Belgium, and Crete and had outlined the strategy and tactics for the use of airborne forces in a hypothetical Allied invasion of France. As an example of his predicted rules of airborne warfare, he projected a seaborne landing exactly where Utah Beach would be, covered by three airborne divisions centered about Sainte Mère-Eglise, Carentan, and the British landing zone near Caen. The book had been published in 1943, and it was likely that by this time a copy had found its way to Germany through neutral countries.

There was a great deal of worry at SHAEF that the Germans might take the example seriously. Their reinforcement of the Cotentin Peninsula near the end of May seemed to indicate that the Germans had taken Miksche's predictions at face value. With D day less than a week away, it was too late to do anything about it except fervently hope that the German move had merely been a routine one. (Although General Student had indeed seen and read a copy of the book, he had taken the map of airborne "landings" in Normandy for exactly what it was—an illustrative example.)

By the first of June the airborne divisions had moved onto the airfields from which they would leave for France. Their area was rigidly isolated by barbed-wire fences and armed guards. The fields were sealed, all personnel restricted, and telephone calls monitored. Once more, mail was held up until after the mission. The field order for the airborne assault was issued the next day, and the briefing of the tug and glider crews began. The briefings were generally considered to be complete and accurate: films of the run-ins to the target and mosaics of the landing zones were shown and discussed thoroughly; maps of the area were plentiful. The only complaint the glider pilots later had was that the aerial photographs seemed to have been taken from such a high altitude that they failed to indicate the small size of the fields, the height of the hedgerows and trees, or the presence of obstacles on the fields themselves. Unfortunately, the photographs did not reveal the flooded areas, which were to come as an unpleasant surprise to paratroopers and glider pilots. There was also a failure to clearly define "hedgerow." To the Americans, this meant a thin hedge of yews or similar bushes, not the high earth-packed barriers filled with tree roots which is the French *bocage*. A glider could roll through the former easily; the latter was a concrete wall.

While the mechanics were painting the distinctive invasion markings (three white and two black stripes, each two feet wide, on the fuselage and each wing), the briefed glider pilots were isolated from the "unwashed." They were not

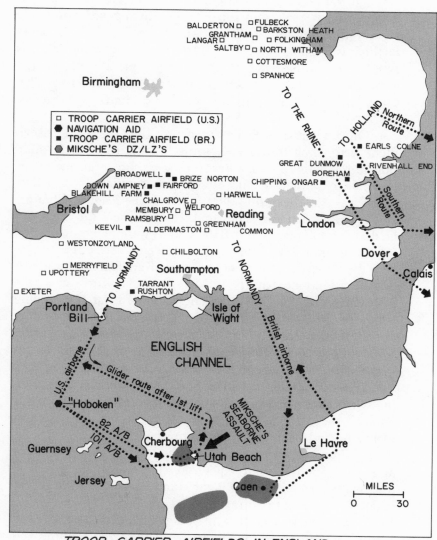

TROOP CARRIER AIRFIELDS IN ENGLAND

Legend:

☐ TROOP CARRIER AIRFIELD (U.S.)
● NAVIGATION AID
■ TROOP CARRIER AIRFIELD (BR.)
⬣ MIKSCHE'S DZ/LZ'S

BALDERTON ☐ ☐ FULBECK
☐ BARKSTON HEATH
GRANTHAM ☐
LANGAR ☐ ☐ FOLKINGHAM
SALTBY ☐ ☐ NORTH WITHAM
☐ COTTESMORE

☐ SPANHOE

Birmingham

TO THE RHINE
TO HOLLAND
Northern Route

EARLS COLNE

GREAT DUNMOW ■ ■ RIVENHALL END
BOREHAM ■
CHIPPING ONGAR ■

Southern Route

BROADWELL ■
DOWN AMPNEY ■ ■ BRIZE NORTON
■ FAIRFORD
BLAKEHILL FARM ■
CHALGROVE ☐
☐ HARWELL

Bristol

MEMBURY ☐ ☐ WELFORD
RAMSBURY ☐
KEEVIL ■ ALDERMASTON ☐ ☐ GREENHAM
COMMON

Reading

London

Dover ●

☐ WESTONZOYLAND
☐ CHILBOLTON

TO NORMANDY

☐ MERRYFIELD
☐ UPOTTERY

Southampton

Calais

☐ EXETER

TARRANT RUSHTON

TO NORMANDY

British airborne

Portland Bill

Isle of Wight

ENGLISH CHANNEL

Le Havre

U.S. airborne

Glider route after 1st lift

● "Hoboken"

82 A/B
101 A/B

Guernsey

Cherbourg

MIKSCHE'S SEABORNE ASSAULT

Utah Beach

Jersey

Caen ●

MILES
0   30

permitted to communicate with anyone who had not been through the briefing procedure. When they had to go to the latrine, they were accompanied by an armed guard who made certain that no unbriefed personnel were using the same facility. In response to one glider pilot's complaint at this supervision during what he considered a private matter, the armed sentry politely informed him not to be concerned "because the next time you piss, you'll be alone in a French field."

On the British airfields the men of the Glider Pilot Regiment were going through the same briefing routine. In addition to the aerial photographs, they were shown an ingenious film taken through a blue filter which simulated what they would see at night during the trip across the English Channel and into their landing zones southeast of Caen. On eight airfields, over 400 planes and 1,100 gliders were being marshaled for the mission. The initial objectives were to seize the bridges over the Orne River at Bénouville and Ranville, to capture or destroy a German battery at Merville which threatened the easternmost of the British beaches, and to clear the landing zones for the following glider lift. The assault on the bridges and on the battery were to be made by *coup de main*; namely, by landing gliders in the immediate vicinity of or on the target in the effort to overwhelm the defenders by surprise.

"Andy" Andrews made his final preparations still wondering why chance had picked him for the "Cloak and Dagger Squad," the *coup de main* on the Ranville bridge. A month earlier he had been in the operations hut chatting with his flight commander and waiting for the morning break for "tea and wads [buns]." The squadron commander had walked in casually and said to the flight commander, "I want you to pick twelve crews to go into special training." Then, turning to Andrews, he added, "I want you as well." In the end, fourteen crews had undergone extensive night-flying training and had practiced massed night landings on a field lighted only by a single "Tee." Later they were briefed on the mission (although no place names were given until the last moment), studying models of the coast and photographs of the area around the bridges.

Just before being confined to camp, Andrews "sneaked out about a hundred yards down a lane on one side of the airdrome to see my wife at our usual meeting place. It was a very difficult good-bye. I made some poor excuses and told some white lies, but I am sure that she guessed. She said nothing, only that she would go home to London the next day."

D day had originally been set for June 5, but the unpredictable weather upset the time schedule. Even as the troop transports were steaming for Normandy and the glider pilots and tug crews were being briefed, the weather was slowly worsening. The forecast for the 5th was for winds up to twenty-two knots, thick clouds below 500 feet, and heavy surf on the Normandy beaches. The winds were much too high for paratroop drops, and the low clouds and poor visibility would make the towing of gliders practically impossible. Eisenhower postponed the invasion for twenty-four hours.

With the gliders and planes loaded, the briefing done, and the drop and landing zones clearly in mind, the troop-carrier men found the last twenty-four hours agonizing. They busied themselves as best they could—cleaning their weapons, studying the routes and the aerial photographs. Glider loads were checked and rechecked. Defiant inscriptions or the names of loved ones were chalked on the glider noses. New words were composed to a British army song and mournfully sung:

> As into the gliders we crawl,
> We're in for a helluva fall.
> No orchids, no violets
> For no-engine pilots,
> So cheer up, my lads, bless 'em all!

As usual, waiting to go was the hardest thing to bear.

5
Leaping the Wall

'Twas on a summer's day—the sixth of June—
I like to be particular in dates. . . .
                                    Byron, *Don Juan*

From the balcony around the squat control tower, one could just see the outline of the planes. Even with British Double Summer Time, the light was failing rapidly.

It was a sight to stir a dramatist's heart and to fascinate a man of the theater. From the crowded observation platform Second Lieutenant Joshua Logan could see the dim blue formation lights on the C-47s and hear the whining roar of their engines as they lumbered gracelessly down the taxiway on their way to the takeoff point. Earlier he had accompanied the photographer who took candid shots in the planes of the paratroopers loaded with all their equipment, their faces painted black or in Indian war paint. In one of the planes Logan had been greeted cheerfully by his first name: one of the blackface troopers turned out to be his younger cousin, Bill Leach, who was jumping with the 101st Airborne Division. It had been a welcome but short reunion, and Logan, who knew the details of the airborne mission intimately, was justifiably worried about what might happen to his young relative.*

As assistant intelligence officer, Logan had come down from Wing Headquarters at Exeter to brief this troop-carrier group on the Normandy drop. After the group operation

* Bill Leach survived the Normandy drop and other combat actions with the 101st Airborne but was killed in March, 1945, on the Rhine crossing.

officer had gone over the details of takeoff times, navigation routes, altitudes, and airspeeds out and back, Logan had explained what was known of the dispositions of the German Army in the Cotentin Peninsula and had gone briefly into escape and evasion techniques. (He was dubious that any of the aircrews could successfully apply his instructions. "I taught escape and evasion," he later told the author, "but when I would talk to these guys, you know they were so American, they were so lacking in any kind of pretense, I thought how could they ever possibly fool a German—or anybody—because they *smell* American.")

After Logan's lecture, the group chaplain took over and asked God to bless the pilots, concluding with a prayer. Suddenly he erupted into, " 'Get in there and kill them! Kill them! Go over there and kill 'em, kill 'em!' " Logan recalls. "He was screaming like that. He went crazy. Scared the hell out of everybody."

With this murderous exhortation still ringing in their ears, the crews left the briefing room for the flight line.

By 11:00 P.M. the field was in darkness except for the last faint touches of the sunset on the horizon. Tension was building up among the people crowded on the control tower. "It was absolutely packed with everybody in the outfit," Logan said, "and also everybody in surrounding outfits. That's the only way they could see the takeoff. The planes were very heavily loaded, there's no question about that. Not only were the paratroopers jammed in there but they had all sorts of guns of various sizes and explosives of all sorts—all kinds of equipment. As they came lumbering by, you had a terrible feeling that they weren't going to get off the ground because they looked so awkward. When that first plane took off and got about two feet off the ground, there was such a sound from that group of people—a kind of wild mixed cry of vengeance and cheering and relief. It was the most extraordinary sound I ever heard in my life. It left a stain in my memory. . . ."

One by one the troop-carrying Dakotas roared down the

runway, climbed slowly into the night, and disappeared. At the rendezvous, they would meet the other paratroop serials that were even then rising from a dozen airfields in England. After assembly, they would head toward their destiny in Normandy.

As the last plane, its lights flickering in the gathering haze, was lost to sight, the mechanics began to move the gliders close to the edges of the runway for the dawn mission. After the bulky craft had been placed nose to tail at the downwind end of the field, there was only the long, tense wait for the planes to return.

The ground crews were still marshaling the gliders, laying out the towropes, and checking the tie-down of the jeeps and guns when the planes came back. At first there was only the distant droning of laboring engines in the darkness, but soon the formation lights appeared in the south. "As soon as we saw them come back straggling in one by one with no sort of a formation at all," one glider pilot reported, "we knew that something had gone terribly wrong. They circled the field once, and from several of the planes red flares were fired, indicating that there were wounded aboard. They were all strung out at different altitudes, and we could tell from the absence of the bluish exhaust flames that several of them were on single engine. I remember that no one said a word, we were so scared. We just stood there on the edge of the field counting them as they came in on their approach. It took over an hour before the last plane landed. Something had gone terribly wrong."

In the crowded, smoky Operations huts the flight crews were carefully interrogated. They were weary, though strangely excited, by their first contact with battle, and surprisingly belligerent at the carefully phrased questions. According to one crew member, "Everything was fine until we hit the French coast. We were flying at about a thousand feet and they told us the overcast would be way above us . . .

and then we ran into this damn cloud bank about five hundred feet thick right at our altitude. As soon as we hit it our
formations broke up . . . some guys tried to climb above it,
some dropped down below it, but most of us followed the
leader right into it. It was so thick you couldn't even see your
wingman's lights and everybody started to scatter. . . ."

Major-General Matthew Ridgway was standing in the
open door watching the formations when it happened. "It was
a beautiful clear night," he told the author, "with a half-moon.
We dropped down to jumping altitude when we crossed the
coast and then—without any warning—we went into a cloud
bank and everything disappeared. You couldn't see a thing,
not even the plane on your wing."

The formations had left the English coast at a promontory called Portland Bill and had flown out over the dark
waters of the Channel to the navigation fix called "Hoboken,"
where they turned left. From the German-occupied islands of
Guernsey and Jersey, there had been sporadic ineffectual antiaircraft fire, but the planes had pushed through until they
could see the dark outline of the Cotentin Peninsula clearly
visible in the bright moonlight.

As the scattered planes maneuvered to avoid the clouds
or opened up as they flew into it, the German guns on the
west coast of Normandy opened fire. It was the first time
most of these troop-carrier pilots had gone through enemy
flak. As one of them described the scene, "God, you never
saw such stuff as they threw at us. It seemed like every German flak unit in France was firing. The sky was filled with the
bright lines of tracers and explosions. I saw the plane ahead
of me take a direct hit in the cabin and it broke apart. For an
instant I could see these little figures dropping down into the
darkness. . . ."

Completely demoralized, they flew on through the night,
trying to find the dropping zones. The pathfinders, who had
preceded them by half an hour, had blundered into the same
cloud bank and had been scattered by the same antiaircraft

fire; there were no lighted Tees or radio aids to help them find the fields. Under the circumstances it was surprising that any paratroopers were dropped on their preassigned dropping zones. Another pilot later reported, "I spotted the Douve River and followed it to what I thought was the junction with the Merderet. Then I timed myself until I saw the lights of the little village at the end of the dropping zone. I gave them the green light and they jumped. . . . There was a plane burning below me and I could see a lot of parachutes in the field, so I figured this was the place. . . . I had no idea where we were, but our orders were to bring no one back, so I gave them the signal to jump. . . ."

Not everyone jumped. There were a few who froze with fear when they looked down into the tracer-filled night and refused to go. Men were wounded standing in the open doorway and blocked the troopers behind them. Burning C-47s carried others to their death. Twelve paratroopers who had slipped in vomit and had become entangled were brought back.

In the flak-filled skies over Normandy many of the pilots had struggled desperately to find the dropping zones, often circling again and again, but later there were to be ugly rumors of some who had signaled the paratroopers to jump even though there was not sufficient altitude for their parachutes to open. According to an eyewitness, the planes had then fled at high speed toward the Channel and England.

Dropped widely over the Cotentin Peninsula, the paratroopers would fight their way through the hedgerow country toward their assembly point. Disorganized and often demoralized, they battled the Germans—and often each other—in the darkness as they tried to carry out their missions. One of these was to secure and mark the two landing zones in which the gliders would be coming in at four o'clock in the morning. But the men who had been assigned to clear the glider landing fields were often dropped twenty miles or more from the proper field. In the confusion and chaos that reigned in Normandy that night, their job was hopeless. There would be no beacons to guide the glider train. The fields were dark, and in the night the now-alerted enemy was waiting.

Not only had the weather briefing been terribly wrong but the aerial reconnaissance prior to the invasion had failed to show that the fields on both sides of the two rivers had been flooded by the Germans. It was into these marshes, hidden from view by the tall grass, that many of the heavily laden paratroopers had tumbled and drowned, a fate they shared with those who had been dropped late after passing the east coast and who had floated into the Channel.

Man fought against man among the hedgerows, trying desperately to distinguish friend from foe. Above this melee of sporadic fire and frantic activity, the first gliders arrived.

Even before the last paratrooper had jumped into the night over Normandy, 102 Wacos loaded with antitank guns, jeeps, and reinforcements had taken off from two American airfields west of Reading. Their most vitally needed cargo was 57-mm. antitank guns; they were the only weapons the airborne would have if the Germans counterattacked with tanks.

Their hands, faces, and necks smeared with powdered charcoal, the glider infantry gathered in the darkness and checked their equipment for the last time. They had taped a popping cricket—a child's toy—to their rifle stocks, the click-click of which would serve as a challenge and an identification in the night. Each man swallowed a Dramamine pill as a precaution against airsickness, to which they were very susceptible since they had ridden in gliders only once or twice. Most of them would have preferred to have taken their chances on parachuting into enemy-occupied France.

As they waited nervously, it started to rain and they huddled under the wings of the gliders and towplanes to keep dry. What they had heard at the last briefing added to their fears: no prisoners would be taken on the first day—a policy the Germans had initiated in Crete. Would captured Allied airborne troops be treated the same way?

At the head of the line, sheltered under the wing of a glider marked "The Fighting Falcon," two men were talking quietly. Brigadier General Donald F. Pratt was the assistant division commander of the 101st Airborne, and he was delighted that he was to glide into France. Originally he had been selected to lead the seaborne component of the division and had hated the idea. He would have preferred to have parachuted with the first element, but going in by glider was his second choice.

The other man was deeply worried. Lieutenant Colonel "Mike" Murphy was not only the senior glider pilot in the European Theater but the man who had been responsible for the training of glider pilots for this mission. An old-time stunt flier who had thrilled prewar crowds by landing a plane upside down on wheels fixed to the top wing, Murphy didn't like the way this mission was shaping up. Originally he had been told that Waco gliders would be used; then he was ordered to train the American glider pilots on the British Horsas. It had been decided that these would be flown into Normandy at first light. Murphy had traveled between the various troop-carrier bases, demonstrating the best techniques for landing the huge plywood gliders in small fields and under poor light. He had stressed the necessity for proper and strict control of airspeed on the approach and had insisted that every glider pilot receive a minimum of five hours' transitional flying on the unfamiliar glider, though he knew even then that it was not enough. "So many Horsas were badly damaged," Murphy told the author, "that the planners got worried."

Then, just before D day, the roof had fallen in on him. Suddenly he was told that the Horsas were out, the Waco CG-4As would be used, and the landing would be made in total darkness. At a meeting with General Montgomery, and the troop-carrier and airborne commanders, Murphy protested strongly that night mass landings with Wacos or Horsas in the small fields in Normandy would mean a 50 percent loss of men and materiel from crash landings. The experience in Sicily was brought up as well as the fact that the American glider pilots had had little experience in making mass landings at night.

General Montgomery listened to the arguments, Murphy recalls, "then he stood up, slapped the table, and said, 'We'll have to suffer it!' " The plans could not be changed; the guns the gliders would carry were vital to the success of the airborne assault. The first gliders would land in Normandy at 0400.

Since a Waco could carry only half the payload of a Horsa, only high-priority equipment and personnel would be taken in on this first glider mission. In Murphy's glider the lashing on General Pratt's jeep was being inspected for the last time by the copilot, Lieutenant John M. Butler, and by the general's aide, Lieutenant John L. May. With all the command radio equipment in the jeep, the glider was 1,000 pounds over the weight limit.

At 0119, the first Dakota towplane taxied out slowly until the towrope was taut and Murphy's glider moved from the edge to the center of the runway. Then, gunning the engines, the Dakota picked up speed; halfway down the runway, Murphy pulled the overloaded Waco into the air and then leveled off quickly to allow the towplane to get its tail down and take off. The moon was bright and, despite an occasional flurry of rain, the fifty gliders and tugs took off without incident, formed in columns of four in echelons to the right over the airfield, and started out on course. Since the flight was to be entirely in darkness, it was to follow the same routes as the paratroop mission had taken earlier that night. This would keep them from flying over the invasion fleet with possible incidents similar to those that had occurred in Sicily.

In glider number forty-nine, the next to the last in the fifty-glider train, Flight Officer George E. Buckley concentrated on maintaining the proper position behind the towplane. The only things he could see were the small blue formation lights on the top wings of the tugs and the reddish glow of the exhaust arresters. Even as he automatically made the small adjustments necessary to keep the glider directly behind the plane and slightly above its slipstream, he worried about what lay ahead, but mostly he was concerned about the night landing. "Even though clear skies were forecast, it was still going to be black as pitch. All my training had been toward dawn or day landings, and the thought of a night landing in a fully loaded glider over strange territory with the Germans waiting below left me quite apprehensive, to say the least." His fears had not been calmed at the detailed briefing where the wing intelligence officer had gloomily announced that the assigned landing zone was "studded with antiglider poles, booby traps, obstacles, and ditches dug across some areas. This information did not help our jitters a bit. . . ."

Behind him a 57-mm. antitank gun was (he hoped) securely lashed down. He could see the red ends of the cigarettes that the three-man gun crew—a corporal and two privates—were smoking; it was too noisy for conversation. The muzzle of the gun protruding belligerently between Buckley and his copilot, Flight Officer William Brunner, only added to his uneasiness. Including the ammunition, rations, entrenching tools, and camouflage net that they carried, they were just at their maximum load. Buckley wondered whether he would be able to hold a slow enough approach speed to land safely in the Normandy fields. He knew that in any crash landing the gun was likely to break loose and crush the pilot and copilot.

"At the instant the wheels of our glider left the ground," Buckley said, "we all shouted and whooped it up. Someone yelled, 'Look out, Hitler; here we come!' " The exuberation had lasted only an instant, and then they had all settled down into a worried, almost sullen, resignation.

Intent on following the blue lights on the tug's wings,

Flight Officer "Tim" Hohmann ignored the gun muzzle that was tickling his ear. Somewhere up ahead in the night was his brother George's glider. Although after constant appeals they had been permitted to serve in the same squadron, it was forbidden for them to fly together on a combat mission. "George and I worried about each other," "Tim" Hohmann wrote the author, "especially if we were separated in combat. I thought about my wife and young son—what it would do to them if I were killed. But after the anxiety and fear came resignation; this was a job that had to be done."

As the train of gliders and tugs droned slowly through the dark skies above the Channel, the pilots could see the silvery wakes of boats headed for the beaches where the landings would begin shortly after dawn. Flying at altitudes between 1,500 and 2,000 feet, the tugs seemed to present no threat to the naval convoys, and they were not fired on by friendly forces. As they passed near the Channel islands of Guernsey and Jersey, there was some sporadic ineffectual antiaircraft fire. The clouds that had done such damage to the paratroop formation were widely scattered now and were no problem to the troop-carrier pilots.

When they reached the west coast of the Cotentin Peninsula, the air armada dropped down to 600 feet. For a few minutes as they flew at low altitude across the dark, eerie landscape, there was a strange silence. "It was a beautiful and peaceful night," Murphy said. "The moon was shining down through the scattered clouds and you could see the tree line and the shapes of the fields. Then, about halfway across the Cotentin Peninsula, the German gunners woke up. We encountered heavy ground fire from that point to the landing zone. I remember watching the tracers making pretty patterns in the dark and thinking of fireworks. Occasionally a bullet would ricochet off the jeep or hit our wings. I called the tow pilot and said, 'These sons of bitches are aiming at you, but they're not leading you enough and they're hitting me!'" The airborne troopers were awed by their first sight of flak: one described it in poetic terms as "beautiful yet frightening—orange balls of fire coming up through the air and arching off in a curve. Always the fire was directed at the towship ahead with its exhaust belching bright blue flames. The antiaircraft fire, though directed at the towplanes, was also in front of us, so we had to pass through it with no parachutes. Our only comfort was to try and get further into our helmets."

Near the end of the column, Flight Officer George Buckley was running the gauntlet of fire for the first time: "Shortly after we crossed the coast of France, small-arms fire and flak started coming up at us. By the time we reached the target, it had intensified to the point where it looked like fluid streams of tracer bullets and explosions in every direction. It seemed so thick that I could not see how it would be possible to get through it unscathed. . . .

"My first reaction to flying through flak at night verged on terror. One feels completely alone up there while every German in Europe zeros in on just you. I can imagine that everyone in the air that night felt the same way. My next step was to try and make myself as small as possible in the seat. I pulled my elbows close to my body, pulled my knees together hoping to protect the vital parts, then tried desperately to pull my head down into my chest. Lastly I squeezed the cheeks of my fanny as tightly together as possible. I probably could have cracked walnuts from the pressure I was exerting. I was even tempted to take my feet off the rudder pedals so that they wouldn't stick out so far.

"The red-lensed glasses I had been wearing to improve my night vision were a waste of time. The minute I took them off, the glare from the flak made things as black as ever. There were several loud snaps from the rear of the glider which indicated small-arms fire going through the fabric. From this point on to the LZ [landing zone] was a matter of minutes which seemed like hours."

As the towplane pilots doggedly held to their course, refusing to allow their formations to be split by the fire, the flak began to score. A C-47 took a direct hit in a wing tank, burst into flames, and smashed into the ground near the village of Pont-l'Abbé. Its glider cut loose at a low altitude and fluttered helplessly in the darkness. By a miracle it managed to crash-land safely. Following the weak radio signal from a "Eureka" placed on the landing zone by the pathfinders, the other forty-nine planes grimly flew through the curtain of fire, suffering heavy damage from small arms and automatic weapons. Twenty-two miles in from the coast they finally saw the flashing green light of the Tee that marked the landing field. Hastily they gave the release signal to the gliders as they passed in turn over the fields. After the release at an altitude of 450 feet, the towplanes dived to treetop level and flew eastward, crossing the shore at the point which at dawn would be known forever as Utah Beach. As they passed over the Saint-Marcouf Islands just off the coast, the roar of their engines spared them from hearing the screams of the detachment of American soldiers that had just landed on the largest island. They were searching for German guns that might threaten the landings at Utah and were at that moment being massacred in the massive German minefields.

In the night dimly lit by the setting moon, the glider pilots fought desperately to land safely in a clear field. They had each been given an assigned traffic pattern, beginning with a sharp ninety-degree left turn off the tow; but, as they swept in their turns with the fields barely outlined below them, they quickly lost sight of the flashing green Tee. Most of them landed in the smaller unsuitable fields outside of landing zone "E." Also, there was a tail wind blowing at twenty-five miles an hour and this, combined with the darkness and the smallness of the fields, made crashes inevitable.

Murphy was the first to attempt a landing: "I spotted the railroad track that was only one-half mile from our field, so I said 'So long' to the towplane and away we went. As we got down to glide speed and the noise of the slipstream dropped, we could hear the machine guns firing. The field I had selected was almost a thousand feet long but completely surrounded by fifty-foot trees. It looked easy because a fully loaded Waco can be stopped in two hundred feet. With my wheels locked and the glider pushed up on the nose skid, we slid for over eight hundred feet on the wet grass and smashed into the trees at fifty miles an hour."

In the crumpled wreckage lay the dead bodies of General Pratt and Lieutenant Butler; Lieutenant May was miraculously unhurt. "I was shoved out the left side," Murphy said. "My body up to the belt was outside the glider with my legs still tangled in the twisted steel tubing. Fifteen feet in front of me was a German tank, and I thought, 'My God! I better lie still.' About five minutes later, it drove off. It went right past all the other gliders that had crashed through the trees—the men were out talking and unloading—and the tank never fired a shot. After that, it took about ten minutes for me to screw my body out of the tubing. When I let myself down to the ground, I just fell because my legs were broken."

Only six Wacos landed on the proper fields, and the second one slid violently through the string of lights that was the flashing green Tee, wiping it out.

"We never spotted the pathfinder lights," Flight Officer George Buckley said. "The green light from the towplane came on. I waited a few seconds, then cut loose and started a circle to the left, hoping we were in the right place. I could just make out the outline of a field on my left which looked clear, but by this time we were so low that we couldn't be choosy. It was this field or nothing. . . . We touched down with hardly a bump, and I thought that we had made it when there was a terrific crash accompanied by loud splintering and tearing noises. We had hit one of the ditches the Germans had dug across the field. It was ten to twelve feet across and approximately six feet deep. The nose of the glider impacted on the opposite side of the ditch, and the shock broke its back. This in turn caused the load to try to break loose, which broke the plywood floor open. Because of our speed we continued sliding across the field, scooping up dirt, weeds, and cow manure through the hole in the fuselage and floor. We slewed sideways and came to a stop."

As the men leaped from the glider and sprawled in the grass, they could hear the ominous sounds of small-arms and machine-gun fire in the fields all around them. Suddenly a glider dropped down out of the night and landed in the same field but on the other side of the ditch, stopping before it reached it. By a happy coincidence, this glider carried the jeep for the antitank gun in Buckley's glider. "The four of us started digging the nose and floor out of the dirt so that we could get the front of the glider open," Buckley said. "While we were doing this, the Germans set off a flare right over our heads, and we all flopped in the grass again. At this moment I recalled what the instructors back in the States had always told us: 'If you're in the open and a flare goes off, freeze in position.' We had flunked the first test already.

"After thirty minutes or so of digging and shoveling, we had gotten the jeep and the gun together to be hooked up. We'd gone about twenty feet when the gun hitch, which was welded to the gun, broke off completely. This gave several of us an opportunity to hurl choice obscenities against war workers at home doing a half-ass job. Fortunately, there was a coil of rope in the jeep, and we jury-rigged a hitch and the gun crew took off on their own."

"Tim" Hohmann was crouched behind a hedgerow covering the unloading of his glider and listening to the sound of gunfire in the nearby fields. He looked at the fluorescent dial of his watch and was surprised to see that the timepiece had stopped. As he shook it angrily, he heard a sound behind him. Turning, Hohmann saw a paratrooper a few feet away, aiming a rifle at his head. Stunned, the glider pilot could only blurt out, "What time is it?" The trooper lowered his rifle, glanced at his watch, and in a surprised tone said, "Five seventeen A.M." Then he disappeared into the night.

Surprisingly, the glider landings were later considered successful, although only six gliders landed on LZ "E." Another fifteen were within a half mile of it, and all except one were within two miles of it. At a cost of twenty-nine casualties, the 101st Airborne was reinforced by six vitally needed anti-tank guns.

On this sixth of June, just before dawn, Normandy was a set of dark stages on which a number of different plays—many tragic, a few comic, and some Grand Guignol—were being acted out. The stages were rigidly compartmentalized by the towering hedgerows among which men blundered about, crawled, giggled, prayed, or moaned in pain. Some died. All over the Cotentin they fumbled through the night, trying to grasp their roles in the improvised dramas. They were learning about war and how to survive.

George Buckley was a smart Massachusetts boy and he learned in a hurry. With the sound of the naval bombardment that was to precede the beach landings in his ears, he started out toward Hiesville, where the airborne command post was supposed to be: "While walking up a narrow lane, I glanced to my left and saw a rectangular opening in the hedgerow with a rifle muzzle pointed right at me. I froze in mid-step waiting for what I thought was sure to come. Nothing happened. The gun muzzle didn't move. I crawled over the hedgerow and looked in. It was a complete bunker dug under the hedge, large enough for four or five soldiers. Its sole occupant was a dead German whose rifle was poking out through the slot.

"A short distance further on I came across a young German by the side of the road. He had been hit minutes earlier. His intestines were in the road. As I stood there looking at him, he died. He was my build, about my age (nineteen), had the same color hair and blue eyes like mine. It could have been me lying there instead of him. I spoke to him very quietly, trying to tell him that I was sorry for what had happened though I knew he would never hear the words. . . . That one German soldier I saw that morning by the roadside all alone left an impression with me which will never be forgotten.

"Shortly after this, I met a glider man with a jeep looking for anyone to join up with him. I volunteered to ride on the hood, serving as lookout while he drove. I felt like Sergeant York or John Wayne until some Germans, hearing the jeep coming, fired a burp gun at us. This burst came so close to my head that I fell off the hood and almost got run over. From then on I walked ahead of the jeep, crouched as low as possible with my head on a swivel. I was learning fast.

"Before we got to Hiesville this happened a number of times. The Germans would hear us and fire and we would fire back in their general direction even though we never came face to face. We had taken so many turns by then that we were completely lost until we met up with four more troopers who showed us the way. They were pulling a wagon loaded with ammo, rations, German mines, and German wooden practice ammo. An argument went on for days about the wooden bullets. Some people claim that they would shatter as they hit you but wouldn't hurt. Others claimed the bullets would penetrate and splinter inside the wound, causing great damage."

While Buckley and his passengers were still digging the antitank gun out of their half-buried glider, four miles to the northwest what was left of the second glider mission staggered over its landing zone. Fifty-two Waco gliders loaded with twenty-two jeeps, sixteen 57-mm. antitank guns, and ten tons of vital supplies had taken off from Ramsbury at two o'clock in the morning, following the route of the earlier paratroop mission to the same fields north of Sainte-Mère-Eglise. The flight had been without incident despite distant fire from the Channel Islands; the radio navigation aids had been picked up and the lights seen at all the turning points. Then, at the western edge of the peninsula, they ran into the cloud bank that had dispersed the paratroop planes but had capriciously spared the first glider mission.

The lead plane and many others, the official history reports, climbed to 1,500 feet, went over the clouds, and let down two or three minutes later through breaks in the overcast. They emerged somewhat scattered and slightly north of course. However, a substantial portion of the serial plunged into the clouds and found itself in such dense obscurity that the glider pilots could not see their own towplanes. Inevitably, that part of the formation broke up, although most of the pilots remained approximately on course.

According to the official reports, "While in the cloudbank, seven gliders broke loose, were released or were cut loose by enemy fire. Two were later located in western Normandy, but the rest were still unaccounted for months later. Further inland the clouds became thinner and more broken, but visibility was still bad enough to cause the premature release of seven more gliders on the west side of the Merderet River. It appears that one or two pilots, catching a glimpse of the flooded valley ahead of them, mistook it for the sea and hastily gave the signal for release. Others behind them saw their gliders descending, assumed the zone had been reached, and likewise released their gliders.

"Once out of the clouds the serial was harassed by small-arms and machine-gun fire. One plane was lost. . . ."

As on the earlier glider missions, the orderly flight pattern was quickly abandoned and it was every man for himself. Under sporadic fire, they glided through the blackness, trying to locate a suitable field in the few minutes of free flight. The only clear landmarks were the town of Sainte-Mère-Eglise and a railroad, so it is not surprising that only twenty gliders landed on the target landing zone; nine others crashed into fields within two miles of the landing zone and three gliders even reached landing zone "E" near Hiesville.

"Safe landings were the exception rather than the rule," the official history continues. "Some twenty-two of the gliders were destroyed and all but about a dozen were badly smashed. Again the principal causes of crashes were the smallness of the fields and the height of the trees surrounding them, but other hazards such as swamps and the rows of posts known as 'Rommel's asparagus' accounted for nearly half the crack-ups. One glider ran into a herd of cattle. The rough landings produced fewer casualties than might have been expected. Only three of the airborne troops were killed and twenty-three injured. Several jeeps broke loose and eleven of them were unusable. The guns were more durable: of the eight that landed within two miles of the zone, all remained intact.

"One effect of dispersion of the paratroops was to provide friendly reception committees on the spot for most of the gliders, even in cases where they missed the zones by a considerable distance. Overjoyed to get artillery, these men [paratroopers] were of great assistance in unloading. They blasted down a wall to get one gun out of an orchard in Ste.-Mère-Eglise and ripped another out of a Waco which had wrapped itself around a tree. By noon, four of the guns were in action at La Fiere and two or three others on the outskirts of Ste.-Mère-Eglise. Though hardly more than fifty percent effective, the mission had given the airborne troops some badly-needed fire power."

Flight Officer John J. Lang of the 84th Troop Carrier Squadron was one of the lucky—or skillful—ones. Along with a copilot and six glider infantrymen, he was carrying a trailer loaded with shells containing white phosphorus, and he knew that a crash landing at high speed would be disastrous. He kept the glider in slow flight, turning until he saw a field about 600 feet long right in the center of the landing zone. Putting his base leg close to the fifty-foot-high trees that marked the southern edge of his chosen field, he slipped the glider down and "landed slow enough so that I didn't have to put the glider on a skid and coasted to the ditch fence row on the other side of the field." Later, when it was light enough, he saw only one other glider that had not cracked up or been demolished. After unloading the trailer, Lang and his copilot decided to stay near the glider until daylight; then the two of them started down the road that crossed the railroad tracks.

"I talked to a farmer who couldn't understand a word we said and vice versa," Lang reported. "About a hundred yards past the tracks, there was a group of airborne and everybody wanted to go down there although we were supposed to assemble near the tracks and to the left of the road. So I started to go by myself . . . and I was dived on by a Messerschmitt shooting up the road. I jumped behind a stone wall and laid there so scared that I shook for about half an hour. When I did start to move, somebody started throwing grenades at me, so I waited and heard some airborne talking on the other side of the wall. I decided to stand up straight and start walking through an opening in the wall. . . . There were about twenty airborne there and I asked if I could go with them; they said yes. They were veterans of North Africa and didn't seem scared or worried about anything. It made me feel real good, but it didn't last. Their lieutenant later told me that I would have to join my own group down on the Merderet. He was downhearted because he only had three of the twenty cannon that they had started out with. The rest were stuck in the mud. He did manage to knock out a German tank; two others got away, but one was burning. Most of our glider pilots were in a barn near there and I asked him if there was anything we could do to help. He said we could form an outer perimeter and he spaced us two at a time around his position. That made me a sort of volunteer for the whole group and I don't think they appreciated it.

"The G.P. who stayed with me got soaked when he landed in the swamp so we spent the rest of D day laying in the sun where the lieutenant placed us. We heard very little and saw a lot less from where we were. Later in the day we were rounded up and returned to the command post. . . . I was helping to guard about three or four hundred German prisoners in a courtyard. The airborne kept bringing them in. They were mostly old men and boys. One moonlit night we made them all lay down and stay down, and when the airborne would bring in new ones they would think their buddies were all laying there dead and would start begging and pleading until they found out they were all alive.

"Finally we marched them back to a field near the beach. On the way we passed Frenchmen who would come out to watch and they would make signs to slit their throats instead of taking them prisoner. I had a C-ration chocolate bar. I gave it to one of the prisoners while they were marching; he took one bite and passed it on. I think about seven or eight of them shared it.

"We were evacuated on an LST. A sailor loaned me a razor and I was shaving when there was an air raid which meant 'everyone on deck' because they closed all bulkheads. But all I wanted to do was get off my whiskers, so I wouldn't quit shaving. I was lucky. Bombs straddled the ship but didn't hit it."

George Buckley also remembered guarding the POWs: "The next morning someone at the CP [command post] asked if some of us glider pilots would take some German POWs down to the beach. They were in the way and might cause trouble again if they got loose or if the situation should worsen. We agreed and started in the direction of the beach in a column with some of us at the head, some of us at the sides, and some coming up the rear.

"I was noted for always asking questions and my question of the day was 'How do we know the road to the beach is open?' Everyone within earshot pretended they didn't hear me and we took off down the road. Some of us were so exhausted by this time after being without sleep for forty-eight hours or longer that we had a hard time keeping up with the POWs, who seemed more anxious to get out than we were. The road to the beach was open.

"That afternoon on the beach we made arrangements to get on board a navy landing ship which was returning to England the next morning. That night German planes flew over and strafed the ship and dropped mines in the area. The next morning a minesweeper was brought in to sweep the area so that we could leave. It struck a mine about two hundred feet off our bow and sank in about four minutes. I did not see any survivors."

The predawn landing in Normandy had scattered the gliders so widely that even those troopers who had escaped serious injury in landing spent hours reaching the assembly point. Broken guns, jeeps, trailers, and ruined equipment covered the hedgerowed fields, and the frustrated airborne troopers found themselves with a large number of wounded to care for. Although the few guns, jeeps, and ammunition that did arrive were welcomed by the hard-pressed parachutists, it was clear that the glider mission had not been a success.

When the last CG-4A glider crash-landed in some hedgerow or catapulted into a grove of trees in the darkness, it was the last Allied glider that would be landed at night on a combat mission for the rest of the war in Europe.

The first daylight glider mission of the invasion arrived over LZ "E" at 9:00 P.M. (British Double Summer Time) on D day—two hours before sunset. Thirty-two Horsa gliders carrying guns, vehicles, and personnel of the 101st Airborne had taken off from Aldermaston and had flown through clear skies over Utah Beach on the east coast of Normandy with a minimum of antiaircraft fire. The landing zones had been cleared by cutting down trees and had been marked with a yellow panel Tee and green smoke. Although the Germans still held out in enclaves two miles north and south of the landing zone, they had withheld their fire until the planes had passed over and had then concentrated on the descending gliders. Fortunately, they were too far away to do much damage. Only five of the huge Horsas landed on the LZ (and two others landed behind the German lines); the rest had a surprisingly easy time. In daylight, in the absence of flak and small-arms fire, glider missions could succeed without high losses. If there was enemy opposition, it was a different story—as the second daylight mission was to show.

The second glider mission in the early evening of D day

was intended to reinforce the 82nd Airborne Division. It consisted of two lifts: one of seventy-six gliders (twenty-two
Wacos and fifty-four Horsas) would land about 9:00 P.M.; the
other fourteen Wacos and eighty-six Horsas would follow two
hours later. Their assigned landing zone "W" had its northern edge about a mile south of Sainte-Mère-Eglise and its
southern point about a mile northwest of landing zone "E."
Like the earlier daylight glider mission, there were no problems with the weather or enemy ground fire en route to the
landing zone.

All during the afternoon of D day a desperate struggle
had been going on for possession of landing zone "W."
Twice the paratroopers had tried to push the Germans back,
and both times they had been stopped cold. At nine o'clock
it was still disputed territory, crowded with snipers and raked
by enemy mortars and 88-mm. guns. An officer tried frantically to get a message back to England to stop the gliders, but
it was much too late. Even as he was radioing the command
ship off the coast, the glider train arrived.

"They came in in a beautiful formation of two-motored
planes," Lieutenant Colonel Ralph Ingersoll later wrote in his
book *Top Secret*. "Behind each, riding high on the end of the
kite string–like towlines, were the gliders. . . . The big formation of transport planes—there must have been forty or
fifty of them in tight Vs—came on as if they were on rails.
They were flying two or three hundred feet high not far
above the treetops."

In a desperate attempt to divert the gliders from the
German-occupied portion of the landing zone, Ingersoll threw
some orange smoke grenades out into the fields in front of
the American position, but to no avail. The smoke clung to
the ground and then dissipated among the hedgerows. In any
case, although orange smoke indicated the presence of
friendly troops, the glider pilots had not been briefed to expect it or did not understand that it indicated fields safe from
enemy fire.

"As they crossed above the road directly in front of us,"

GLIDER LANDING ZONES IN NORMANDY

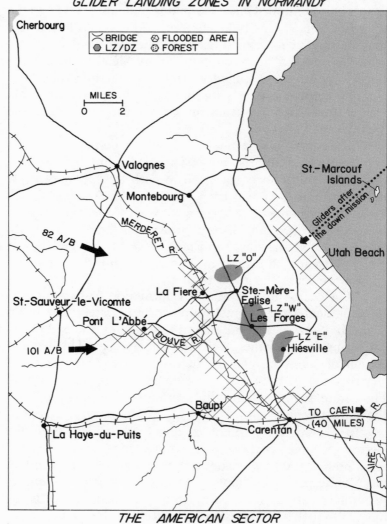

Cherbourg

BRIDGE   FLOODED AREA
LZ/DZ   FOREST

MILES
0   2

Valognes

Montebourg

St.-Marcouf Islands

Gliders after the dawn mission

Utah Beach

82 A/B

MERDERET R.

LZ "O"

La Fiere

Ste.-Mère-Eglise

LZ "W"

St.-Sauveur-le-Vicomte

Pont L'Abbé

Les Forges

DOUVE R.

101 A/B

LZ "E"

Hiésville

Baupt

TO CAEN
(40 MILES)

La Haye-du-Puits

Carentan

VIRE R.

THE AMERICAN SECTOR

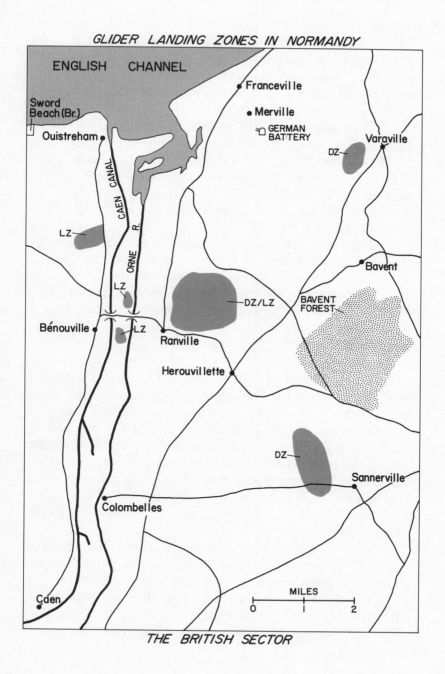

GLIDER LANDING ZONES IN NORMANDY

ENGLISH   CHANNEL

Franceville

Merville

GERMAN
BATTERY

Varaville

DZ

Sword
Beach (Br.)

Ouistreham

CAEN CANAL

ORNE R.

LZ

LZ

Bavent

BAVENT
FOREST

LZ

DZ/LZ

Bénouville

LZ

Ranville

Herouvillette

DZ

Sannerville

Colombelles

Caen

MILES

0   1   2

THE BRITISH SECTOR

Ingersoll continued, "the lead glider let go its kite string and all the kite strings behind which had been tightened black against the sky now floated loose. The whole hilltop began to crackle with small arms fire up towards the planes. The [enemy] battalion had held its fire waiting for us but the glider invasion was too much for it."

Under intense fire, the glider pilots searched frantically for a landing spot. Ingersoll watched helplessly as they "beat the air over our heads like monstrous birds, then crashed into trees and hedgerows. . . . They pancaked down on the road . . . skidded crazily and stopped." Some had to fly through an oily column of smoke where a Dakota had plunged burning into an orchard.

As the tugs maneuvered overhead to escape the barrage, the gliders came to rest, some directly in front of the German positions. One landed almost under the muzzle of a German 88. Its crew calmly got out, raised the nose, and unloaded a jeep into which they packed their equipment. As if unaware of the battle that was going on all around them, they drove unmolested across the field, through an opening in a hedge, to the American lines.

It was all over in ten minutes. "The survivors filtered past us supporting the limping, carrying the wounded. There were more still alive than seemed possible," Ingersoll marveled.

By now it was almost midnight and D day was ending. Since the glider pilots had presumably slept in bed the night before, they were detailed to stand guard. As they dug their foxholes in the dark fields, the dazed glider pilots counted heads; it was hard to believe that so many had escaped. "We had taken one helluva beating," one of the survivors wrote. "Casualties ran high."

Because of the widely dispersed landings, the efforts of the glider pilots to rendezvous at an assembly point were unsuccessful. Despite instructions to get back as quickly as possible, they usually stayed with the unit they had brought in, often serving as CP guards or in a foxhole on the firing line. "The most uninhibited individualists in the Army," the history of the 101st Airborne called them. "There seemed to be something about flying a glider, or being selected for that job, that freed a man from the ordinary restraints of Army life. Those who wanted to fight, fought like lions. Those who wanted to go back . . . managed to get there before anyone else. . . . [The glider pilots] were usually right up front during those crucial hours when the need for men is greatest. But they successfully defied all attempts at organization."

Shortly after midnight on June 6 six Halifaxes towing Horsa gliders droned through patchy clouds toward the French coast fifty miles east of the Cotentin Peninsula. Inside the gliders were packed six platoons of the British 6th Airborne Division, plus a detachment of engineers whose job would be to disable the demolition charges on the bridges across the Orne River and Caen Canal. After seizing the bridges, the *coup de main* party would clear the landing zones for the gliders which would be coming in in the early evening, bringing the rest of the division. The mission was a critical one, for the bridges formed the only link between the seaborne landing and the paratroopers who would be coming down east of the river.

In one of the Horsas, Sergeant "Andy" Andrews turned the controls over to his copilot and turned to look at his passengers. "There were just two of them," he recalls, "looking rather stern and very young sitting in the two jeeps loaded with special radio equipment. With their blackened faces and bulging airborne smocks, they looked like the cast of a musical production waiting in the wings for opening night." As they approached the French coast, they ran into what seemed at first to be mist but was actually smoke from the bombing of the coastal gun battery at Merville preceding an attack by another glider and parachute mission. The smoke became thicker, and Andrews took over the controls again since "I didn't fancy landing in the Channel at any time, especially this night."

The smoke soon disappeared, and almost at once the

tug pilot said on the intercom, "Oh, there are the two houses—bang on time too." Just as he had seen it in the film shown at the briefing, Andrews spotted the two houses dead ahead. "It was a very comforting sight and a great relief."

As they crossed the coast at 5,000 feet, the five glider crews (one Horsa had lost its way) could see the parallel white streams of the Orne River and Caen Canal. Six miles inland would be their objective: the bridge that spanned the two waterways. One by one the five Horsas released and floated silently toward their distant target, "to make certain" —as an official British history claimed—"they would arrive at the bridges alone and unheralded, like thieves in the night."

Andrews said good-bye to the tug pilot and pulled the rope release. "There was the familiar jerk with the wind gradually receding to the background and the speed dropping to a modest eighty miles per hour. My copilot was intently watching an ack-ack battery on our right whose tracers seemed to be a bit too near. . . . I put on half flap and saw another Horsa well below us flying towards the flak. Just a second later it switched on its emergency lights and illuminated a small row of trees between ourselves and the green Tee which defined the field in which we were to land. I had to forget it as I concentrated on my approach, but my copilot said it seemed to crash into some trees to the right of the Tee marker. Then there was a little bump and another. It must have been something like a ditch. One wheel seemed to stick and started to veer the glider around; I applied opposite rudder and braked quickly and no sooner had we straightened than we stopped."

Andrews and the glider that had crashed into the trees had landed four hundred yards from the bridge over the Orne River near Ranville, but the third glider had come in very close, practically on the approaches to the bridge. The platoon it was carrying rushed the bridge and overwhelmed the few defenders. In spite of the loss of two of its three gliders, the first *coup de main* assault in Normandy was a success.

At the Caen Canal, the three gliders landed very close to

the bridge approaches, one less than fifty yards away. The troops immediately rushed the bridge under heavy fire and within fifteen minutes had driven off the German defenders.

Meanwhile, Andrews, his copilot, Sergeant Paddy Senier, and the two airborne troopers were struggling to get the tail off their Horsa. They had taken off the nuts which held the tail on, but it refused to budge even when the copilot jumped on top of it. "It was the oddest tug-of-war I have ever competed in," Andrews wrote. "One Horsa Mark I and four tired and sweating airborne types. The glider won and, while we sat back exhausted for a moment, it sank back quite contentedly for all the world as if it were back in England. I thought of using the charge to blow the tail off; but, apart from the noise and the fact that at present we were undisturbed, the type of equipment we were carrying decided me against it. Just as we picked up the handsaw, we heard the sound of approaching aircraft and then right above us the air seemed to be full of parachutes . . . for the next five minutes we were busy dodging kit bags which dangled from the feet of heavily loaded paratroopers. One even landed on the tail of the Horsa but nothing happened. . . . A plane caught fire, lit up in flames and crashed."

As Andrews and his copilot sawed away at the reluctant tail, they heard the sound of a hunting horn and knew that the paratroopers were attacking the bridges.

At the Merville battery, however, nothing went right. The position itself was formidable: four 150-mm. guns in concrete emplacements with walls six-and-a-half feet thick, its roof covered with thirteen feet of earth, steel doors barring its entrance, and the approaches covered by many machine guns. The entire position was fronted by a minefield one hundred yards deep and surrounded by barbed wire. It had been estimated that the battery was protected by over two hundred German soldiers.

The preparations for the assault had been meticulous. Six hundred men of the 9th Battalion Parachute Regiment had practiced attacking a reproduction of the battery both by day and by night. They were to drop accompanied by five gliders carrying jeeps, antitank guns, explosives for blowing the wire, mortars, six-pound guns, machine guns, etc. When they were in position and the attack begun, three gliders manned by volunteers carrying fifty-eight paratroopers and Royal Engineers would crash-land directly on top of the battery. They were to be guided in to a pinpoint landing by a "Eureka" radio transmitter placed by one of the initial attacking party.

Everything had gone wrong. The airborne troops and the five gliders had been scattered over a wide area by strong winds, and at three o'clock in the morning only 150 of the 600 men and none of the equipment carried in the gliders were ready for the attack. The aerial bombing had been useless, missing the battery completely but almost wiping out a reconnaissance party that was advancing to probe the defenses.

Knowing that the heavy guns would wreak a terrible havoc on the troops landing on the nearby beach, the paratroopers attacked. Under a withering fire and supported by only one machine gun, they rushed the outer defenses, throwing grenades and yelling. Just then two gliders appeared overhead (the third had broken its rope and had landed safely back in England). Hopelessly the paratroopers watched the Horsas circling in the darkness waiting for a signal. But there was no "Eureka" to guide them—it had been accidentally destroyed in the landing—and there were no flares. Finally, putting their trust in RAF navigation, the two glider pilots cut off. One mistook a bombed village for the battery and, by the time he realized his mistake, was too low to reach it. His glider came down a quarter of a mile away, and its passengers rushed to aid the assault. The second glider landed only fifty yards from the perimeter.

After a bitter fight at heavy cost to the attacking force—50 percent of its men killed or wounded—the battery was stormed. It was then discovered that the guns were not the large-caliber weapons they had expected but 75-mm. field pieces, which nevertheless could have caused serious casualties among the landing troops on the beach. It was, as Chatterton described it to the author, "a V.C. [Victoria Cross] job."

Shortly after three o'clock in the morning, the *coup de main* parties were reinforced by the arrival of almost fifty gliders carrying the commander of the 6th Airborne Division, Major General Richard N. Gale. Seventy-two gliders had started out, but some broke loose over England, three came down in the sea, and fourteen were scattered far from the correct landing zone. The glider fleet had been led by Lieutenant Colonel Iain Murray and had flown through low clouds and rain to reach the embattled troops struggling to hold their gains and to prevent a German counterattack on the left flank of the seaborne landing. The British paratroopers dug in and held on doggedly, awaiting the arrival of the main lift that evening.

"There was plenty of light on the resupply mission," Ernie Lamb recalled. "June the sixth was just a fortnight from the longest day of the year—if in fact it wasn't the longest day. We flew parallel to the Caen Canal at an altitude of 800 feet and I could see the gliders of the *coup de main* mission, one of them right up against the bridge itself. I was flying a Hamilcar on my first operation and carrying a unit of the reconnaissance squadron. They were known as the 'tentacles' of the army (although some of the chaps used another word instead of 'tentacles'). There was very little flak and I picked a field farthest from the river since it had no antiglider poles in it. It was long enough for a decent landing and I touched down at about ninety miles an hour, remembering to keep the tail down before I braked. Overturning a Hamilcar is fatal since the whole load would come down on the pilots. . . . We jumped down from the cockpit, let the air out of the tires and the oil out of the landing gear struts to allow the bottom of the glider to settle to the ground. This made it easier to get the ramp out and unload the vehicles. As we

138 / The Glider Gang

were doing this I saw a Tetrarch tank rumble out of a Hamil-car directly into the path of another landing Hamilcar. It was 'knocked for six' and pretty well battered but the Hamilcar was able to glide on to a safe landing with its undercarriage broken."

Tom Pearce was copiloting a Horsa carrying twenty troops and ammunition. The pilot, Sergeant Les Frater, had just lowered full flaps and was making a steep descent to a landing when, out of the corner of his eye, Pearce saw the wing of another glider. "Glider right!" he yelled. But it was too late. There was a horrible ripping sound as the other Horsa crashed into them from below. For a split second Pearce could look down into the cabin of the other glider and see the white faces staring up at him. Then the gliders slid apart. "This was all at about six hundred feet," Pearce told the author. "Les took the flap off to regain flying speed and we dived towards the ground hoping that the elevators were going to work so that we could round out. They did and, putting full flap on again, we landed somewhat sideways at about a hundred miles an hour.

"As we came to a shuddering halt, Les turned to me and said, 'Time for a cup of tea, Tom.' There were two flasks above our heads and one was still intact. When we tried to get out of the cockpit, we found that the doors were jammed, so I grabbed an ax and started chopping the windshield. It was like trying to cut through six-foot-thick ice. It just sprayed back at me. Then the cabin door opened and one of the chaps in back said, 'It's all right. You can get out here. In fact, you can walk out.' As we passed through the door we saw that the cockpit was the only intact part of the glider. The sides of the fuselage had been ripped and torn asunder."

The field was filled with tall corn, over the tops of which Pearce could see a large heap of plywood which was all that remained of the glider they had collided with. "We started rushing across to see if we could help when suddenly there was a low hissing noise and one of the airborne troops yelled,

'Delayed mortar bomb!' We all fell on our faces and there was a long, long silence but nothing happened. So we started to creep up slowly, and in the middle of the wreckage was the twenty-man dinghy which we carried for the Channel crossing. It was inflating itself with an ominous sound like an angry snake."

The crew of the crashed glider (two men from Pearce's own squadron) and the four gunners they had carried were all dead.

While the 246 gliders of the evening resupply lift were slithering to a halt in the fields around Ranville, the Germans were frantically trying to find the range with mortars. "Andy" Andrews crawled carefully through the exploding bombs to a hill overlooking the landing zones. His professional admiration was aroused by the sight of the fields filled with gliders; it had been a perfect example of a massed landing. Then he looked over to the right where his own glider stood. He was shocked to discover that what he had thought was a locked brake that had caused him to swerve on his landing run had actually been the Horsa wing crashing over an antiglider pole. "My luck must have been terrific, for the glider had only touched this one pole and had steered a course between the others at night without my having known that they were there."

The deepest penetration of German-occupied France was made by Staff Sergeants John Potts and Bill Jones. When their Horsa crossed the French coast, Potts was worried by the absence of flak, and it occurred to him that there might have been a serious navigational error. Three or four minutes later the flak hit them. "Incendiary or tracer bullets hit the port wing," Potts wrote to the author, "and set the wood on fire, but the real damage was a direct hit upon the cabin between Jones and myself. I was hit along the right arm and shoulder, but Bill was untouched and kept the glider on station behind the tug. The next burst severed the towrope and we were in free flight. . . . I could clearly see a field of landing size below the port wing and both of us put our hands to the wheel, turned into the field and were down with light flak still trailing us. We all made a hasty exit from the burning glider. We were certainly in the wrong place but where were we? The troops decided to move away from the target area and Jones and I started to look at the glider. Almost at once we came under small-arms fire. I dropped down behind one of the glider's wheels, Jones took the other and we started to fire back. Soon there was a further burst of fire accompanied by grenades and the unmistakable 'stonk' of a mortar. I remember a real crack of a noise, a flash, and that's all. I do have faint recall of being dragged somewhere but my first hazy recollection was someone saying, 'For God's sake, look at his face. He needs a doctor now!' Little did I realize it was my face. There were German voices and some rather rough material was wound around my head. I also remember some foul coffee, obviously German, and a rather good cigarette, obviously English."

After being photographed, Potts was taken for interrogation. "The German officer was very courteous and very correct. He asked nothing about the invasion and I vaguely recall that I then thought that the landings had failed. He reprimanded me for being a member of a sabotage mission and went on about these unsoldierlike activities of the British special forces. As night fell we were put into trucks and taken to Amiens. It was an English-speaking German who informed us enroute that we had landed east of the Seine River in the midst of the vast armies that von Rundstedt was holding to repel the real invasion. . . . Later I thought it was rather comical: just seventeen airborne men against von Rundstedt."

In the prison in Amiens, Potts's wounds were treated. A few days later they were told that the Germans were satisfied that he and Jones were bona fide pilots and not saboteurs and that they were to be handed over to the Luftwaffe. They were also told for the first time that the invasion had been successful and the fighting was continuing. From Amiens the two glider pilots were sent to Frankfurt, the first stop on their way to Stalag Luft 7 in Silesia (ten months later they would be liberated by the Russians advancing on Berlin).

On June 11 the German radio on its European service boasted of the capture of "British Sergeant John Denis Potts, 5391767, who was wounded and taken prisoner in the area of Le Havre." "They might at least have gotten it right," John Potts complained to the author. "I was a *staff* sergeant."

Fifty miles separated the Americans in the Cotentin Peninsula from their British comrades near Caen, but both, by exemplary courage and dogged determination, had fulfilled their missions and had helped pierce the Atlantic wall behind which the Germans had hoped to consolidate their earlier victories. In doing so, the Allied airborne forces had added another tenet to their growing doctrine: with control of the air it is possible to carry out airborne operations successfully in daylight.

This principle, won in storming the Channel coast of France, was now to be tested on the French Riviera. Before leaving England, the American glider pilots packed the belongings of their comrades who were dead or missing in Normandy. It was a task that was to become all-too-familiar. "Before we finished," one recalls, "we had gone through the uniforms and kit carefully to make certain there was nothing that would cause pain or embarrassment to his wife or family: contraceptives, love letters from or photos of English girls if the guy was married, even address books—all these were thrown in the trash can. I couldn't help wondering if my friends would be doing this for me after the next mission."

6
Campaign on the Riviera

For three weeks the glider pilots lived in tents on the edge of the Italian airfields—a sunlit paradise. After months of the damp grayness of England ("I missed the English summer; I was in a movie that afternoon"), Italy, warm, colorful, and friendly, was almost a recreation area. Those whose airfields were close to the Mediterranean would drive down in trucks to swim; at Orbetello, where the cliffs overlooked the beach, the village girls would throw down clusters of grapes to the soldiers cavorting nude in the water. But this was no vacation; they were here on business—and their business was war.

Originally the invasion of southern France—a seaborne landing between Saint-Tropez and Sainte-Maxime covered by an airborne landing—was planned to take place at the same time as the landing in Normandy. Unfortunately, the shortage of landing craft made this impossible and, although Churchill and Montgomery pleaded insistently that the landing in Provence be canceled, Eisenhower, strongly supported by General Marshall, insisted on its necessity. Their argument was that, without a separate threat to the German army in the south of France, the drive out of the Normandy beachhead would have to drop off combat divisions along its right flank to guard against an attack. This would seriously weaken the striking power of the Allied spearhead. Besides, it was known that the supply situation would soon be critical, and the seizure of Marseilles would permit resupply of the American armies on the right flank. The operation was code-named "Anvil" (later "Dragoon"), and the airborne phase was to be carried out by the 1st Airborne Task Force. This was a provisional group of 10,000 parachute and glider infantry already in the Mediterranean theater but reinforced by troop-carrier units—towplane crews and glider pilots—which were flown down from England to Italy by way of North Africa. The combined airborne task force was to be commanded by an American, Major General Robert T. Frederick.

While the Americans and British were closing the trap at Falaise in Normandy, preparations were under way at the airfields in the vicinity of Rome: D day on the Riviera would be August 15, 1944. One of the units whose men, guns, and vehicles were being loaded into gliders was the highly decorated 442nd Combat Team, Japanese-Americans who had written a brilliant record in the mountain fighting in Italy. The fact that the parents of many of these nisei soldiers had been interned spurred them to prove their loyalty by the outstanding combat record of their unit. This was to be their first airborne invasion and, although they had spent a few hours as passengers in gliders, like most glider infantrymen they were not too happy about the fragile craft. Most of them would have preferred to take their chances dropping by parachute, but now they would have to go with their antitank guns and jeeps.

The mission had actually begun at one o'clock in the morning of D day when nine pathfinder planes had crossed the coast of southern France, on time and on course. However, once past the shoreline they flew over a layer of fog which, clinging to the terrain, hid all the landmarks except the tops of the highest hills.

The morning parachute mission encountered the same litany of untoward events as in the Normandy assault, but this time a treacherous ground fog played the role of the unforeseen cloud bank on the Normandy coast. The pathfinders had been dropped blind as far as fifteen miles from their landing zone and were unable to set up the navigational aids by the time the paratroop planes came in. Only one troop-carrier group made anything resembling the proper drop. The group leader spotted hilltops jutting above the fog which he recognized from the sand-table model he had studied. Judging their position by this unusual landmark, he gave the green light to the paratroops, all of whom landed within half a mile of their drop zone. The other groups were not so fortunate. They scattered their paratroopers over the fields, vineyards, beaches, and rooftops miles from the drop zone. One serial even dropped its troops on the town of Saint-Tropez, and some parachutists drifted out to sea and drowned.

The predawn glider mission had taken off from the Italian airfields at five o'clock in the morning. It consisted of thirty-five Horsas flown by British glider pilots and forty Wacos flown by Americans; the cargo was mostly artillery for the British paratroopers. By the time the Horsas had reached Corsica, the mission had been canceled because of fog, and the Horsa serials turned around and returned. The American towplanes circled the landing zones for an hour, hoping that the fog would clear. Finally, at 9:30 A.M. thirty-three Wacos were released (one had broken its towrope and landed in the sea; another had disintegrated over the water, killing all aboard).

The big glider mission ("Operation Dove") of the day began in the afternoon. In the van were the thirty-five Horsas which had aborted their landing earlier in the day, followed by a parachute mission of forty-one planes. After that came 332 Waco gliders carrying a complete glider infantry battalion plus guns and support troops, a total of 2,250 men with large amounts of materiel. Takeoff and assembly, which began around 3:00 P.M., was slow owing to the thick dust kicked up by the towplane propellers at many of the airfields. But finally the long towplane-glider train formed and flew north along the Italian coast, crossed over Elba and the northern tip of Corsica, and headed for landfall just north of Saint-Tropez.

Major Generals James M. Gavin, Maxwell D. Taylor, and William C. Lee in a photo taken after the war.

A lineup of Waco gliders at an English airfield just before taking off for Normandy.

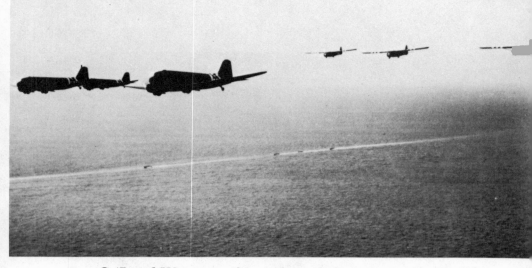

C-47s and Wacos pass the naval assault force crossing the English Channel to Normandy on D day.

C-47s release Waco gliders over LZ "W" in Normandy.

A Horsa and two Waco gliders in a hedgerow-lined field in Normandy on June 6, 1944.

The wreckage of Lieutenant Colonel Mike Murphy's glider in which Brigadier General Don Pratt and the copilot were killed.

This Horsa glider crumpled its landing gear and jammed its doors when it touched down in Normandy on D day. The American airborne passengers hacked through the wooden sides to get themselves and their vehicle out.

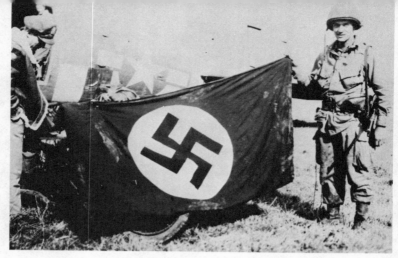

Flight Officer Joseph Mendes, glider pilot of the 434th Troop Carrier Group, displays a Nazi flag captured in Holland.

After colliding with anti-glider poles, this American Waco sits crumpled in a field near Sainte-Mère-Eglise.

The author (left), copilot Flight Officer Bud Klimek (right), and two nisei passengers before the flight to southern France.

Clouds of dust mark the paths of Waco gliders landing in vineyards and hopfields north of Le Muy, southern France, on August 15, 1944.

Antiglider poles in southern France, August, 1944.

Guarded by glider pilots, German prisoners are marched to the POW camp at Le Muy.

In Le Muy, French Resistance fighters and American glider pilots fire on a German sniper in the church steeple.

On passing Corsica, they encountered the first serious delay. The lead Waco glider developed a serious vibration in its tail, and the towplane pilot turned away from the formation. Faithful to their training, the entire group turned with their leader and headed back toward Italy. Finally the glider cut off and ditched in the Mediterranean, after which the group realized its error, turned around, and took up position again—not at the head but in the middle of the formation. Several more ditchings occurred during the eighty-five-mile flight to the French coast.

The unexpected turn by one group ended the carefully planned time interval between formations. Soon, planes were slowing down to keep from overrunning the serials ahead of them and—worse—planes were speeding to catch up. Flight Officer "Willie" Haynes of Pawhuska, Oklahoma, watched anxiously as the airspeed needle crept higher and higher. The Waco glider was "red-lined" at 150 miles per hour; being towed above that speed meant imminent structural failure. Several times copilot Haynes called the lieutenant colonel flying the towplane and asked him to slow down, but the speed kept increasing. When the needle moved above the "red-line," he picked up the telephone for another urgent request. At that instant the glider off his right wing disintegrated, hurling the two glider pilots into the sea.

Horrified, "Willie" Haynes watched the debris floating down, then whispered menacingly into the telephone, "Listen, you son of a bitch. I'll give you until I count ten to slow this thing down and then I'm going to shoot your goddam right engine out. One, two, three . . ."

As Willie's admiring pilot, Flight Officer Douglas Smith, told the author, "There must have been something in his voice that convinced that 'light' [lieutenant] colonel that he meant it, because before he reached 'eight,' we were below the red-lined speed."

The author, who was flying the third glider in the 439th Group serial, vividly remembers the crossing of the coast. A large number of warships were standing off the Sainte-

Maxime–Saint-Raphaël area bombarding the town. Smoke from burning houses and installations had blown out over the water, forming an appreciable haze at an altitude of about 800 feet. It was over this inadvertent cloud layer that the troop-carrier planes and gliders flew. Naval antiaircraft discipline had been tightened appreciably since Sicily; nevertheless, nervous gunners could still view the planes overhead as a threat. Although a clear channel had been designated for the troop-carrier planes to cross north of the naval area, faulty navigation caused them to fly through the northern edge of the forbidden area. As the author looked down at the impressive display of warships, he saw a heavy cruiser whose topside guns suddenly opened fire.

A split second later, there was a loud banging noise in the rear of the glider, which shuddered as though a heavy door had been slammed against its tail. The Waco fell off uncontrollably on its right wing and dived several hundred feet, still attached to the towplane. It took the frantic efforts of both the author and his copilot to get the right wing up and the glider level, but no amount of elevator seemed capable of stopping the steep dive. Finally, it was the pull of the towrope jerking the nose of the glider upward that stopped what seemed to be a fatal plunge. The bewildered glider pilots found themselves at the controls of a glider flying nose high and yawed to the right, at such a steep angle that it seemed to be hanging suspended from the towrope.

At this point the pilot turned to shout a warning to his passengers, two Japanese-American artillerymen. He saw that they were sitting calmly in the front seat of their jeep, smoking cigarettes and watching the frantic maneuvers with mild interest. Obviously, they had heard all the horror stories of the erratic glider flying and the madness of the glider pilots during the Sicily and Normandy invasions. Fellow airborne troopers and the glider mechanics had taken great pleasure in regaling them with the stories of these disasters during their few hours of orientation flying. Clearly they viewed all this wild maneuvering and frantic flying as standard operating procedures for gliders on a combat mission.

The heavily wooded hills to the east of the town of Saint-Raphaël rise to a height of over 800 feet along the route that the tug-glider train was flying. From its position 200 feet below its towplane, the stricken glider was clearing the treetops by a bare fifty feet at times and suffered the further indignity of being hit by small-arms fire from scattered enemy troops on the slopes below. The popping sound of bullets ripping through the taut canvas could be clearly heard, but the pilot and copilot were too busy keeping the glider under control and the passengers did not recognize the significance of the sound.

From the point where they crossed the coast to landing zone "A" (two miles west of Le Muy) is a distance of approximately twenty miles or ten minutes' flying time. Later the author compared notes with the copilot, and we agreed that it was the longest ten minutes of our lives. Every time we thought we had stabilized the glider, it would hit an air current from the hills below us, lurch, and try to fall off on its right wing. It was only by pure muscle that we were able to keep it level, even though we seemed to be flying sideways to the path of the towplane. Our main worry was what it would do when we finally cut off tow. It was clear that only the upward pull of the towrope was keeping the glider in level flight; what happened when we cut off and were in free flight was uncertain, and we sweated about it all the way to the landing field.

Enemy opposition was minimal and, except for some sporadic small-arms fire, the sky armada was undisturbed as it flew over the rolling hills parallel to the Argens River valley. The fields were a mélange of green pastureland and brown vineyards. But already the consequences of the unexpected turn of the lead serial near Corsica were beginning to show up. The planes in the rear had started to overrun the leaders and had climbed to higher and higher alti-

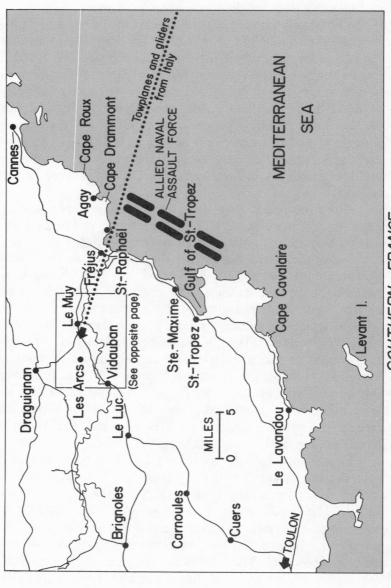

SOUTHERN FRANCE

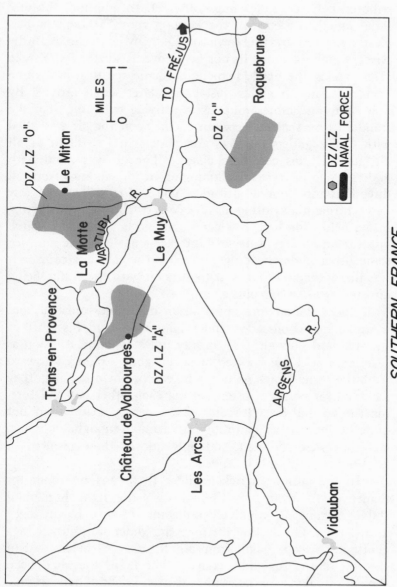

SOUTHERN FRANCE

tudes to avoid collisions. By now the glider train was distributed between 1,000 and 2,500 feet. In addition, the first serial failed to recognize the landing zone, although it was clearly marked by the town of Le Muy and the Naturby River, which ran along its northern edge. Realizing its mistake after passing the fields, it made a 180-degree turn and came back, releasing its gliders just as the later serials arrived. By now more and more groups were arriving with less than the standard time-spacing between them. Soon the air was filled with C-47s, gliders on tow, and gliders in free flight at all altitudes. It was complete chaos. "The air was filled with gliders," one pilot recalls, "plunging in for landings from all directions and from all altitudes. You had to weave your way down through a gyrating mass of Wacos all intent on getting into a field. You had to select a suitable landing field, watch out for antiglider obstacles, and keep a sharp eye out for some other glider heading for you on a collision course. It was like Piccadilly Circus at high noon with the traffic being directed by an insane policeman."

Under the circumstances all air discipline vanished, and it was a rare coolheaded glider pilot who held his craft to the standard slow glide of seventy miles an hour. As soon as a suitable field was spotted, a dozen gliders plunged toward it at the same time. As they circled for their landing, they jockeyed for position, often cutting each other out and forcing the cursing loser to settle for a nearby field, often not quite as long or as tempting. Amazingly enough, only two collisions were reported, and only one of these resulted in fatalities to crew and passengers.

In the author's stricken glider there was no room for maneuver to avoid a collision. With the right horizontal stabilizer gone, it would be impossible to turn to the right at any time. On cutting off tow, the glider was turned in a gentle left sweep, luckily from an altitude well below that of the rest of the tug-glider convoy. The fields they had been shown on aerial photographs at the briefing had seemed almost ideal, but it was only on closer inspection that they spotted "Rommel's asparagus"—antiglider poles up to six inches in diameter, set in long rows fifteen to forty feet apart and tied together by wires which would trigger mines at their bases when hit. (Not until later was it learned that the Germans had not had time to fuse the mines.) Throwing anxious glances in all directions, the glider pilots dived down into the fields and maneuvered wildly to avoid a nose-on collision with the antiglider poles. The author was one of the lucky ones. As he made his final turn to land, he found an open field about 600 feet long in front of him. In spite of fifty-foot-high trees at the approach end of the field, he managed to slip the glider with full spoilers touching down at ninety miles an hour. Once the wheels were on the ground and the glider was lurching at high speed toward the hedgerow at the far end, he put the glider up on the skids and shuddered to a halt five feet from an earthen embankment. All around him gliders were diving down and landing in clouds of dust with rending crashes as wings were taken off by the glider poles and noses buried into hedgerows.

(In the hectic weeks before the invasion, it had been discovered that there were less than one hundred serviceable Waco gliders in the Mediterranean theater. In a frantic attempt to assemble and flight-test the gliders for the mission, it was decided not to provide these with the Griswold nose, a heavy tripod of iron bars welded to the nose of the CG-4A glider which acted as a battering ram in knocking down obstacles during landing—especially since only 40 percent of the requested modification kits had arrived. So the gliders that plowed into the poles in the vineyards of southern France were not protected by the Griswold device.)

On the British landing zone, things went much better. In spite of their exhaustion after seven hours of flying (having flown almost to the French coast and then back to their base at Tarquinia, Italy, because of the morning fog), they had hastily reassembled the towplanes and gliders and had returned in the early afternoon at the head of the air armada. Ground opposition had been very light, and the only difficulty was in safely landing the large cylindrical Horsas in the small fields and vineyards. Thirty-six Horsas (one had aborted early in the flight with aileron problems) brought in troops and guns to support the British paratroopers of the 2nd Independent Parachute Brigade. In the main the landings were highly successful and, although some glider pilots were injured in the landing, only one (Staff Sergeant W. R. Jenner) died of injuries suffered in the crash of his glider.

Even after thirty years some of the glider pilots could be profane about the antiglider poles and the pileup of towplanes and gliders over the landing zone. Second Lieutenant Ellsworth Dewberry was one of them: "And then right after the Normandy invasion, they flew the whole goddamned outfit right back down to Italy to prepare for the invasion of southern France. That was really a piece of cake; there was no opposition. There were not even any Germans there. The goddamned boyscouts could have made a beach landing there and taken it. It was really ridiculous. However, they were so confident we were coming, every available field on our map was scattered with glider poles. There was no air opposition, no ground opposition. I had a green copilot . . . he never had any experience in flying gliders but he saved my ass 'cause we were coming in and I was sweating it out because everything was really all fucked up. Groups releasing on top of groups, it was pretty much wing to wing. . . . Well, you know how it was . . . they didn't stagger us in right. I come in on the objective with another group right ahead of me within seconds, trying to land. I was trying to watch out for people on each side on my wing and I told the boy to try to pick a landing spot for me—my copilot, a young kid. And I was still trying to keep an eye on both wings and at the same time tried to spot a good place 'cause I had a map in my mind. They'd given us that map bullshit, you know, on the briefing, and I had a beautiful field picked out. It just looked delicious. If I could duck these sons of bitches crowding me on right and left. I come in real nice and easy from about 500 feet. . . . It looked beautiful until we got down to about 200 feet and the kid, my copilot, said, 'Jesus Christ, it's full of poles!' . . .

"I always did think that they landed these goddamn things too fast. You could mush them bastards in at fifty miles an hour real easy with a full load. A lot of guys come in sixty, seventy, eighty miles an hour and actually those CG-4As—you could mush them in real nice at fifty miles an hour and a lot of people didn't realize that.

"I don't like to pat myself on the back but I was a pretty sharp pilot, one of the few things that I was good at. I saw these glider poles at around two hundred feet when this kid pointed them out to me so I had airspeed of about sixty then and I saw a peach orchard, a little peach orchard right beyond the glider poles and I could feel I still had a little bit of pressure on the stick and I got over those glider poles at about fifty miles an hour and piled right into these peach trees. And it was beautiful, really beautiful . . . I didn't scratch anybody, I didn't get hurt, the kid didn't get hurt (I call him the kid; he looked to me about twenty years old and at the time I was twenty-nine or thirty). . . .

"After we got down on the ground there wasn't a god- damn German within twenty miles! That was a real fucked-up abortion that we shouldn't even have tried. We lost a lot of boys hitting those glider poles 'cause they had it taped out real sharp. They knew exactly where we were coming and every open field was scattered with these goddamn telephone poles. We could have gotten a beach landing in there and taken that whole coast but I guess somebody wanted to use their airborne. . . . Well, that was southern France."

On the western edge of landing zone "A" stood a lovely château called Valbourges with a spacious terrace and deli- cate windows, a seventeenth-century edifice in the midst of the turmoil and bustle of a twentieth-century war. Gliders con- tinued to plow through its vineyards even as others were being unloaded. Out of their gaping maws came jeeps to be hooked to cannon and to trailers; then they drove off as the glider infantry moved into the surrounding hills and up the valley to capture Trans-en-Provence, which stood like a cork in the pass that led to Draguignan.

More accustomed, perhaps, to cavaliers in plumed hats or the King's musketeers, the gray walls of the château looked down disapprovingly on the mass of sweaty and dusty young men in their strange helmets, field jackets, and baggy pants who rushed about setting up telephone wires and digging foxholes on the verdant lawn. "Shortly after we assembled at the château, which was our rendezvous," someone recalled, "two grinning paratroopers drove up in a German staff car with three prisoners, a German colonel, his aide, and his driver. When they marched grimly out of the car and up the steps into the château for interrogation, I looked in the back; there was blood all over the seat."

Several hundred other German prisoners were brought in and parked temporarily in the field in back of the château. To the astonishment of the American airborne, they were not the old men of the "stomach and ear" divisions—rejects suffering from ulcers and deafness—that the briefing had told them to expect. Instead, they were young, vigorous soldiers in their early twenties who had been sent to southern France for a rest after service on the eastern front. According to the paratroopers who brought them in, there had been practically no fighting to the death and the German prisoners seemed to accept their captivity with equanimity. It was only when a glider pilot handed them a week-old copy of *Stars and Stripes* with a map on the first page showing the rapid Allied advance out of the Normandy beachhead that the mood of the young prisoners became somber and even bitter. They had not been told of the Anglo-American victories in northwest France.

The German officers were impeccably dressed and invariably arrogant; they were convinced that their captivity was temporary and that a massive German counterattack would soon free them. Thoroughly briefed on the Geneva and Hague conventions, they knew their rights as prisoners of war to the last detail. One protested to the paratroop sergeant in charge of the guard detail that he had been placed in the same enclosure with the enlisted men; as an officer he was entitled—even as a prisoner of war—to a separate place of confinement. The sergeant listened politely to the long tirade, then, slipping into the Yiddish of his native Bronx, informed the flustered officer that his request would be granted. He had him put in a nearby pigsty.

It was 7:30 P.M. (British Double Summer Time) before the last glider rolled—or crashed—to a halt in the vineyards around the château. By the time they had been unloaded and the jeeps and guns sent on their way, it was dusk. The glider pilots dug their foxholes on the lawn to guard the airborne command post in the château. Never one to sneer at comfort in the midst of a war, they lined the foxholes with parachutes, dragged the collapsible rubber dinghies from their gliders, and inflated them to serve as comfortable beds during the chilly night that was rapidly setting in. For those who couldn't be bothered digging foxholes, there was a long irrigation ditch running through a nearby vineyard which they promptly occupied and furnished to their satisfaction.

Soon it was dark and the night sky was filled with millions of stars. The fog on this cold, windless night formed in the hollows among the trees—the same fog that had frustrated the paratroopers and glider pilots of the dawn lift. The night was silent except for the murmur of voices as they discussed the events of the day. The excitement was slow to dissipate, since for many this had been their first combat mission. "Did you see those poles—those damn telegraph poles?" "Yeah. A Frenchman told me the Germans paid him to plant them in his field, but he made sure that they weren't planted too deep so that they would fall down at the slightest blow. Well, the two that I hit didn't fall down." "Did you see Captain Brown in the barn over there? Broke both his legs when his glider crashed into a tree. They keep reassuring him that they won't have to amputate. . . ."

The hours passed, the fog thickened, and soon the murmur of voices died away. Some men slept while others took the first guard watch. Soon the only sound was the off-key whistling of "Deep in the Heart of Texas" by a Lone Star State loyalist.

It was a nervous night and few slept. The moon came up over the low-hanging fog at 3:15 in the morning and bathed the stately château of Valbourges in silvery hues. Except for the incessant song of the cicadas and the occasional burst of fire from the direction of Le Muy, it was very quiet. Inside the château, the owner, a British citizen named James Stevens, who had lived most of his fifty-four years in France, tried to stay out of the way of the airborne, busily setting up their command post. He had filled the château with his friends, relatives, and a few local inhabitants who had moved from the coastal area the previous week to what they thought was complete safety in the isolated château. Now they found themselves in the very midst of a combat zone, surrounded by grim young men with black-painted faces and a ferocious air. Behind the château Stevens had ordered beds of hay to be laid for the wounded.

Huddled in his foxhole, Second Lieutenant Charlton W. "Corky" Corwin was feeling guilty about one of the injured men. After landing, he had run over to a Waco that had crashed nearby and lay crumpled upside down, its nose buried in the soft earth. The dazed passengers told him that the pilot was still inside and, even as he questioned a trooper with a broken leg, a feeble voice from deep in the wreckage pleaded, "For God's sake, Corwin, help get me out." Startled that the injured man had recognized his voice, Corwin had tied a rope to the glider fuselage and the other end to a jeep; as the jeep slowly backed off, they were able to raise the fuselage about four feet. Corwin crawled under and worked his way carefully toward the front of the Waco, knowing that, if the rope broke, he was dead.

"All I could see was dirt," Corwin told the author, "and as I dug into it about two inches, I felt his body. Spreading the dirt back, I finally uncovered him, working carefully, since he was probably hurt internally. Just as I was ready to move him, I hesitated . . . I flinched . . . thinking of the glider hanging above me. In that instant, someone crawled in next to me and jerked the man out. Later we heard that the injured man had died; he was a glider pilot I had flown with in training.

"I felt very guilty. If I had not flinched and had continued to move him slowly, he might have lived."

That night the glider pilots heard the strange sounds of ripping cloth from surrounding fields. At first light they could see paratroopers and glider infantrymen cutting the Army Air Force insignia from the glider fuselages and wings; these were spread on jeep hoods as identification to friendly aircraft. Many of the gliders were stripped of their instruments by souvenir-hunting soldiers.

The next morning, after a breakfast of K rations and hastily brewed coffee, the glider pilots were ordered to take the prisoners to the division POW enclosure near Le Muy. By the time they started out, the fog had burned off and it was another bright summer day, perfect weather for a stroll in the Provençal countryside. They lined the prisoners up in the center of the road in ranks of three and, with a guard on each side about twenty yards apart, set off down the rural road. The prisoners were glumly quiet, and the glider pilots were amused to see that many of them were carrying packed valises. Obviously, they had been prepared for their captivity.

As there was still some resistance in Le Muy, the prisoners were turned over to the military police short of the town. One German officer had barricaded himself in the steeple of the church and was firing on anything that moved on the main road past his hideout. The glider pilots went into action behind a stone wall and, with several French Resistance men, kept up a steady fire on the church steeple until the paratroopers were able to reach the main entrance to the church. It took two hours for the German officer to surrender. By that time word was passed that infantry from the beach had been spotted; the road to the coast was open. This was all the encouragement the glider pilots needed, for their orders had been to make their way to the coast and take any convenient ship to Corsica, where they would be picked up by their squadrons.

In small groups they marched or hitched a ride down to the coast, most of them arriving at Sainte-Maxime in the late afternoon in time to observe a German air raid on the ships massed in the harbor. There were no ships leaving for Corsica until the next morning, so, with the ability of good soldiers to make themselves comfortable, they moved into the deserted resort hotels facing the bay and slept in the rooms intended for peacetime tourists. The next day the author, with three of his squadron mates, was ferried out to a landing ship that was leaving shortly for Corsica. On the way he spotted a heavy cruiser not too far away and asked the ensign its name. It was the U.S.S. *Tuscaloosa*—the only American heavy cruiser in the fleet—and he filed that name away in his mind.

For such a hastily improvised airborne operation, the paratroop and glider landings in southern France were a model success. Although enemy opposition had been negligible, the smallness of the fields and the presence of the antiglider poles had extracted a harsh penalty: eleven glider pilots were killed and thirty injured. Over one hundred of their passengers had been seriously hurt in the crash landings in the vineyards on the hillsides. Though the amazing Waco glider once again proved its durability—there was very little damage to the guns, jeeps, and trailers that had been brought in—one troop-carrier wing later reported that of approximately four hundred gliders only two were still serviceable after the landing and only twenty-six could be salvaged. How many of the others might have been saved if the airborne had not cut out their insignias and stripped them of their instruments is not known.

Although the glider pilots were not aware of it at the time, their run-in over the coast had been made under the critical eye of Winston Churchill, who had been aboard the British destroyer *Kimberley*, and of Secretary of the Navy James Forrestal, who had watched from the bridge of the command ship *Catoctin*. In addition, the operation had included Second Lieutenant Jean-Pierre Aumont of the Free French Forces, who was serving as a liaison officer with the American Army. On the flank of the convoys, Lieutenant Commander Douglas Fairbanks, Jr., had led a diversionary gunship action to fool the Germans as to the actual landing site.

Among the casualties of "Operation Dragoon" must be included a forty-four-year-old Free French aviator who had disappeared on a reconnaissance over southern France two weeks earlier. He had begged special permission to keep flying in the attempt to obtain information on the disposition of German forces that would oppose the landing. His name was Major Antoine de Saint-Exupéry, the internationally known author of *The Little Prince*.

Within the next few days, most of the American glider pilots were taken by ship to Corsica and then flown back to their airfields in Italy. But some decided to take advantage of the vagueness of their orders to do some impromptu tourism in southern France and Italy. For the next month distraught MPs were rounding them up from such far-flung places as Marseilles, Toulon, Rome, and Naples. To a man, they claimed that they had become hopelessly lost trying to find their way back to their home airfields, and although there was a great deal of suspicion as to their motives—since many were found in very disreputable houses—no charges were pressed. Instead, they were corralled and flown back to England.

Many of them arrived just in time to be thrown into the desperate battle that bears the name "Market Garden."

7

Too Many Rivers to Cross

"Operation Market Garden" was really three separate battles, bitter, prolonged, and uncoordinated struggles to get the stalled Allied armies moving again before winter. Strung out over sixty miles from the Belgian-Dutch border to the lower Rhine, it would involve two American and one British airborne division, comprising about 35,000 men, engaging as many of the enemy in six days of brutal fighting before the issue was decided. After their breakout from the Normandy beachhead and their headlong pursuit of the broken German armies, it was inconceivable to the Allied commanders that the Germans would be able to put up a strong defense short of the Rhine River. The plan—probably one of the most imaginative and daring of the war—had been conceived by the usually cautious General Montgomery: an airborne carpet would be laid in front of the British troops on the Meuse-Escaut canal line, opening a narrow corridor for them through central Holland (this was "Market"). Capturing vital bridges across seven rivers and canals would allow the British XXX Corps to plunge forward through Eindhoven, Veghel, Grave, Nijmegen, until it reached the town which was to give its name to the battle, Arnhem. This ground offensive was called "Garden."

To the British, ending the war in 1944 was vital. They had been fighting for five years and their manpower was exhausted. Montgomery had been battling Eisenhower for some months to give up his strategy of an advance to the Rhine on a broad front and to put his supplies and resources into an advance in the north on a narrow front (under Montgomery's command, of course). Having failed to shake the Supreme Commander's resolve, Montgomery had then proposed the commitment of the newly organized 1st Allied Airborne Army,* in advance of his own 21st Army Group, to open a path through Arnhem onto the north German plain, thus outflanking the Siegfried Line and making the crossing of the Rhine at other points largely academic. To this plan Eisenhower quickly agreed, since he himself was under pressure from Generals Marshall and Arnold for a more imaginative use of the airborne divisions. Finally, the idea of a "mass vertical envelopment," which had intrigued the American chief of staff and head of the Air Force (and which they had failed to obtain in Normandy), was to be attempted. This time the northernmost airborne divisions would be far in advance of the ground troops.

Directly in front of the British XXX Corps, the U.S. 101st Airborne Division would capture the river and canal crossing in the Eindhoven-Veghel area. The vital bridges at Grave and Nijmegen would be the responsibility of the U.S. 82nd Airborne, while farthest north and responsible for the capture of the Arnhem bridge would be the British 1st Airborne Division. Still smarting from its experience in Sicily and anxious to emulate the brilliant work of its rival—the British 6th Airborne Division—in Normandy, the 1st Airborne Division was being led by a new commander, Major General "Roy" Urquhart, who had never led an airborne division before. Because of his lack of airborne experience, Urquhart allowed himself to be persuaded by the RAF that a landing in the immediate vicinity of the Arnhem bridge

* Activated in August, 1944, 1st Allied Airborne Army was commanded by Lieutenant General Lewis Brereton, with Lieutenant General "Boy" Browning as his deputy. It was made up of the U.S. XVIII Airborne Corps comprising the U.S. 82d, 101st, and 17th Airborne Divisions; the British Airborne Corps comprising the British 1st and 6th Airborne Divisions; the U.S. 9th Troop Carrier Command; the 1st Polish Parachute Brigade; and two RAF Troop Carrier Wings.

was impracticable because of intense enemy flak and the unsuitability of the marshy ground for landing heavy gliders. The only other landing area was a heath eight to ten miles northwest of the bridge. This, then, was selected for the airborne assault. It was a tragic error.

Why was Arnhem to be a British objective? With two American and one British airborne divisions committed to the operation, the odds would seem to favor sending an American division to Arnhem. However, in early September Montgomery had planned an operation called "Comet Two" involving British airborne forces dropped in the Nijmegen-Arnhem area to seize the river crossings. Although this was later canceled because of bad weather and stiffened enemy resistance, the British had studied the terrain in the Arnhem area carefully and had drawn up preliminary plans for the airborne assault. Since "Market Garden" was a strengthening of "Comet Two," it was logical that the British should select Arnhem as their objective. Also, for the equivalent number of towplanes, the British Horsas and Hamilcars could bring in more guns and vehicles in a single lift than the American Wacos. If the rumors of two German panzer divisions refitting near Arnhem were true, antitank guns would be vital. In addition to these military reasons, there was a psychological one: "Boy" Browning had been selected to lead the combined American-British airborne forces. Therefore, it may have been felt that national pride required that the toughest job, the spearhead, be given to a British airborne division since the entire operation was to be under a British commander. (General Eisenhower told his naval aide that the British had been very insistent on being given Arnhem as a target.)

While the final plans were being drawn up and distributed, the glider pilots got ready for the mission. The indications were all there for the experienced eye to see: the troop-carrier planes had been taken off resupply runs to the armies in the field; the glider mechanics were working fever-

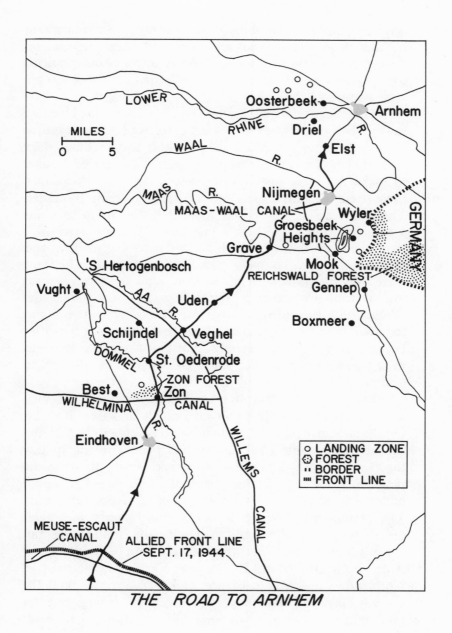

MILES

0   5

LOWER

RHINE

Oosterbeek •   • Arnhem

Driel

WAAL   R.

Elst

MAAS   R.

Nijmegen

MAAS-WAAL CANAL   Wyler •

Groesbeek
Heights

Grave   Mook •

REICHSWALD FOREST

'S Hertogenbosch   Gennep •

Vught •   Uden •   Boxmeer •

AA   R.

Schijndel •   • Veghel

DOMMEL   • St. Oedenrode

ZON FOREST

Best •   Zon

WILHELMINA   CANAL

R.

Eindhoven

GERMANY

WILLEMS   CANAL

LANDING ZONE
FOREST
BORDER
FRONT LINE

MEUSE-ESCAUT
CANAL

ALLIED FRONT LINE
SEPT. 17, 1944

THE ROAD TO ARNHEM

ishly preparing, assembling, and inspecting the maximum number of gliders; and an enclosure had been prepared on the airfields for the reception of the airborne. Soon the fields were sealed, and a silence seemed to settle over them. People were waiting for the orders.

The glider pilots were veterans now. Those not bloodied in the Normandy hedgerows had received their baptism among the vineyards of Provence. A few had become cocky and arrogant, but mostly their experiences in combat seemed to make the men quiet—even reserved. By now they knew their strengths and weaknesses and those of their comrades. There was an acknowledged hierarchy: the more missions a man had flown, the higher his status. The real aristocrats were the very few who had flown Sicily, Normandy, and southern France. To have put their courage to the test, their lives in the balance three times and to have survived was to win great respect. Those who had just joined the Glider Pilot Regiment or had just arrived from the States felt that they were being watched, that there was a barrier between them and the veterans. Not that their reception was in any way unfriendly, but it was clear that they still had to prove themselves on a combat mission.

In spite of the outward appearance of calm, the men were edgy and tense; it didn't take much to start a fistfight. On the airfield at Membury Flight Officer Kenneth Hinkel and Second Lieutenant Adolf Riscky had been drinking quietly together until an incautious word had set them throwing punches at each other. As someone explained, "It was a mixture of nerves and a fairly large bottle of Beefeater gin." The bystanders let them work off some energy and their dislike for each other until a Thompson submachine gun got into the act, and then they quickly stepped in and broke it up. Both Hinkel and Riscky had already crash-landed in Normandy and southern France, and their anxiety about the coming operation was building. Hinkel, the youngest glider pilot in the squadron, had long had a premonition about this mission. In Italy, before taking off for southern France, he had said that "he'd make out in that one, but wouldn't survive another invasion," Flight Officer Douglas Smith recalled. "He was just a kid. He cried softly all night before the takeoff. Riscky was strangely quiet."

On the morning of September 17, 1944, the skies over England were clear. An early morning fog had dissipated an hour before the scheduled takeoff, and only wisps clung in the valleys. Over the Channel the weather had been reported excellent, and only over the Continent would there be any problems; although the visibility there was greater than five miles, a thick cumulus layer hung at 2,500 feet. This would be serious for the British gliders, which normally flew at that altitude—twice as high as the American tugs. The malevolent fates that determine the fortunes of war had decided to give the Allies almost perfect weather for the first day of the airborne invasion of Holland, but the plan called for three days of good flying weather. The clear skies and excellent visibility on the first day added to the feeling of optimism and hope, but it would prove to be a trap.

From their airfields north and west of London, the American troop-carrier groups began taking off just before 10:00 A.M. With unprecedented speed, C-47s carrying paratroopers rose from the runways and began the long circular route about the airfields to allow the later planes to catch up. Behind them more planes pulling Waco gliders lumbered into the air. As usual, the glider pilots wore no parachutes, and on this mission the American gliders carried no copilots. Loaded with troops, jeeps, and artillery, they bounced along at the ends of the long towropes with an airborne soldier sitting in the right-hand seat.

As the groups formed and headed for the assembly point, the inevitable accidents began. Towlines broke, cargoes shifted dangerously, and gliders caught in their towplanes' slipstream oscillated wildly; soon three gliders broke loose and floated down to safe landings in English fields. All their cargo was retrieved and sent on later lifts into Holland.

It was an awe-inspiring sight. With a thundering roar, wave after wave of planes—Dakotas, Halifaxes, Stirlings, some carrying parachutists and some towing gliders—swept through the skies toward the Channel coast. Ahead of them almost three thousand Allied bombers and fighters were racing to attack the German flak defenses along their route. In the largest daylight assault of the war, over 2,000 planes and 600 gliders were bringing 20,000 men, 500 vehicles, and 330 cannon to open the corridor for the Allied sweep to the Rhine.

They crossed the English coast at two separate points east and northeast of London. The Nijmegen lift was on the northern route, with the British on their left headed for Arnhem. In the American column Colonel Chatterton flew a Horsa carrying General Browning; behind him were thirty-seven Wacos and Horsas with the rest of Browning's headquarters. The British glider train for Arnhem—478 Horsas and Hamilcars—had suffered heavily from mishaps even before leaving England: twenty-three gliders had broken loose and their cargoes, including the jeeps of the reconnaissance squadron, would not be in Arnhem on the first day. To General Urquhart, flying in a Horsa piloted by Lieutenant-Colonel Iain Murray, this was to be a very serious loss.

On the southern route, five hundred C-47s (seventy of them towing gliders) swept across the coast headed for a landfall near Dunkirk. Unlike the planes in the northern column, which would be under enemy fire as soon as they reached the Dutch coast, the formation carrying the first elements of the 101st Airborne Division would be over friendly territory until they crossed the front lines on the Meuse-Escaut Canal. After that it was only a short run to their drop and landing zones near Zon. To the veteran paratroopers and glider infantrymen it sounded like a "milk run."

The soft green patchwork fields of England disappeared as they flew out over the Channel, which now claimed its share of the losses. As the glider pilots struggled to maintain their position without the aid of a copilot, towropes were overstrained and broke. Gliders splashed down in the calm sea, and their crews could be seen standing on the wings and waving to the formations overhead. Air/sea rescue launches headed quickly toward them. In addition, a Waco that started to disintegrate ditched safely. Otherwise, the flight was uneventful, and soon the coast of Holland appeared on the horizon.

Lieutenant Colonel Charles H. Young, commander of the 439th Troop Carrier Group, remembered crossing the Dutch islands very well. "About five miles inland from Schouwen, we saw bursts of flak off to the left ahead, short of a column of Horsa gliders at which they were shooting. Fighters gave us excellent support; four of them shot up a gun position on a docked ship at the east end of Schouwen right under our noses before they could fire a shot at us. Every direction we looked, up, down, or sideways, we saw airplanes. It's a thrill to be part of an operation so gigantic.

"I never had a sensation before like I had that day. It could be approximated by tying a person to a wall and shooting at him with a machine gun from a distance of 175 yards for ten seconds. Just before reaching our drop zone, 500 feet above the ground, I saw a crew of Germans run to their 20-mm. guns and fire at us as we flew directly over them. We could see the whitish-yellow flames at the gun muzzles and the tracers went by our cockpit on both sides at the same time and it sounded like people beating on the airplane with sledgehammers. It's hard to describe—you want to duck but there's no place to duck. You get mad but you don't have anything to hit back with. You're scared—bad—and none of us deny it. I looked back at my crew and the paratroopers and they were looking at me. You wonder how much of it you could stand. . . . I saw two planes go down in flames just before they shot at us. The second looked like he had an engine on fire. It smoked badly and someone in his formation called, 'G for George, you're on fire. Bail out!' "

As the planes and gliders carrying the 101st Airborne swept over the front lines, the flak began. Flight Officer Joe Poindexter was so fascinated by the sight of a fighter plane zooming down to knock out an antiaircraft gun that he did not realize that his glider had been hit until he smelled hot metal. He turned and asked the medics sitting in the jeep behind him to take a look in the back and see what damage had been done, but "they were stiff with fright and did not answer." The airborne staff sergeant who was flying in the copilot's seat loosened his safety belt and crawled back to make an inspection. He reported that a section of the wing between the aileron and the fuselage had been blown off back to the main spar. Poindexter wiggled the controls and saw that none of the cables had been cut so he held on grimly, crash-landing safely in his assigned area.

As the formations approached their landing zone north of the Zon forest, the antiaircraft fire became intense and accurate. Soon the air was filled with burning troop-carrier planes. Sixteen were shot down, most after their paratroops had jumped, and six more crashed after releasing their gliders. Stung by the criticism of their conduct on the Sicily and Normandy missions, particularly about their unwillingness to face flak, the troop-carrier pilots were determined to get through to the drop zones as ordered. One Air Force historian wrote, "This time enemy fire had almost no effect on the delivery of the paratroops. The formations held tightly together and the pilots of the damaged planes coaxed them along with a skill and a courage which had the paratroops openmouthed. One colonel was so absorbed in watching the struggle of a badly damaged plane to reach its zone that he almost forgot to jump."

"Don't worry about me," the pilot of a burning plane told his flight leader. "I'm going to drop these troops in the DZ." He kept his word—and crashed in flames immediately after the drop. At least three other pilots stayed at the controls of burning aircraft and gave their lives to ensure their paratroops an accurate drop.

Flight Officer Gale Ammerman grabbed the phone and warned the tow pilot that gasoline was streaming out of his right-wing tanks. There was a pause while the pilot considered the situation, then he answered, "We're going towards the drop zone as long as the engines keep going." Ammerman recalls that the courageous pilot "split the drop zone down the middle but did not make it back to England."

As one glider approached the release point and the flak began, the airborne trooper sitting in the right-hand seat took off his helmet and put it between his legs. To the questioning stare of the glider pilot, he said calmly, "Hell, if I'm hit there, I'm dead anyway."

In spite of the losses, the mission was over 80 percent successful. The 101st quickly assembled its men and vehicles and moved out to secure the bridges.

After the initial flak from barges and gun emplacements over the Dutch coast, the formations carrying the 82nd Airborne to the Nijmegen area had a relatively quiet trip—until they made their turn at Grave. Then enemy gunners in the Reichswald Forest just over the German border sent up a barrage of light flak and small-arms fire. Since the unarmored troop-carrier planes still lacked self-sealing fuel tanks, they were extremely vulnerable. Ten planes were quickly shot down and 118 others were hit. But the pilots persevered, and the drops and releases in general were very good. Although only six gliders reached the correct landing zone, all the others came down within a mile of it, delivering all the guns without damage. As Flight Officer John L. Lowden was about to make his landing inside a fenced field, the airborne sergeant sitting next to him remarked quietly, "I wouldn't presume to fly for you, but I think you're about to land in a minefield." Lowden released the spoilers and stretched his glide to the point of stalling, just barely making it out of the danger area.

Colonel Chatterton landed his Horsa glider with flak bursting all around him. The glider smashed through a power line, ripping off the nose wheel, and came to rest in a cabbage patch behind some small cottages. Getting up from the beer crate on which he had been sitting, the immaculately dressed General Browning tucked his swagger stick under his arm and set off resolutely for the nearby German frontier. He was determined to be the first British officer to urinate on German soil. (Contempt for the enemy's homeland is expressed according to nationality, not individual temperament: the Americans spit on it; the British and Commonwealth soldiers urinate on it; and the French defecate on it.)

Meanwhile, Chatterton was watching the American gliders land. Unlike the British system of preselecting landing sites for each glider, the Americans were coming down from all angles, wherever there was a clear space. "It was a fantastic sight," Chatterton later wrote. "The Germans were even more staggered than we were and all firing ceased."

To Chatterton's relief, they had landed among an American airborne artillery unit. Pulling the guns from one glider and the jeeps from another, the Yanks connected the two together, drove them into a nearby woods, and were soon shelling the enemy batteries that had been harassing the landing troops.

Second Lieutenant Arthur Kaplan landed his glider in a field near Chatterton's. Under sporadic mortar fire, he helped unload an ammunition trailer, then accompanied his passengers toward the rendezvous point. As they passed a barn, they heard suspicious noises inside and crashed through the door, rifles ready. "There—in one of the stalls—a paratrooper was making love to a very willing Dutch girl," Kaplan recalls. "He was quite profane at being interrupted, so we apologized and left. I was really amused by this incident. The guy couldn't have been on the ground more than an hour."

By the time the British glider train started its approach across the lower Rhine to the broad fields west of Arnhem, thirty-nine gliders were already missing. Twenty-three of these had broken loose over England and their cargoes could be expected in a later flight, but unfortunately these contained most of the jeeps of the reconnaissance squadron which was to have reconnoitered the road to the Arnhem bridge. Now the bridge would have to be attacked blindly. One Horsa had gone down in the Channel; seven had broken loose over Holland before reaching the initial point, and, having fallen in hostile territory, had to be assumed lost. Engine trouble on the tow aircraft had forced three to turn back. One had been shot down over Schouwen—the only loss to antiaircraft fire. There had been surprisingly little flak on the flight from the coast to the lower Rhine; and as they approached the landing fields, they were surprised at the lack of hostile fire from the vicinity of the Arnhem bridge. A *coup de main* attack on the bridge had not been planned because of the belief that antiaircraft fire would be heavy enough to result in prohibitive losses. Except for some scattered small-arms fire, no enemy action troubled the formation as they reached the release point.

One by one, with unrivaled precision, the big wooden gliders cut off and turned slowly to set their pattern for the approach. The RAF bombing in the vicinity of Arnhem had undoubtedly been very effective, but the smoke from the bombardment, combined with the natural haze, bothered some of the glider pilots. In addition, the wind was light and variable, and there was a tendency to overshoot the landing fields. With their huge flaps lowered, the Horsas floated down to precise landings, except for a few which failed to stop and crashed into the tall trees that outlined many of the fields. The most tragic accident involved two Hamilcars whose wheels dug into the soft soil, flipping them onto their backs. Since the pilot and copilot are in a Plexiglas-enclosed cockpit that protrudes from the top of the glider and since the heavy load is directly below them, the turning over of a Hamilcar is almost invariably fatal to the crew. Other Hamilcars coming in later and seeing their two companions on their backs in the field quickly chose other landing spots and came in safely. The two seventeen-pounder guns in the overturned Hamilcars were lost.

As each Horsa landed and shuddered to a halt, the crew rushed to the back to cut the cables before unbolting the tail. Except for distant small-arms fire, it was strangely quiet on the landing fields. The only sounds were made by hundreds of glider pilots hammering furiously at recalcitrant mounting bolts. Finally, the tails were removed and the cargo brought out.

In spite of the loss of most of their jeeps, the reconnaissance squadron moved out for the bridge. The glider pilots and the rest of the airlanding brigade remained to protect the area for the next glider lift.

At the end of the first day the planners at 1st Allied Airborne Army were still optimistic about the results. The daylight delivery of men and materiel by parachute and glider had been largely successful, with acceptable losses in planes and gliders, and the opposition (except for the surprising absences of flak at Arnhem) had been as expected. It seemed that the reinforcements of the second- and third-day lifts would give the airborne divisions the punch necessary to capture all their objectives. But the delicate fabric of the "Market Garden" plan was already beginning to unravel.

The Guards Armored Division had been stopped short of Eindhoven, and their next river crossing, the bridge at Zon, had been blown up before it could be captured. This inevitably meant a delay while bridging equipment was brought up to span the river. The vital bridges at Nijmegen and Arnhem had not yet been taken, although they were still intact and paratroopers were approaching to secure them. Ignored by the Allies—despite Dutch underground reports that identified them and their location—two German panzer divisions had been refitting in the area northwest of Arnhem and were even now preparing to attack the British Airborne Division.

And now the weather, the critical element in the "Market Garden" plan, began to change. As rain and low clouds swept in over the Channel, fog began to form over the English airfields.

On Monday—D day plus one—uncertainty in the

weather caused a great deal of confusion. Originally it had been planned to send the missions over the northern route. When the meteorologists predicted that the northern fields would be covered by fog in the early morning and that rain and low clouds would cover the route until afternoon, General Brereton ordered the mission sent over the southern route. By late morning the southern route was unusable because of low ceilings, and the route was again hastily switched back to the northern one. Takeoff was to be delayed until shortly before noon in the hope that the weather would clear.

At Aldermaston Flight Officer Dale Oliver was sitting at the controls of his Waco, vaguely unhappy; he sensed that something was wrong. Looking back at the jeep that was his cargo, he wondered if some of the ropes were loose despite his having checked them shortly before. Oliver got out of the glider and walked around it for another complete preflight inspection, "thinking whatever bothered me would manifest itself. We were parked on the grass but even so the tail seemed to sit slightly lower than it should. Since the towplane engines were beginning to turn, I ran quickly to look under the left stabilizer and noticed a wrinkle in the fuselage fabric and a minor bend in the tail wheel strut. I unzipped the inspection flap and when I looked upward inside the vertical fin area, I almost fainted. The inside construction was broken and mangled, none of which showed from the outside. Evidently the ground crew, when they parked the 'beast' for takeoff, had braked too suddenly, putting the nose down on the ground. Being loaded heavily, the tail had then slammed back to earth. I'm certain that the structure would have lasted only a few minutes in flight." Oliver's cargo was hastily transferred to another glider at the tail end of the serial.

Right on schedule, the planes and gliders started to take off for the second-day mission. The British put their serials into the air from fields with peaceful names like Great Dunmow, Down Ampney, and Blakehill Farm. The

Americans, including those who had moved up to northeast England from the south, took off from Spanhoe, Saltby, Chilbolton, and a dozen other airfields. At the assembly point they formed into three lanes to cross the North Sea: the right-hand lane was the resupply for the 101st in the Zon area; the center lane was intended for the 82nd Airborne near Nijmegen; and the left-hand lane was going to Arnhem.

As they flew to the assembly point and then out over the sea, the usual troubles began. Towropes snapped; gliders caught in a slipstream of other planes became uncontrollable and released. One Waco disintegrated, spilling its human cargo like broken dolls. A fear-crazed soldier ran forward and pulled the rope release in one glider. Over the Channel there were ditchings, and the air/sea rescue launches rushing to the downed gliders were a welcome sight. Those gliders which had broken loose over England and had landed safely had their cargoes quickly trucked back to the nearest airfield, where they were loaded on reserve gliders and sent off by themselves to follow the mission into Holland.

As they crossed the Dutch islands of Schouwen and Walcheren, the flak began, much of it from barges in the estuary. Fighters dived down to engage the antiaircraft guns. Sergeant Jim Davies was at the controls of a Horsa filled with medical supplies, medical personnel, and a jeep when they crossed the Dutch coast: "The weather was bright and sunny. I was flying at the time and watching tracer bullets coming up along the rope between the glider and the tug. Suddenly the tug peeled off in a dive and the rear gunner opened up onto the ground. There I was hanging on, wondering if I could get the glider into such a tight turn. Later I asked the Australian power pilot what he was trying to do and he told me that he forgot that he had a glider on tow and had just peeled off like a fighter."

Shedding gliders intermittently along their flight path as towropes were shot through, the towplane formations flew into Holland, then separated to head toward their different areas. At Arnhem the landings were now to be made in the face of sporadic antiaircraft fire. Sergeant Tom Pearce, still badly shaken by a narrow escape over Walcheren when tracer shells had narrowly missed him, had a second close call shortly after release. "In the landing area, we cast off," he said in an interview. "Very shortly after that we heard a loud crack, which didn't seem to affect anything. We didn't know what it was, so we just went on ahead and landed—made quite a good landing. Then, while the troops were unloading our gun and trailer, I walked around the back, and in the tail of the Horsa was a huge dent as if a giant had pushed with two fists gently just so far and then said, 'Well, that's enough.' This must have been from the concussion of the exploding shell we had heard, although we didn't realize what it was at the time. My first pilot later told me that there was a hole in the port wing about a yard square from the same explosion."

It was while moving into position with other glider pilots to defend the landing areas that Pearce saw what he called "the most spectacular arrival of a Horsa glider I have ever seen. They were casting off at about two thousand feet, and right close to a Horsa was a black burst which was obviously antiaircraft fire. The glider immediately went into a vertical dive; I thought it was doing something like four hundred miles an hour. I thought it was going straight in, but suddenly at about five hundred feet it leveled off. The strain of the pullout was so great that it broke the back of the glider. It traveled along through the air in this V shape with the rear of the fuselage at a sharp angle to the rest of the glider. It went along for three or four hundred yards and then hit into a plowed field. The cockpit broke loose and barreled along the ground like a huge top. The two pilots who had been strapped in got out without a scratch, but the four men in the back, the gun crew, were flung out of the sides of the Horsa. The only one who was hurt had a fractured ankle."

Meanwhile, in the Zon area Dale Oliver's glider was one of eleven to arrive out of the eighteen in his squadron that had left England. The serial arrived at the landing zone, Oliver said, "precisely on point and at absolutely prescribed altitude of five hundred feet despite torrential ground fire. My wingman carried the 57-mm. antitank gun for my jeep, and he was to stay on my wing all the way down. Unfortunately, I had to make a very steep turn to a good strip of ground, and he was unable to follow. Thus one more jeep-gun unit was split up. My touchdown was a near disaster, for the field was soft loam. I went hub deep immediately and stopped so suddenly—tail high—that the nose scooped up the dirt like a snowplow. The deceleration slammed the rear panel of the pilot's seat into my back, and I was afraid my spine was broken. The only thing that saved me was the tension of my flak vest."

As he got out of the glider, Oliver saw a C-47 billowing smoke and crashing in flames just north of his landing spot. A second plane on fire flew close by. "The pilot climbed it steeply to about eight hundred feet, at which point it began to stall out. Just at the peak of its stall, two figures shot out of the cockpit overhead hatch and both chutes were seen to open."

Flight Officer Joe Poindexter also saw the C-47s dropping in flames around them: "One of them came into the landing zone towing a Waco. It had one engine on fire and was flying at about 200 feet. As soon as the glider released, the plane went into a steep climb at approximately 500 feet and the radio operator and mechanic bailed out. Their chutes opened perfectly but they were so close to the C-47 that the flames disintegrated their chutes and they fell to their deaths. At about the same time the C-47 stalled out and crashed."

The crashing of the towplanes endangered the men already on the ground. Dale Oliver was standing on the road alongside the landing zone when he saw a C-47 coming from the east paralleling the road at less than a 500-foot altitude: "As I watched, his right engine suddenly shot a streamer of flames—like a red crepe ribbon stretching back—and then one figure shot from the fuselage, his chute popping open immediately. The tip of that gaseous ribbon barely flicked his canopy, collapsing it and killing him. Almost simultaneously—as if the pilot had fallen forward against the control wheel—the plane rolled on its back and the nose started down. At that moment I yelled to everyone on the road, 'Hit it!' They all vanished into the ditch. Having seen it head almost vertically for us, I felt compelled to run to my right. All of this must have happened in a flash, but even as I began to take my first long step, I thought, 'You'd better take one last look. It might be drifting to where you're going, Oliver.' But then I sensed I'd better get off the road and drop into the ditch which was a few feet behind me—I remembered that ditches were our only security and better than the womb.

"As I began my whirl, I did look up and saw two monstrous steel discs—the propellers going full bore. I was sighting along the inverted belly of the ship like rifle gunsights, from the radio antenna cone beneath the nose back to the tail wheel. I dropped right where I was . . . the props went on each side of me, and had I dropped a thousandth of a second later, I am sure that the top of the inverted cockpit would have struck my head.

"The strange thing is that I heard no unusual noise, simply a loud smothering sound that said 'C-R-U-N-C-H' . . . and then silence, except for the crackling fire from the ditch and various color flares going off from the fuselage. When the plane had crashed, the fuselage had been high enough above the road to allow me four or five feet of space between the plane and the ground. I was directly under the very center of the fuselage or a point about where the trailing edge of the wing would be with the wings to either side of me. As I started to crawl away, the fuselage—now weakened by the fire—fell across the road but, being inverted, the rudder was pointing down. It was the inverted vertical fin which held long enough for me to crawl out."

As the shaken Oliver pulled himself from under the burning plane, another glider pilot came running up, shook his hand, and said, "Man, I didn't think I'd ever see you again!"

In the Nijmegen area the gliders were saved from disaster by the delay in takeoff and the bravery of the paratroopers. Early in the morning the Germans had attacked out of the Reichswald Forest and had captured the LZs. If they still held them when the gliders arrived, there would be a massacre that would make what happened on LZ "W" in Normandy seem like a "milk run." Hastily gathering his last reserves, General Gavin threw them into the battle to beat the enemy back. "A mid-morning counter-attack by the division," Gavin later reported, "drove the Germans to the approximate line of the forest, thus driving them from the LZ but not denying them the opportunity to place considerable flak over it and small arms fire upon it." A message was sent to England warning the glider pilots to land on the western edge of the LZ, where they would be safest from enemy fire, but it arrived too late. The gliders were already on their way.

"The tugs and gliders," Gavin's report continues, "arrived during considerable flak and ground fire. Those landing on the west side of the LZs generally landed unscathed. Those that landed on the portion near the Reichswald Forest were generally pretty well shot up."

The troop-carrier formations had already suffered heavily in the flak-filled corridor from the Dutch coast to Nijmegen. Ten planes had been shot down and their gliders lost over enemy-held territory. They had arrived over the target area desperately looking for the smoke signals and colored panels that would indicate the landing fields. Very few glider pilots spotted any sign that the LZs had been reached. As soon as they could see the fighting on the ground, they slipped the ropes and glided down as slowly as they dared. Ripped by small-arms and automatic weapon fire, some managed to stop after a ground run of as little as fifty feet by adroit use of arrester parachutes. Others, coming in too "hot," dug their skids or wing tips into the dirt to keep from hitting an obstacle. As the paratroopers covered them with volleys at the German positions, hundreds of Wacos slithered across the disputed fields, shuddered to a halt, frantically unloaded jeeps and cannon, then fled to safety in the American lines. It was confusion and chaos. It bore no resemblance to a military operation, yet strangely enough it was highly effective. In spite of the wholesale damage to the gliders—"They littered the fields like broken matchsticks," General Gavin told the author—only twenty cargoes were lost from enemy fire on the LZs.

The biggest loss was the unexplainable failure of many Wacos to release over the fields now so clearly marked by hundreds of gliders. General Gavin stood helplessly in front of his headquarters near Groesbeek and watched twenty-five gliders sail overhead, carrying the precious guns of one of his field artillery units deeper and deeper into Germany.

Because of navigation errors and flak damage to lead aircraft, several of the serials were unable to spot the landing fields so close to the edge of the Reichswald Forest. They overflew the zone and continued into Germany before releasing their gliders. Some of the gliders, with their passengers and cargo, were lost completely, but other troopers were able to defend themselves on landing and to make their way back to friendly territory with or without their cargoes. Typical of the latter were the men of the 320th Field Artillery Regiment, who defended their position until nightfall and then pushed on ten miles north to the American lines, bringing with them 160 airborne, 22 glider pilots, 10 jeeps, and 2 cannon. In another case, the Germans destroyed the gliders by shelling shortly after they landed, and the troops and glider pilots dispersed and found their way individually back to the friendly lines.

When night fell on Monday, September 18, Browning could have had little cause for optimism at his headquarters near Nijmegen. The British XXX Corps was still waiting for the bridge at Zon to be completed. The vital bridge over the Waal remained in German hands and might be blown up at any minute; the 82nd Airborne could spare no troops to take it until their precarious hold on the Groesbeek heights overlooking the Reichswald Forest was secured. As the battle that morning had shown, it was entirely possible that they would be driven back. But worst of all was the uneasiness over the lack of communication with the 1st Airborne Division at Arnhem. The failure of the radios kept Browning in the dark as to the true situation around the Arnhem bridge and what help might be needed to secure that crossing over the lower Rhine.

Unknown to Browning and to the staff of the 1st Allied Airborne Army in England, what was developing at Arnhem was a debacle.

On the third day, victory again seemed to be in the Allied grasp. At six o'clock in the morning, the British Guards Armored Division crossed the Zon bridge and thirty minutes later reached Veghel. By eleven o'clock they had passed through Grave and were within sight of the bridge at Nijmegen. But in spite of this, the situation was still critical. The narrow corridor was being cut at various points along its length by determined German counterattacks. Gavin's 82nd Airborne had not yet received its reinforcements of glider infantry, which were needed to take the now strongly held Nijmegen bridge. To the north at Arnhem, the British airborne were being pushed back by the attacks of two German panzer divisions, reinforced by hastily gathered troops. One British battalion under Lieutenant-Colonel John D. Frost was clinging precariously to the northern end of the Arnhem bridge under direct artillery and mortar fire, a rain of steel that was rapidly diminishing their numbers. The situation was clearly desperate and would require desperate measures.

Now the weather turned against the Allied commanders. Fog, haze, and low stratus clouds hung over English airfields, the Channel, and Holland. Visibility at many points was reduced to one-half mile or less. Normally such weather would have grounded all aircraft, but the need to resupply and reinforce the three airborne divisions fighting to hold open the corridor to Arnhem was so vital that the decision was made at 1st Allied Airborne Army Headquarters to send the gliders over the southern route. The only concession to the weather was to delay the takeoff from ten in the morning to three in the afternoon in the hope that the fog would burn off and the weather would improve.

It did not improve; it got worse.

The nightmare of that desperate attempt to get through to the embattled airborne can be guessed from the formal words of the official history: "Glider pilots, unable to see their tugs, had to guide their craft by the tilt of the towrope and by telephone conversation with the plane crew. At most points over the Channel, it was possible to get under the clouds by going down to about 200 feet, but even then the visibility was generally half a mile or less. Many gliders broke loose, cut loose or were brought back; the whole last serial was called back after it was well out over the Channel." Most of the gliders were released to land at the first airfields sighted after recrossing the English coast, but the 436th group elected to fly back to its base at Membury.

As they approached the field under a low, threatening ceiling, Second Lieutenant Robert Dopita, the copilot of one of the tugs, saw a tragic scene. Two Waco gliders that had released ahead of his plane and were now flying just below him at an altitude of less than 700 feet suddenly turned and rammed head on. For a split second the two intermingled gliders seemed to hang in the air and then broke apart. A jeep—its driver still sitting rigid at the wheel and his passenger slumped beside him—tore out the front of one of the gliders and tumbled to the ground. Bodies spilled out from the wreckage like toy soldiers out of a great box, turning over and over, arms and legs outspread as they fell. The two gliders crashed a short distance apart, and one of them burst into a brilliant white flame from the phosphorous shells it had been carrying.

The hot-tempered words and threats made over a "bottle of Beefeater gin" had come true. By a startling coincidence,

Hinkel and Riscky had killed each other—and had taken six glider-borne troopers with them.

Flight Officer George Brennan was flying one of the gliders in the 442nd Troop Carrier Group that did not receive the signal to turn back and that doggedly flew lower and lower, determined to get under the clouds and through to Zon. "We flew across the Channel at an altitude of thirty feet," Brennan recalled, "the tug prop blast kicking up a spray over our windshield. I saw five gliders of earlier missions bobbing in the water. There was an artillery sergeant sitting in the copilot's seat and he was understandably very nervous, but I had my hands full trying to follow the towship and so there was no chance for small talk. I was carrying three troopers and a jeep loaded with 105-mm. artillery ammunition. The jeep had about ten jerricans of gasoline slung around the body and I couldn't help wondering what would happen if we took a direct hit. We crossed the coast at Dunkirk and the C-47s had to climb to clear the buildings in the city. The rest of the way we went in at two to three hundred feet at about 120 miles per hour. There was a lot of small-arms fire all the way in.

"As we got close to the landing zones, the flak really became thick. A twenty-millimeter shell passed through my left foot and exploded over my shoulder. It took part of my foot and a fragment split my left hand. Later fragments hit my left elbow, chest, stomach, right side, buttocks and fractured my jaw. The gas cans had been punctured and were leaking, along with oil from the jeep's crankcase. The gas and oil soaked the floor and collected under my feet. A tracer caused this to flash and my face, eyes, and hands were burnt. The sergeant got singed and took a flak fragment that perforated his right thigh and went into his scrotum. Needless to say this made him very apprehensive. He was single and from conversation prior to takeoff, I gathered that he liked the British uninhibited approach to sex.

"Without a copilot, with my left foot and hand useless, my eyes less than effective, and in a semiconscious state, I hit the tow release, and by the grace of God made a good short landing in a small plowed field near Veghel."

As Brennan and the sergeant crawled out through a hole in the nose, there was sporadic fire aimed at the glider. Urging the sergeant to hurry, Brennan started to crawl toward a ditch, but his companion calmly dropped his pants to examine his wound. According to Brennan, "His exact words were, 'I want to see if all this hurrying is worthwhile.' He had a large perforating wound of the right thigh that had penetrated the scrotum, but it didn't geld him and naturally he was very relieved."

Ordering the two uninjured airborne troopers to make their way to the landing zone, Brennan and the sergeant crawled down a ditch, waded a small stream, and made their way into a barn. "A farm-wife type came and gave us each a glass of hot milk. Of all the barns in Holland we had picked one belonging to Nazi sympathizers. The lady had three sons in the Dutch S.S. and she sent her twelve-year-old son to tell the Germans that we were hiding in the barn. A German paratroop officer and noncom arrived, examined us, gave us each a cigarette, then left. They told the lady we didn't have long to live, and to leave us alone. What happened next is fuzzier. I remember S.S. types coming in, kicking me in the face and ribs, and then disappearing after taking our watches, first aid kit, and cigarettes. I too figured I didn't have long to live and while one of them had his face close to mine asking questions, I spat in his face. I think perhaps this explains the kicks. I made a career of being stupid." After the Germans left, Dutch Resistance men arrived and removed the two wounded Americans.

One of Brennan's squadronmates, Flight Officer James Swanson, had been shot down at the same time. "A burst of 40-mm. flak ripped off the rudder and the left wing tip, and killed one of the troopers. Machine gun fire hit the towship, walked back along the rope and into the glider cockpit, knocking out the tow mechanism. Down we went into a large beet field."

With German soldiers coming across the field to capture them, Swanson and his passengers fled in the opposite direction. A Dutch patriot corraled them and hid them in a barn. A short time later, George Brennan was brought in, badly hurt—"you couldn't lay a hand on him without touching a wound," Swanson recalled. It was clear that Brennan needed medical attention immediately, but moving him to a hospital past the German patrols was a problem. "They put him in a two-wheeled horse cart," Swanson said, "dressed as a pregnant woman, complete with head scarf and lipstick. His 'husband' drove him past several German checkpoints without a hitch."

"I remember being carried in a farm cart that was loaded with straw and manure," Brennan wrote the author, "then waking up in a white elevator and seeing an 'Otis Elevator' sign. Later I learned I was in a maternity hospital, operated by Catholic nuns in the town of Schijndel, and that it was the headquarters of the local underground. I was in surgery for a long time while they plugged all the holes. They had a problem deciding whether to leave my foot on or to lop it off. They finally left it on.

"I was placed in a ward with a bunch of pregnant women, and my stomach was built up so that I looked about eight months in foal. My face and hands were bandaged, and my jaw precluded any conversation. German patrols came through the ward every day, and whenever they stopped at my bed and asked questions, I just groaned. One of the nuns would give them a tongue lashing and hustle them on. When it came time for my 'delivery,' the nuns moved me to a private room and hung a large T.B. sign on the door. After that no Kraut would come nearer than thirty feet."

Worsening weather forced the cancellation of the glider missions that were supposed to bring the 325th Glider Infantry Regiment to the hard-pressed 82nd Airborne near Nijmegen. The arrival of the British tanks had failed to win the bridge over the Waal. The Germans were dug into old Dutch fortifications in a park at the south end, and their artillery stopped the tanks and the paratroopers with heavy losses. Rather than run the risk of further failure, General Gavin proposed to send one battalion across the river in rubber rafts to attack the north end of the bridge; at the same time the British tanks would renew the attack at the south end. To do this, he would have to withdraw a battalion from the front lines holding the Groesbeek heights at a time when it was under constant attack.

The glider pilots were bivouacked west of Groesbeek, and it was there that Major Hugh Nevins, the glider officer of the U.S. 50th Troop Carrier Wing, received an order shortly after 9:00 P.M. to report without delay to the division command post. He arrived there fifteen minutes later to find General Gavin and his G-3 huddled over a map. "Major, I have a tough problem and you can help," Gavin said. "I want your pilots to relieve the Five Hundred and Fourth Regimental Combat Team on line duty. Your job will be to close the gaps in the lines that the Five Hundred and Fourth will make when they pull out." He indicated on the map the area, overlooking the rail line to Mook and facing the Reichswald, that the glider pilots would have to hold when the paratroopers were pulled out to make an attack on the Nijmegen bridge. "I pointed out to the general," Nevins said, "that our firepower was limited, as my pilots were armed only with .45 caliber pistols and our heavy weapons were M-1 rifles and grenades. He chuckled wryly and said he realized that, but that it had to be done. He asked when we could get into position, and could I possibly make it before midnight. I said I believed we could; then I saluted and made my way back through the dark to my command post. It was a grim and fearful undertaking, and I really was not as confident as I had inferred to General Gavin.

"It was completely overcast now and pitch black. I sent runners to the Group glider pilots asking them to wake their tired men and quietly gather about the command post. It was now after ten P.M.

"I spoke quietly to the assembled pilots. I literally could not see them in the dense blackness. After pointing out the need and the seriousness of the situation, I asked for two hundred ninety-five volunteers. I don't know how many stepped forward, but with tears in my eyes, I selected the first two hundred ninety-five men in the line, touching and counting each man. I was very proud of all of them.

"Holding hands in the dark, we two hundred ninety-five underarmed, shaky men moved quietly to the rendezvous with the regimental combat team commander. From there, as two paratroopers were pulled out of each double foxhole, I replaced them with two glider pilots. We moved quickly along the entire front and completed the exchange just before midnight. We manned these positions for the next thirty-six hours, until noon on the twenty-first.

"The Germans were now increasing pressure from the Reichswald, to our left front. Most of the steady incoming fire was small arms or machine guns, but 88s, mortars, and the dreaded screaming 'Nebelwerfers' [eight-barreled heavy mortars] fell on us methodically at about hourly intervals day and night. The single most devastating ordeal was lack of sleep for thirty-six straight hours. We were already tired, and lack of rest was really worse than the enemy fire. Fortunately, there were no direct enemy infantry assaults on our position. Several were made to our left and came against the Third Battalion area. We would see them and then pray that they would not shift our way.

"The single most terrifying memory for me was a tank attack in broad daylight. I was checking glider pilot positions overlooking Mook on the twenty-first. To my horror, eight huge Tiger tanks, looking like enormous crawling prehistoric monsters, were creaking up the railroad around our right flank. If they got behind us, they would slaughter us piecemeal. Over the field phone, I alerted battalion and division command posts, asking for antitank support as quickly as possible. I'm sure my voice was shaking.

"Within twenty minutes I was watching, fascinated, as two bazooka teams stalked the lead tanks. With amazing courage and efficiency, they crept right up to the first three tanks silhouetted on the railroad above them. At ranges of less than fifty yards, they literally detonated the first three tanks. Considerably relieved, I watched the remaining five tanks back up to the first crossing, turn about, and hurry back to the Reichswald.

"About noon on the twenty-first, we were relieved. I led the weary, red-eyed, unshaven glider pilots back to our area, and we fell asleep on the nearest level ground. We had suffered just twelve casualties, and only two dead."

During the next three days, the bad weather—fog, haze, low ceiling, and visibilities as low as a thousand yards— doomed the "Market Garden" operation. Only a few scattered gliders were able to fly and to reach their landing zones; on two of the days all glider missions were canceled. The efforts of Troop Carrier Command to resupply the embattled airborne divisions in spite of the worsening weather were unsuccessful; only a pitifully small amount of food, ammunition, and gasoline was recovered. In addition, the Germans constantly mounted strong counterattacks against the shaky corridor and succeeded in cutting it at several points. The Allies were forced to divert troops and tanks from the drive to Arnhem in order to keep the road open.

By the third day it was clear that the battle for the Arnhem bridge had been lost. Although a rapidly dwindling number of Red Berets under Lieutenant-Colonel Frost still held the northern end of the bridge, all attempts to reinforce them had failed. Under a withering fire from artillery tanks and mortars, the British airborne had clung desperately to the few houses close to the bridge and had kept the enemy at bay. One by one the houses were set afire and the defenders—those still alive—were pushed into a smaller and smaller area. Frost himself was badly wounded and, among the remaining 115 men, there were few who were unhurt. Their ammunition and food almost gone, they kept looking desperately for the reinforcements which never came. The next day they surrendered.

Everything seems to have gone wrong after the landings

that had begun so hopefully on Sunday. General Urquhart had been cut off and forced to hide for a critical thirty-six hours. The men who had had to remain on the landing zones to secure them for the second lift could not be used in the battle to reach the bridge. The railway bridge and pontoon bridge which might have been used to allow XXX Corps to cross the Rhine were destroyed even as the airborne reached them. By the time the second-day lift had come in, the alerted Germans had been reinforced and the lightly armed British airborne was now faced by two panzer divisions. All subsequent attempts to break through to the highway bridge and relieve Frost failed, with heavy casualties to the British. After its commanding officer was severely wounded, Lieutenant-Colonel Iain Murray took over an airborne brigade.

The last attempts to break through to the bridge were bloodily repulsed in the streets of Arnhem, and Urquhart—who had returned and resumed command—ordered a defensive perimeter to be set up west of the town around the suburb of Oosterbeek. Divisional headquarters were at the Hartenstein Hotel in the center of the defense perimeter. The pullback often had to be made in the face of enemy attack and under constant mortar fire which caused many casualties. When the perimeter was finally established, those glider pilots who had assembled at the rendezvous were ordered to defend part of the eastern rim. "All the other glider pilots," Colonel Murray told the author, "had remained with the units they carried in their gliders. I found that these men were serving in positions of responsibility and the units didn't want them to leave."

The glider pilots' dogged defense of their section of the perimeter is part of the gallant story of Arnhem—"a world name like Mons," as Colonel Chatterton called it. From foxholes and from houses they fought off the enemy, who was often either just across a small field or just across the street in another house. For five days and nights they repulsed every attempt to break in and overrun their positions. The Germans threw tanks, self-propelled guns, and an incessant barrage of shells and mortars against them, but they fought off the attacks, dug in deeper, and held. The perimeter was reinforced by a number of Polish parachutists and a few hundred men from an infantry division who crossed the river, but this did not change the final outcome.

Tom Pearce was with the glider pilots who dug in near some cottages on the outskirts of Oosterbeek. They had no sooner taken their positions than the Germans started mortaring them. "They were using eight-barrel mortars," Pearce told the author, "which we called 'moaning minnies.' You could hear them fire from their position three miles away and follow the shell through its flight until it seemed to be coming down right upon you. One of the chaps had dragged a settee out of a house and was lying on it. When we heard the shells, of course he dropped like everyone else into a trench. One shell dropped through the settee and lifted it right over the roof of the house into the garden at the back."

The Germans kept pressing in closer and closer, and the sniping was incessant. Sergeant "Andy" Andrews had pulled some tree branches in front of his foxhole to keep from being observed by the enemy, who occupied a row of semidetached brick houses less than a hundred yards away. At night they could hear the Germans talking. "One of them started whistling," Andrews recalled, "and the tune seemed vaguely familiar. After a few bars I realized that the last time I had heard it was when we were fighting some German parachutists in a little town in southern Italy. . . . I wondered if the whistler had been my enemy there too."

The next day during a lull in the firing Andrews was startled to see a German soldier walking along the hedgerow on his side of the road. "He was hatless, hands in his pockets and tunic open. He seemed to be looking through the hedgerow as if searching for berries or birds' eggs. My rifle was uncovered and I calculated the range at forty yards. I looked through the sights and I knew I could kill him whenever I wanted to but I never squeezed the trigger. I lowered my gun and watched as he calmly strolled back the way he had come."

"Andy" Andrews was shaken by the experience. He couldn't understand why he had not killed the German. Shouldn't he have been angry at the death of his friends, the bombing of London? Was it because he might have been the whistling "friend" from Italy? He remembered the scene in the film *All Quiet on the Western Front*, which he had seen as a twelve-year-old boy. At the end, a German soldier, reaching out from a trench to catch a butterfly, was shot by a French sniper. That movie had had a great effect upon him.

The firing went on day and night, and narrow escapes became commonplace. Louis Hagen was firing his Bren gun from a second-story window at a burned-out house across the street from which the Germans were sniping and throwing grenades. Suddenly there was a terrific bang and he jerked his hand back covered with blood. "A bullet had entered the flash eliminator," he told the author, "split it open and, by some miracle, ricocheted off again without going into me." The gun was still serviceable, so he wiped off his hand and went back to firing.

Hagen's dogtags gave his name as "Lewis Haig"—a precaution against his being identified as a German national and executed if he were captured. Since landing, he had not only been constantly under fire but had volunteered for night patrols to reconnoiter the enemy's positions. Often he was able to crawl close enough to hear the Nazi officers cursing their men for refusing to attack and to hear the privates calmly inform their superiors that "if attack is necessary, why go ahead, Herr Leutnant, and attack—but we're staying under cover." The aggressive tactics of the British airborne, even as they were being slowly driven back to the Oosterbeek perimeter, had caused heavy losses in the German ranks and made them leery of coming to close quarters with the Red Berets.

A sensitive, perceptive observer, Hagen (who would later write a book, *Arnhem Lift*, about his experiences) told the author that "you can't predict how a man will act in a battle like Arnhem. It wasn't the tough, profane type that turned out to be the best soldier in the end. It was rather the more thoughtful, the more sensitive, the more gentle chap—the man who did not kill because he enjoyed killing but who did it because it was necessary and only when it was necessary.

"The tough guy on the parade ground is not the bravest soldier in the field. The ones who acted ferocious back in England, who did not have the intelligence or the sensitivity to admit that they were afraid—as we all were—who swore and boasted to mask their fears . . . in Arnhem, I found these men cowering in the cellars afraid to come out because the mortars were falling."

From a second-story bedroom in one of the houses, a glider pilot lieutenant was firing a PIAT (Projector, Infantry, Antitank—a spring-loaded bazookalike weapon) with Sergeant Tom Pearce acting as loader. They were firing through a hole in the roof toward a crossroads where the Germans would turn their tanks. The PIAT shell had a range of only 120 yards, but it could stop a tank. "I loaded it," Pearce recalled, "and he laid what he thought was the correct angle and fired. The angle wasn't steep enough and the shell, instead of clearing the gable of the house next door, hit it and exploded some twelve feet in front of us. All I can remember is a huge red nasturtium that I once painted in school, getting larger and larger. I woke up twenty-four hours later in a cellar where the wounded had been put. I was sitting in a chair, smoking a cigarette. I found out that the lieutenant was unhurt, but he was killed in the fighting later."

On Monday, September 25—the eighth day of the battle for Arnhem—Urquhart informed Browning of the desperate situation. Unless the 1st Airborne Division could be reinforced immediately, it would have to be withdrawn. Although the bridge at Nijmegen had been taken on the 21st by the gallant Anglo-American assault, the Guards Armored Division had been stopped cold by German 88-mm. guns on the only usable road to Arnhem. Browning gave Urquhart permission to evacuate the perimeter.

Early in the evening, glider pilots reconnoitered the

evacuation route down to the river, laying white tape along its path. The word was quietly passed to the different groups fighting on the perimeter, telling them the order in which they were to move back. "It's a funny thing," Tom Pearce recalls, "we were told to black our faces and we were already dirty enough with nine days' growth of beard and not having washed or shaved in all that time. They also told us to wrap our boots with toweling and curtains from the houses to keep us quiet.

"At eleven P.M. we crept out of the house. It was very dark with low clouds and a drizzling rain. It was so dark we had to catch hold of each other's coattails to ensure that we stayed in the right party on the right path. In a single file we crept through the woods following the white tapes . . . we went across a field and passed a slit trench out of which came two Germans with their hands on their heads. We obviously had no way to take prisoners, but we couldn't shoot them because of the noise, so we made them walk in front and when we came to a crossroad where the tapes went right we said nothing and let them continue on the other road thinking that we were still behind them. I've always wondered how far they went. . . . In the darkness you could see mounds which were dead cattle, bodies which were dead men, and hear cries, 'For God's sake, help me!' We didn't dare leave the file because then we would have been in the same position."

The anguished scream of pain from out of the darkness was too much for Sergeant Jock East; he left the line and crawled forward to help. "It was an old buddy of mine, Jim Fairgreaves, who was badly wounded, his face all bloody," East recalled. "I tried to move him but he's a big chap, so I went back to the line and asked for a volunteer to help bring him in. I found one and we managed to get Jim into the line of troops waiting to be ferried across."

On the riverbank hundreds of exhausted men stood quietly in line waiting for the little motorboats that would ferry them across. The Germans were suspicious that reinforcements were crossing and sent mortar shells at random against the riverbank, but the men were too tired to care. From the

Before taking off for Holland on September 18, 1944, Brigadier General Anthony C. McAuliffe, then artillery commander of the 101st Airborne Division, gives last-minute instructions to the glider pilots and towplane crews of the 434th Troop Carrier Group.

Men of the 325th Glider Infantry receive a final briefing before the Holland operation.

Coffee and doughnuts are served on the flight line before takeoff for Holland.

A glider pilot checks a trailer loaded with munitions as men of the 17th Airborne Division prepare to cross the Rhine.

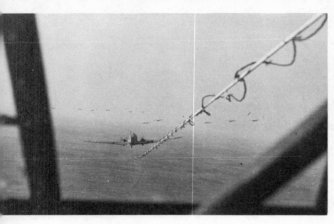

C-47s and Wacos approaching the Dutch coast en route to Nijmegen. A telephone line is wrapped around the towrope.

A B-24 bomber on a resupply mission flies over Dutch fields filled with CG-4A gliders.

Dutch civilians greet glider infantrymen of the 101st Airborne Division near Zon, Holland, on September 18, 1944.

Paratroopers dropping near Grave, Holland, on September 23, 1944. Gliders of the first- and second-day lifts are in the fields below.

Lieutenant-General Miles Dempsey greets General Gavin in Holland. In the rear is Lieutenant-General "Boy" Browning.

Lieutenant Richard K. Fort guards a truckload of German prisoners in Holland.

Glider pilots, paratroopers, and British tank men examine a captured German staff car in Veghel, Holland, on September 19, 1944.

other side of the river friendly troops fired an occasional stream of tracers to define the channel across which they should cross. There was a feeling of helplessness, even of fear. Tom Pearce watched the man next to him trying to dig a foxhole in six feet of mud with an airborne fighting knife whose blade was no wider than a pencil. "He was acting by pure instinct and training. As soon as you stop, dig in."

In the night, punctuated by the explosion of mortar shells and the screams of the wounded, the evacuation moved agonizingly slowly. There was some confusion as to the orders about the wounded. Those who had been unable to walk had been left behind in the care of the medical officers and a chaplain to be surrendered to the enemy, but the motorboat crews insisted that they had orders to take no walking wounded across. When Jock East and his friend Jim Fairgreaves got to the boat, some of the men objected. "I threatened them with my rifle and bayonet," East wrote the author, "and we got Jim into a boat. I held on to the side as I did not want them to think that Jim was taking my place. . . . On reaching the safe bank I was met by a Dutchman who helped me drag Jim to safety and assured me that he would see that he was taken to a hospital. . . . It was only later that I learned that Jim was permanently blind."

"I was on the last seat in the boat," Pearce said in an interview, "and there wasn't room for Captain [J. G.] Ogilvie and Lou Hagen. They were both expert swimmers and Captain Ogilvie said to Lou, 'Come on, we'll swim. Anybody else who's a strong swimmer can make way for the chaps who can't swim to get on the boat.' That was the last we saw of him because he was volunteering to swim the Rhine, which is tidal and wide, with a bullet in his shoulder, his kilt on, and a Sten gun still wrapped around his neck. Although he was a Scottish long-distance champion in his youth, he didn't make it."

Hagen also almost drowned in the strong current. At first the air in his battle smock kept him afloat and swimming was easy, but gradually this buoyancy was lost and the wet uniform started to drag him down. Refusing to panic, he let himself sink slowly while he got rid of his Sten gun, hand grenades, boots, and steel helmet. After that, swimming was easy. He looked around for Captain Ogilvie, but there was no sign of him. When he got to the far bank, he was furious when two enthusiastic soldiers dragged him from the water and tried to apply artificial respiration.

Only one quarter of the over ten thousand men in the 1st Airborne Division were evacuated from Arnhem. Of the 1,300 glider pilots one-half were killed or taken prisoner, a loss that was to have serious consequences for the regiment.

When "Andy" Andrews was flown back to his airfield in England, it was to a depressing scene: "We went to our Nissen huts where a fire was burning; blankets and sheets had been made up into comfortable-looking beds. There were only two of us alone in a hut that held twenty-six beds. It was too much. The empty beds and ghosts made staying an impossibility. Without a word, we dumped our kit and rifle on the bed and left."

"A world name like Mons," Chatterton had called Arnhem, and just as that gallant British defense in August, 1914, had produced its legends (such as the story that Mons had saved the French Army), so the legends of Arnhem began to grow. For many years afterward it was reported that the British airborne attack had been betrayed by a Dutch Resistance leader who was a double agent. It is now known that this man was completely unaware of the fact that Arnhem was one of the objectives when he left the Allied lines. Another legend that persists even today in British accounts of the battle concerns a briefcase containing complete "Market Garden" plans which was found on the body of an "American officer" in a Waco glider shot down near General Student's headquarters at Vught. British authors persist in writing that the discovery of the plans contributed to the debacle at Arnhem, whereas, in fact, Student transmitted them to higher headquarters, where they were ignored as a plant. Since the Waco was an American glider, the story of the "American officer" who was careless enough to carry operational plans into combat is now part of the legend of Arnhem, but the fact is that no one knows the identity or nationality of the dead officer. Part of Browning's headquarters staff flew in Waco gliders, one of which was shot down in the area of Vught.

Another legend is that the Americans refused to accept Arnhem as an objective. When Chatterton insisted that the story was true, the author wrote General Gavin. In his answer, Gavin said, "I can assure you that the Americans were never asked to accept Arnhem. Based on a discussion that took place in the office of General Brereton on Sunday afternoon, September 10, 1944, it was my impression that the objectives were related to the location of the troops and the troop-carrier airfields. . . . Immediately following the meeting they took me to their headquarters . . . and gave me a great deal of the intelligence that they had. . . . Arnhem looked reasonably good, aside from the depth of the penetration. They had but one bridge to get and good landing zones south of it."

As for Eisenhower's remark to his naval aide that the British had insisted on taking Arnhem as its objective, General Gavin wrote, "Frankly it has always been my impression that he, Eisenhower, was not familiar with what he was talking about. The implication that has come through to me was that he wanted to make the point that they asked for Arnhem to save us the burden of the most difficult mission of all, and this simply is not so."

Failure on such a vast scale must find either a reason or an excuse. An unrepentant Montgomery blamed Eisenhower for failing to divert all supplies to him. Browning blamed the 1,000 American glider pilots he said were in the Nijmegen area; he told Chatterton that if they had been better prepared and organized for a ground combat role, they could have been used to take the Nijmegen bridge earlier or at least to release a paratroop regiment to do the job. In his letter, General Gavin wrote, "The glider pilot problem was a very serious and troublesome one. The glider pilots with the British airborne effort had been given ground combat training and they were prepared to fight as infantry. In the American army, the glider pilots lived and worked with the Army Air Corps. Despite that, I rounded them all up and committed them to action near Mook—some of them without weapons, telling them to take their weapons from our dead and wounded or from the Germans. They never quite got over that, but I had to use them. . . . Prior to that action, the view held by the Americans was that once they landed their job was done and since linkup would occur very soon they would be taken out by the Army Air Corps to fly other missions. But my need at Mook was too great and besides, they were willing and proved to be good fighters. I never did have one thousand. Your figure is closer, less than six hundred. Most of our copilots were troopers from the infantry and artillery who had never flown in a copilot's seat."

In spite of the recriminations of betrayal and of failure of the Americans to adequately support the operation, today it is clear that two critical mistakes were made: one, failure to land in the immediate vicinity of the Arnhem bridge, and two, failure to take into account the evidence for the presence of the two German panzer divisions refitting in the area.

"I wanted to put fifty gliders in a *coup-de-main* on the bridge," Chatterton said. "Twenty-five would certainly have survived and the seven hundred fifty men they carried could have seized the bridge. But the army couldn't understand it. . . . They called me 'a bloody murderer' for even suggesting it."

Browning, who was shown aerial photographs of German tanks in the Arnhem area before the attack, dismissed them with the casual remark that they were probably not ready for action. There was a great optimism about the "Market Garden" operation which failed to take into account the surprising German recovery after the headlong flight from France. So the British 1st Airborne Division went into Arnhem and, after a courageous fight, was wiped out. Even its number disappeared from the Army list.

The division found its grave in the city with which its name will always be linked.

8
Winter Siege

At the sound of boots pounding down the corridor, "Corky" Corwin sank deeper into his sleeping bag and wished that his hangover would go away. Yesterday had been Christmas, and a great deal of alcohol had been consumed by the glider pilots of the U.S. 96th Troop Carrier Squadron in Orléans. Corwin had had more than his share, and on this freezing morning he wished that the pounding steps would stop. Through an alcoholic haze, he heard a door being opened and a question asked, followed by the angry sound of insults and curt refusals. The door slammed and the footsteps came down the hall to the bedroom in which Corwin and five other glider pilots were sleeping off their celebration. As he walked through the door, the squadron glider officer looked around uneasily. "I need a volunteer for a combat mission. One glider and two glider pilots. Anyone want to go?"

There was no answer. He began to call out the names of the men in the room and drew three sharp noes. Finally he asked, "Corwin?"

"Corky" Corwin shook his head trying to clear it and stalled for time. "Where?" he asked. "I don't know" was the blunt answer. Corwin thought it over for a moment. "O.K. I'll go."

The squadron glider officer sighed with relief and told him to report to the Operations hut in half an hour. Then he quietly closed the door and left.

As the footsteps retreated down the corridor, Corwin was suddenly struck with the horrifying thought that he had violated one of the sacred rules of military service: never volunteer!

By the day after Christmas, 1944, the Battle of the Bulge had reached its height. Ten days earlier the sudden German assault through the Ardennes had broken the three weak American divisions holding that front and had torn a huge hole in their lines. Through this gap the German armored divisions swept, spread out, and raced for the Meuse River. Their objective was Antwerp and the North Sea. If successful, they would split the Allied armies in northwestern Europe and force the British in the north of the trap to a second Dunkirk.

To prevent this, Eisenhower had thrown in his precious strategic reserve: the 1st Allied Airborne Army. From their camps in the region of Reims, the U.S. 101st and 82nd Airborne Divisions, only two weeks out of the fighting in Holland, were trucked hastily into Belgium. The U.S. 17th Airborne Division was flown by Troop Carrier Command from England to the Continent, and the British 6th Airborne was to follow by sea. The desperate situation in Belgium and Luxembourg forced Eisenhower's hand. He was no longer able to keep back the airborne divisions as a constant threat that the Germans would always have to take into account in their defensive planning. Hitler's "last throw of the dice" threatened to wipe out all the Allied gains since they had broken out of the Normandy beachhead five months earlier.

On the night of December 20 the "Screaming Eagles" of the 101st Airborne found themselves surrounded at Bastogne. The Belgian town was a critical communications junction where seven highways and three railroads converged and was the key to the battle. General Brereton wrote in his diary, "Because of the terrain and weather, the side that controls the roads and communications networks will win. The Ardennes area is heavily forested with evergreens, broken by a network of deep ravines, narrow valleys, and steep hills. Snow storms and heavy drifts make travel even on roads difficult."

Pounded on all sides of their rapidly shrinking perimeter by four crack German divisions, the "Screaming Eagles" fought back desperately. Their supply situation was soon critical: gasoline for tanks and vehicles was very low and artillery ammunition even lower. Soon it was only ten rounds per gun except for one battery. Even worse, early in the siege their field hospital had been overrun by a sudden German attack and all its medical personnel captured. Over four hundred badly wounded paratroopers were now crowded into a small civilian hospital in the town which could handle only half that number. Many of these men were in critical condition and needed surgery, but the surgeons had been taken away as prisoners of war by the Germans in violation of the Geneva convention.

In the absence of the division commander, Major General Maxwell Taylor, who was in Washington, D.C., the division was being led by Brigadier General Anthony C. McAuliffe. It was he who on December 22 gave the famous one-word reply "Nuts!" to the German demand for surrender or annihilation. Now he called for an air resupply to keep his troops fighting.

For the next two days troop-carrier planes taking off from English airfields on instruments and flying through fog and mist struggled to keep the garrison at Bastogne supplied. Forced to fly low to find their target, they were easy marks for the German gunners waiting along their flight paths. Guided by the navigation aids set up by two pathfinder teams that had dropped on the morning of September 23, the airlift managed to airdrop 300 tons of supplies while losing eight planes. The French airfields to which several troop-carrier groups had moved were clearer, but the pararacks by which the supplies were dropped and the specialized teams needed to pack them were not available on the Continent. However, there were gliders recovered from the Holland operation and, since the critical items were gasoline and artillery ammunition, which could not be parachuted, "Operation Repulse" now turned to the glider pilots in the desperate effort to maintain the "hole in the doughnut" that was Bastogne.

From Orléans, Corwin and his untested copilot, Flight Officer Benjamin "Connie" Constantini, were towed in their glider to a fighter base at Etain, near Verdun. Waiting for them were two surgical teams, thirteen men in all and all volunteers. "I gathered the medics around," Corwin wrote in a letter to the author, "and told them that if we crashed their best bet was to hold on to the fuselage tubing. There were no seat belts for them. They sat on the benches with all the surgical equipment and blankets piled up in the middle."

The flight from Etain to Bastogne took only twenty minutes. As the tug and glider cruised through the smooth air, the two glider pilots checked the landmarks below them on their maps and watched for the yellow smoke that would mark the landing field. The airborne would also put a white "L" panel on the field to guide them.

Suddenly a thick column of yellow smoke appeared dead ahead, and the green release signal flashed from the navigator's dome of the towplane. But the smoke was coming from a burning truck, farmhouse, and haystack, and Corwin refused to release. He was certain that the navigator in the tug had made a mistake, since Bastogne was not yet in view and the landing field was due west of the town.

"Corwin, I saw the panels!" Constantini yelled and pointed back to a spot they had passed. "I just put my trust in God and Connie," Corwin wrote, "hit the towrope release and turned the glider around. There was a big snow-covered field surrounded by woods just barely within gliding distance. The landing was so smooth, I didn't even feel the wheels touch, but when we stopped rolling, we were face-to-face with a cannon barrel sticking out of the woods."

Luckily the gun was manned by 101st Airborne artillerymen. After the medics had been driven to the hospital, Corwin and Constantini were taken to the division command post in the center of the city and turned over to Intelligence. The G-2 officer pointed out that they had landed on the very edge of the southern defense perimeter and that the panels they had seen were intended to mark friendly troop positions to the Allied bombers. The Germans held the far end of that particular field.

"However," the officer continued, "you were very lucky. When the Germans saw you arrive, they clobbered the field you were supposed to land in with shellfire!"

When the word came back that Corwin's glider had landed safely after encountering very little flak, the second mission of the day was being prepared. Ten gliders were being loaded with jerricans of gasoline, and twenty glider pilots were being briefed. It is only when they got down to the flight line and saw the cargo that they realized what they would be carrying. "From then on we worried about incendiaries, praying we wouldn't encounter any," Captain Wallace F. Hammargren, the glider operations officer of the 98th Squadron, later wrote.

It was almost three o'clock in the afternoon when the gliders and towplanes rumbled off the runway, quickly assembled, and headed north. The snow-covered countryside beneath them looked peaceful—like a Christmas card. The towplanes droned steadily through the cold, clear air. Behind them the gliders bounced at the ends of the 300-foot ropes, maintaining position carefully.

Soon the landscape unrolling slowly below them changed. They could see the charred remains of farms, some still burning; the twisted wreckage of tanks, trucks, and other debris of war—all a startling black against the snow. They were now following the fighting path of Patton's armored columns pushing slowly toward Bastogne.

"At five P.M. the ride began to get a little more exciting,"

Captain Hammargren recalled. "We first noticed flak coming up from our left, looking like Fourth of July Roman candles in the dusk. Then it began to arch towards us from the right as well. Below we could see houses and barns burning.

"I could see the flak marching up towards Lieutenant Dick Baly in the second position. It struck his glider, knocking out a four-foot section of the left wing and damaging his left elevator. Later I learned that it had grazed his steering column and blown off the panel over his head.

"At about the same time, however, I was having trouble of my own. The Germans decided it was time for me to cut loose from the tug ship so they put a piece of flak through my towrope a foot in front of the glider's nose. That foot of rope was still hanging there when I landed.

"Fortunately I was over the landing zone when the rope was shot away, so I made my 360° pattern and landed. . . . We immediately jumped out of the glider and hit the ground, taking defensive positions and watching the figures which we saw running towards us. The situation around Bastogne had been so confused we weren't sure that we were in the right place or that the area was still in friendly hands. In the dusk it was impossible to tell whether these guys were Americans or Germans so we kept our fingers on our triggers and waited. When they got close enough we could see that they were Americans all right.

"A major came up to me and asked, 'What are you carrying?' 'Gasoline,' I replied. 'And the other gliders?' 'All gasoline too.' 'Thank God,' he said. 'We're down to the last drop.' "

Trucks quickly arrived and the glider pilots helped move the gasoline from the gliders. The pilots were taken to a long stone barracks, where they slept that night on the floor. At least some of them slept; many of them complained that the guns were making too much noise.

The next day the news spread that an armored column had broken through the perimeter from the south and that the road out was open, but the ordeal was not over yet. Shortly after noon the glider pilots stood in front of their barracks and watched the 439th Troop Carrier Group being cut to pieces as it struggled to bring its gliders into the perimeter.

The 439th Troop Carrier Group had been flying the 17th Airborne Division from England to Belgium when the second glider resupply of Bastogne was announced. Flight Officer Eric "Case" Rafter remembered it very well. "One group of paratroopers came in planes and stayed overnight. They were heading for the front and the idea was to have them sleep in the C-47s down at the field. Most of the glider pilots, power pilots, and enlisted men went down to the planes and invited them to sleep in our warm tents. The paratroopers were glad to do this and also for a couple of drinks that were handed around. After the paratroopers had gone on . . . all the glider pilots were called out to the company street and informed that an airborne division had been surrounded by Germans and that they had to be resupplied from the air by glider. Captain John Neary [91st Squadron Glider Officer] called out the names of the pilots whom he had 'volunteered' to go on this mission. As I had only flown one mission, I was one of the 'volunteers.' And in general it was considered fair to even up the missions so those of us who had only one mission were sure to go into Bastogne."

Flight Officers Paul Hower and Waverly Jarvis were asleep in the tiny one-room cabin they had built out of soggy planks from glider boxes. They had celebrated Christmas the night before with their friends, eating leftover food packages from home and sampling various local vintages. As usual, they had missed breakfast and that day had even skipped lunch. "A loud and incessant pounding on our door finally roused us," Hower recalled. "A sergeant from Operations informed us that we were wanted immediately. In answer to our questions he said all he knew was that there would be a mission that afternoon." From reading *Stars and*

Stripes, Hower and Jarvis knew that the Allies were in a lot of trouble around Bastogne. They had heard rumors of at least one earlier glider resupply flight. They dressed quickly and went down the hill to the Operations hut.

The briefing was quite skimpy, since not too much was known about the area that the 101st still held. Although the weather was forecast to be cold and clear with excellent visibility, there were ominous reports about flak around Bastogne. "I went down to the flight line," "Case" Rafter said, "and got into the seat of the glider. It was filled with 155-mm. ammunition. I asked the men who had packed the glider if it would explode if it were hit. One said 'yes' and the other said 'no.' I noticed that all the fuses had been stored near the tail. This was very encouraging because the detonation, if it went off, would probably not reach me, assuming it did not set off the ammunition. On the other hand, it occurred to me that it would not have a very beneficial effect on the way the glider would fly."

A few minutes before takeoff the mission was suddenly canceled and rescheduled for ten o'clock the next morning. Glider pilots went back to their tents to sweat out the night. Flight Officer Francis L. "Bud" Carroll debated whether to write to his mother. "I had written to her the day before and I didn't mention the mission, so I said, 'Well, if I get packed, she'll know about it anyway so why bother her?' " Hower found that he could not get to sleep, so he decided to read. Since the electric light might bother his tentmates, he lit a candle and started to read Mark Twain's *A Connecticut Yankee in King Arthur's Court.* He found that the book calmed his fears.

The next morning the glider pilots dressed for combat. Hower said his own outfit consisted of "wool socks, combat boots, overshoes, sweat pants and shirt, olive drab shirt and pants, wool knit sweater, some tight-woven rain repellent pants, combat jacket, leather-palmed wool gloves and wool knit cap." While dressing, he thought, "I may be tired and even hungry, but I won't be cold." In his musette bag he put extra socks, chocolate bars, a toilet kit, four packs of cigarettes, extra clips for his machine gun and .45 caliber pistol, and hand grenades. On his pistol belt he attached a canteen and a first-aid pouch, in addition to the pistol in its holster. He decided against taking a shovel since it would be of little use in frozen ground. His gas mask he had thrown away in southern France. In the mess hall he pushed away the food and settled for a cup of coffee; then he walked down to Operations where the trucks took the glider pilots to the flight line.

When "Case" Rafter climbed into the pilot's seat of his glider and attached his seat belt, three friends were present to help him put a flak suit over his flying gear. "I felt a cool breath of air in the rear and found that my shirttail had come out. Nothing could be done about this and one of my friends said to me, 'Whatever you do, Rafter, don't let the Germans capture you.' Thinking that he had some inside information on Germans executing glider pilots, I asked him why. He replied, 'If the Germans get you, they'll know we're at the bottom of the barrel.' This was not exactly encouraging but later I thought it was pretty funny. . . ."

There was a delay when it was found that the plastic windshields of the gliders were covered with frost. The crew chiefs tried scraping the frost off, then using hydraulic fluid, but nothing worked. Finally it was decided to wait until the sun came up and melted the frost off the windshields. At 10:30 in the morning the first towplane rumbled out to the center of the runway, moved forward slowly until the slack in the towrope was taken up, and then sped down the runway and into the air.

Standing alone in a snow-covered field a hundred yards from the end of the runway, a tall, white-haired chaplain in a rumpled uniform made the sign of the cross in the freezing air as each tug and glider roared over him. Father John M. Whelan was beseeching divine protection for his "boys."

Being forty-sixth in the line of fifty gliders, Bud Carroll

saw the rest of the formation taking off. "There were no aborts
. . . everybody went off as scheduled, and it's a funny thing
going on your first mission. . . . I've had the rope break loose
on me about half a dozen times in training. Now flying off
into combat, I wanted to see that thing break again. You
know you're not going to cut off because you're committed,
and you can't back out.

"As we flew along over France it was cold and awfully
lonesome in that glider and I did some very, very hard praying. There was only one glider pilot in each glider. I suppose
they figured there was no sense losing two glider pilots in one
mission. In about two hours we approached the scene of the
battle. You could see that the little towns we were passing
over were all smoky from the fighting. It is wrong for a man
to be as scared as I was at that moment. . . ."

As usual, the first gliders received little flak; it took time
for the Germans to get the range. "Over Bastogne," Rafter
said, "I looked down and saw a broad rolling field. The orders
were to tow the gliders in at five hundred feet; but there was
a tendency on the part of the tug pilots to fudge a little, to
come in a little higher, to get away from the antiaircraft fire.
We came into Bastogne at about seven hundred fifty feet over
the ground. Over one of the burning villages, I felt a distinct
explosion beneath me. My glider was lifted fifteen or twenty
feet into the air, but I easily corrected this and drew no
ground fire after that. I dove my glider a little too fast so that
I came in much faster than I should have. . . . However, the
ground was frozen and inside the Bastogne perimeter. On the
field I landed on, there was no snow, so the fast landing did
no harm. I did plow through a barbed wire fence which fes-
tooned my glider, but I landed in perfect shape. I then got
out all by myself with no other gliders around, and a paratrooper came walking over to me wearing the 'Screaming
Eagle' insignia of the One Hundred and First, so for the first
time I knew which division had been surrounded."

Strung out in a single column, nose to tail, flying at slow

speed and low altitude, the towplanes and gliders were easy targets for the German gunners. Unable to take evasive action, the Dakota pilots doggedly flew into the withering fire. Soon the planes started to fall. Paul Hower was hypnotized by the sight. "The Germans had our altitude down to a foot. Where there was nothing, three black puffs suddenly appeared and I heard 'whump-whump-whump.' I was so scared I couldn't have told you my name. How I admired the courage of our tow pilots flying into that flak! We could see planes coming back, we saw other planes going down, their altitude so low the chutes didn't have time to open before they hit the ground."

Plane number thirteen was piloted by Lieutenants Joe Fry and George Weisfeld. Ten miles from Bastogne, their C-47 took a direct hit in the cabin and burst into flames. Fry ordered the crew to bail out; the radio operator and crew chief jumped immediately, but copilot Weisfeld said quietly, "Joe, I'll stay with you until you're ready to leave." The two men struggled to keep the burning plane flying until their glider could reach the landing zone. As soon as they felt the jolt of the glider releasing, Fry shouted, "Let's get out of this son of a bitch before it blows up!" While his copilot ran through the blazing cabin and leaped out the back door, Fry put the plane on automatic pilot, strapped on his chest parachute, and turned to follow. "By this time," Fry wrote to the author, "the cabin was a mass of flames. I closed the door, jettisoned the top hatch and climbed out, praying I would not fall into the props. I was surprised that there was so little wind blast and I was able to crawl on my hands and knees on top of the plane until I reached the navigator's bubble. The next thing I recall is looking up at several shroud lines of my parachute hanging loose in the breeze and seeing the plane burning below me. Then I hit the ground."

Watched by the airborne troopers from their firing pits, Fry had slid off the fuselage and had hit the left horizontal stabilizer of the plane. The impact burst his chest chute, the shrouds wrapping around the stabilizer, leaving Fry dangling helplessly in space as the burning plane plunged toward the ground. A few seconds later the C-47 blew up. The stabilizer broke off, and Fry floated down to be picked up by the paratroopers and dragged into a foxhole.

The glider he had been towing, piloted by Lieutenant John D. Hill, landed safely with its cargo of shells. Hill was waiting at the first-aid station when a badly burned Joe Fry was brought in.

One by one the unarmored C-47s flew through the barrage like ducks in a shooting gallery. One by one they started to fall; thirteen of the fifty towplanes were shot down, many of them in flames. Towropes were cut by bullets or released as the tugs started to dive. Soon the air was filled with gliders coming down in enemy territory.

"Directly ahead of us," Paul Hower remembers, "was a huge black cloud of flak. There's no way to get through. I thought, 'Why don't they turn, go around, do anything, except fly into that cloud?' The cutoff point was only about a minute away, when suddenly my towplane went into a steep bank and I thought, 'Oh, boy, we're getting out of here. I don't know where we're going, but we're getting out of here.' Then, just as suddenly, the towrope comes flying back at me and I hastily hit the tow release lever to get it unhooked from the glider. At about 200 feet I saw an open field in front of me and start my approach but the glider won't land.

"For the first time since we started getting flak I did some meaningful thinking. I looked at the airspeed indicator and saw that I was going 150 mph! There is no way a glider can be landed at that speed. I pulled up and saw another open field off to my left. The new approach took me over a patch of trees and there must have been a German with a Mauser rifle behind every tree. There was a constant splat-splat-splat of rifle fire through my glider. . . . I finally got into the field and rolled to a stop on the frozen ground. I grabbed my machine gun, jumped out the far door and raced around the tail, firing at a small shed nearby in case there were any Germans in it. I was still getting rifle fire from the woods I had just flown over.

"Two more gliders floated in to a landing about a half a mile away. While they were still rolling, an 88 ack-ack gun on top of a hill opposite us started shooting. I saw one glider pilot blown out the door of his glider by a big blast of orange fire. His glider shuddered and spun around. Next the 88 hit the other glider and blew it up. Now they started shooting at my glider and the third round exploded it. The ground just seemed to shudder."

When the 88 started shooting, Hower thought for a moment of hiding in the small shed. Instead, he crouched down in the open field behind a small mound of dirt covering some vegetables. It was a wise decision. The last round of the 88 blew the shed apart. Overhead, Hower saw two fighter planes zooming in at ground level straight toward the 88. They didn't spot it, but the 88 stopped firing so as not to give away its position. "Anyway," Hower said, "there really wasn't anything left for them to shoot at.

"I saw a German halftrack come out of the woods and head for a shellhole from which a white handkerchief was waving. A glider pilot came out of the shellhole and climbed into the halftrack. As I watched, they captured another glider pilot. I consider going over there but I didn't want to surrender although the rifle fire was scary. While I'm trying to make up my mind, the halftrack pulled back into the timber.

"The rifle fire suddenly quit and the silence scared me almost as much as the firing. For some reason or other I looked back in the direction from which I had landed. Coming over the hill, nicely spaced as infantry are taught, were eight or ten Germans. The thought of trying to shoot it out with them left me about as soon as it started. Besides I'd forgotten to replace the clip I'd used up on the shed. I rose to my feet, dropped my Tommy gun, raised my hands, and started walking towards them. One of them aimed his rifle at me several times, each time the barrel getting bigger and bigger until it finally looks like a stovepipe. I thought. 'I wonder how Glennis will make out being a widow.' After a quick body search for more weapons, a mere lad takes me back to a small village—my first stop on the way to Stalag Luft I.''

From the forty-sixth glider near the tail end of the mission, Bud Carroll watched the planes being shot down. "I was always fascinated by airplanes," he wrote. "I love airplanes and I hate to see them go down. You see one in trouble, spinning down. . . . I followed at least three that went right down into the ground and puff! There were no parachutes. At 400 feet you don't have much time. . . .''

Then the barrage closed around them, and his towplane took a direct hit on the vertical stabilizer. "It was a big flash and the rudder went flying and floating through the air. The plane immediately pulled up in a steep climbing turn, out of control . . . and I let him pull me out. I followed him out of the flak and then I cut loose.''

Carroll spotted a farmhouse sitting in an open field with very few trees around. He headed toward it as the only place likely to give him cover when he landed. "Suddenly," he said, "there were tracers and incendiary bullets going right in front of the glider. Only about a dozen of them, but whoever was shooting at me was saying, 'Halt, you're not going anywhere.' Well, you can't take evasive action with a glider. You're just a clay pigeon—you have to keep going down. Then this guy started to strafe the glider with machine guns and I could hear the bullets going through the fabric, bing, bing, bing, and every once in a while it would hit the metal frame and went whee! whee! There was a burst right up through the copilot's seat which was nothing but plywood. Luckily I didn't have a copilot, but wood splinters flew through the air. . . .

"I looked down and spotted him in a fortlike structure made of hay and covered with snow. I could see the spurts of fire from the machine gun coming up at me, so I turned around and just then I saw high-tension wires right in front of me. My first reaction was to pull up and as I did, the wheels rolled right across the wires. . . . I shoved the nose down, heading for the farmhouse.

"At that instant the bullets came through the side of the glider and across my lap. They were just creasing my leg in several places. One of them pierced my hip, another ripped into my thigh, and I started to pass out. I was very weak but I remembered to keep the glider level, hoping it would fly itself down. That's the last thing I remember.

"When I woke up, I was on the ground with shadowy figures all around me speaking German. They were pulling me by my armpits out of the wreck, out from under three-thousand five hundred pounds of 155-mm. shells. I fainted again. When I woke up the second time, I was on a stretcher in an open truck. I looked up at the blue sky, and all I could hear was the far-off sound of guns. I passed out again, and when I came to for the third time, I was on a stretcher on the floor of a barn.

"Later they brought in another glider pilot from my out-fit named Kaiser. He didn't say anything, he didn't look down at me . . . he was hurt pretty bad. But then, finally, his eyes focused on me, laying on that stretcher, and he said, 'Carroll, what are you doing here?' Crazy words, but that's the only thing he could think of.

"Then the young kid who shot me down—he couldn't have been more than seventeen or eighteen—came in with my musette bag. He was smoking my cigarettes and chewing my candy bars, and he said to Kaiser, who could speak German, 'Your comrade spun in,' and he just shook his head that I was alive to tell about it. My ankle was busted, and all swollen up, and I had split my head a little; otherwise, I was in good shape. An American officer came into the barn—a C-47 navigator. I couldn't talk because I was in shock, but Kaiser asked him how far Bastogne was. The navigator said, 'Four minutes.' At one hundred fifty miles an hour, four minutes is not too far.

"In this barn there were two German medics, a German

officer, and a Belgian farmer who just went about his business not saying a word, doing his daily chores with a bucket in his hand. After a while, I was taken to a schoolhouse and put on a table. The German doctor and one of the medics were going to operate on my legs, so they poured ether on gauze over my nose. The medic wanted to get it over in a hurry, so he slit me once on my right leg. I let out a yell, so he gave me a second dose of ether and put me to sleep. When I woke up my leg was bandaged with a big pad of gauze. They had taken the bullet out. Later I remembered that as they were giving me the ether, the doctor was asking me questions: where had I come from, how many gliders were in the mission. He was interrogating me at the same time that he was administering ether, and I just said, 'I don't know.' He told me to count to ten and all the time he was trying to get information out of me. We just sat in that barn for about two days, munching on black bread, and then we were moved. . . ."

Thirty-five gliders landed within the Bastogne perimeter, bringing in fifty-three tons of sorely needed supplies, chiefly artillery ammunition. Fifteen glider pilots landed in enemy-held territory and were either killed or captured. Thirteen towplanes were shot down, and four more were so badly damaged by flak that they crashed-landed during the return trip. Not all the captured troop-carrier personnel were as well treated as Hower and Carroll. Second Lieutenant Lester J. Epstein parachuted to safety when his C-47 was shot down. After the Battle of the Bulge was over, in January, his body was found in a shallow grave not far from Bastogne. His head had been crushed with rifle butts.

On the second floor of the Bastogne police jail, in the southeast corner of the town, about eight hundred German prisoners watched morosely as the formations of C-47s and gliders roared over. To Technician Fifth Class George Allen of the 101st Airborne Division Intelligence, it was obvious

that they were deeply impressed, especially when he over-
heard one of the POWs say bitterly, "How can you defeat an
enemy who can do things like that?" They had not seen the
Luftwaffe for months, and now, for the first time, they felt
that the war was lost. Allen went downstairs to check on the
officers in the lockup on the first floor. Orders had been received that the prisoners were to be sent out of Bastogne,
along the road opened by Patton's armored column.

When "Case" Rafter arrived in the town square, he had a
bottle of fortified North African wine given him by a grateful paratrooper. The first man he shared the bottle with was
Lieutenant John Hill of his squadron, who had flown into
Bastogne behind Joe Fry's burning plane. Fry was being
treated by the medics for facial burns, and Hill was standing
by to see if he could be of any help to the man who had so
gallantly saved him. Fry didn't want to go through the hospital system as a wounded man from Bastogne; he wanted to
get back to the 439th where he could be treated while being
with his friends. Rafter and Hill took charge of Fry, who still
had melted aluminum all over his flight jacket, and got him
into the truck convoy that would take the prisoners out of
Bastogne.

"The prisoners were a pretty rough-looking bunch,"
Rafter remembered, "and I was suspicious that they might try
to escape. So I kept them as far from me as possible, and
covered them with the Tommy gun. One of them came up
and asked me for something to eat. He could speak a little English, having been a prize fighter in Cuba. I gave him all the
food I had tucked away for a long stay in Bastogne, and he
distributed it to the others. They were quite grateful, and
didn't make any attempt to escape, especially after they saw
all the tanks along the road we were traveling. When we got to
Luxembourg the prisoners were put on trains and we were
housed in a building which was heated and had been a pool
room. I crawled under the pool table and slept very happily,
being very glad to have gotten over the mission. From Luxem-

bourg we got on a train to Paris, arriving there the next morning. Joe Fry was beginning to hurt from his burns, so Hill and I took him to a civilian French doctor who gave him some morphine for his pain and refused to accept any pay for so doing."

"The supplies brought in by gliders and dropped by C-47s," General McAuliffe wrote in a letter to the author, "particularly ammunition, played a vital role in the defense of Bastogne. . . . The volunteer surgical teams that came in by glider saved many lives."

The 439th group had gone into Bastogne in squadron order, with the 91st leading and the 94th bringing up the rear. Seventeen planes and fifteen gliders were lost. Of the fifteen glider pilots who failed to return, eight were from the 94th: four were killed and four taken prisoner. When one of the survivors returned to his hut at Châteaudun, he was astonished to find the beds occupied by replacements. Furious, he drove them out in the snow, threatening them with a pistol.

Then he sat down on his cot and cried for his friends.

9
The German Rhine

All over France and England the troop-carrier airfields were sealed up, shut tight against prying eyes on the outside and loose tongues inside. Telephone service had been restricted to only command personnel, and even these calls were monitored; all outgoing mail had been set aside and stored.

The mission was on.

The airborne troopers had moved in during the night and had been placed in enclosures on the edge of the airfields; at that point, all traffic in and out had been stopped. Elaborate security precautions had been taken in their move from the staging areas; to prevent identification, all insignia and other markings had been removed from their uniforms and equipment, and the bivouac area was surrounded by armed MPs.

Confined to their squadron areas, still unaware of their destination, most of the glider pilots were resigned, worried, or apathetic. Only the "virgins" who had never flown a glider into combat seemed concerned that they might miss what everyone believed would be the last airborne operation of the war. After so much hard training, they were worried that they might be left out. They hovered around the squadron Operations hut, waiting expectantly to see who would be chosen to go.

When the list was finally posted and his name was not on it, Flight Officer Wesley Hare went to the senior glider officer to complain. As he recalls it, "I was left off the list to go, but I went around bitching to everybody and telling them I wanted to go, but no luck. Finally, I gave up trying. I thought, 'Well, I'm not going, I won't do anything more about it.' On the morning before the mission, I went in to see the captain, and told him I was sorry to give him so much trouble about wanting to go, and he said, 'You're going! Your name is on the list—and I'm going too.' So, we went to the briefing."

On the night of D minus one (March 23, 1945), the briefings began. The combat crews of the 439th Troop Carrier Group assembled in the town theater at Châteaudun, south of Paris. The doors were guarded by military police to prevent any unauthorized personnel from entering. Crowded into the orchestra and balcony seats of the small hall were the pilots, copilots, crew chiefs, radio operators, and glider pilots. Although this affair was strictly "by invitation only," dress was informal: leather flying or Eisenhower jackets, khaki sweaters and pants, cowboy boots, crushed garrison hats, overseas caps, mufflers, silk scarves—anything was acceptable. There was a nervous chatter as they waited to learn what their job would be.

The briefing was given in a thorough manner by the Operations officer, a major who had celebrated his twenty-eighth birthday over Normandy. Using a huge map that filled most of the stage, he reviewed the group and wing assembly plan. After takeoff the next day, the tugs and gliders would form over the airfield, then fly directly to the rendezvous near Pontoise. There they would meet the three other groups of the 50th Troop Carrier Wing. The four groups would fly directly by way of Saint-Quentin to Wavre, where they would join the echelons of two other troop-carrier wings and the British. The flight to the initial points (where the final turn would be made before the run-in to the landing zones) was traced out, and the landing zone (LZ "S") just north of

Lieutenant John D. Hill and the glider he flew behind a burning towplane into Bastogne.

Waco gliders on double tow en route to the Rhine, March 24, 1945.

A Waco glider after it collided with a tree while attempting a landing near Wesel.

Above the smoke obscuring the landing zones near Hamminkeln, Germany, Liberator bombers drop supplies to the British airborne twenty minutes after the assault began.

British service troops established a rest camp on the west bank of the Rhine for returning glider pilots.

Staff Sergeant H. N. "Andy" Andrews near Hamminkeln, Germany, on March 25, 1945. The broken chin strap and webbing were the result of his being thrown through the smashed nose of his Horsa glider on landing.

Glider pilots of the 439th Troop Carrier Group ready to board trucks and recross the Rhine. Standing (from left to right): Flight Officers Pat Doran, John Bonds, and John Bennett. Kneeling: Flight Officer James Seifert, Lieutenant Thomas Berry, and Flight Officer John Schumacher.

Wesel was pointed out. The flight was to be made at an altitude of 1,000 feet, dropping to 600 feet after leaving the initial point, at which height the gliders would be released.

The latest intelligence on enemy dispositions in the area was given, and it was pointed out that the elaborate preparations and smoke screen on the west bank of the Rhine, as well as the reports by British newspapers, meant that the enemy was not unaware of the coming assault. The weather forecast was favorable: visibility of at least two miles in the Wesel area and four miles elsewhere, with winds of about ten miles per hour. There would be a thick haze in the early morning, but this would clear before the beginning of the airborne assault, which had been set at ten o'clock the next morning.

A captain from Intelligence spoke briefly on escape and evasion techniques. He warned the combat crews not to expect the help that they had received in Normandy, southern France, and Holland, for here everyone not in an Allied uniform would be an enemy—civilian and soldier alike. He sounded grim.

Colonel Charles H. Young, the veteran group commander, talked about the necessity of tight formation flying, in order to get the gliders into their landing zone in good shape. He ended by saying, "I am sure what you are going to do tomorrow will be an important contribution towards a rapid ending of the war."

The correspondent of the *Chicago Tribune*, Larry Rue, who was to fly the next day in one of the gliders, remembered the crowded hall:

"There were two solemn occasions at this briefing. The first was at the very opening, when the Protestant chaplain came out on the stage and prayed to God to give those going on the mission the strength, the skill and courage successfully and safely to perform their dangerous mission on the morrow. The second solemn occasion was when the Catholic chaplain, Father John Whelan, closed the briefing. He got on the platform in what cannot be described as a perfect military getup. His pants were too long, so they were rolled up over his shoetops, which were muddy. His hair was closely cropped. He is one of the most popular members of this group, and whenever anyone does him a favor he promises to have him elected mayor of Peoria. He stood for half a minute until dead silence reigned, and then began:

" 'O Father, Your mercy and their courage and skill is all they will need.' He blessed everyone, and wound up without a break, looking at his wristwatch:

" 'I want every Catholic present to have complete absolution. We haven't much time, so I wish all Catholics immediately to go up in the gallery for Holy Communion, while the Protestants can conduct their services downstairs.'

"Half of those below went upstairs, while half of those packing the galleries came down. That such a strong religious spirit pervaded that tough gang of boys came as something of a revelation."

Actually, it was not so much "strong religious spirit" that motivated the men, but great respect bordering on fear. Father Whelan was over six feet tall, weighed two hundred pounds, and was an amateur boxer. He practiced a form of "muscular Christianity" that permitted no arguments.

In the trucks that took them back to the sealed-off airfield, the glider pilots were very quiet. They were thinking of the red dots that had been so liberally sprinkled over the assault sector, each one indicating a known German antiaircraft unit. Most of them were veterans, and they knew that for every flak unit that could be identified from an aerial photograph, there were a dozen or more hidden in haystacks, in farmhouses, and elsewhere, which had not been seen. There was a gut feeling that this would not be the "milk run" that the English newspapers had predicted.

In the darkness at the back of one truck, a glider pilot spoke thoughtfully. "My father was here in France in nineteen eighteen. He was wounded in the Argonne. When he heard that I was going overseas, he wrote to me and said that if I ever got to the Rhine, I should spit in it for him." There was a pause, and then he continued, unsteadily, "I just hope I have spit left."

There was little sleep at any of the airfields that night; the nervous tension and apprehension that always preceded a mission drove away the desire to sleep. Men checked their equipment, cleaned their weapons, or sharpened knives and bayonets. Some wrote letters home, trying to erase from their minds and from their words the thought that this might be a last message. Some felt the need for company and gathered in their tents or rooms to talk quietly about the coming battle. In one squadron the glider pilots gathered around a guitar player, listening to country music. For others there was an overwhelming need to be alone; in solitude they studied the photographs of the landing fields, as if to discover in the lacework of lines or in the various grayish tints the fate that awaited them. There were those who wandered down to the landing strip, where the planes and gliders had been marshaled, and checked their loads again and again. There was little margin for error in the loading of a Waco CG-4A; a shift of as little as four inches in the position of a jeep or a cannon would send the glider and its cargo into a dive from which there could be no recovery. Unwilling to return to the barracks area to face the barrage of wisecracks and jesting with which the men were hiding their fears, some of the glider pilots simply walked in the darkness around and around the inside perimeter of the airfield until it began to get light.

Someone turned on a radio, trying to find some music with which to pass the time. A broadcast from Radio Berlin blared forth, saying, "Allied airborne landings on a large scale to establish bridgeheads east of the Rhine must be expected. We are prepared."

Switching hastily to the Armed Forces Network, the men heard a commentator reading a proclamation from General Eisenhower to the German Armed Forces:

"The Supreme Commander of the Allied Forces has come into possession of a secret order, issued by the German

High Command on October 18, 1943. . . . This secret document orders the execution of Allied airborne soldiers.

"The Supreme Allied Commander thereby addresses to you the following strict warning: . . .

"The execution of uniformed airborne troops and parachutists is an offense against the recognized laws of warfare. . . . All persons—officers, soldiers and civilians—who have any part in the ordering or carrying out of the above-mentioned order issued by the German High Command will be severely called to account and punished according to military law. . . . The excuse of having 'only carried out orders' will not be recognized."

Amid a barrage of curses, the radio was hastily turned off.

There would be little sleep that night. There was too much to think about.

Like, how deep is the damned Rhine?

Fifty miles upstream from the fateful bridge at Arnhem, the Rhine curves south past the thirteenth-century Hanseatic city of Wesel. The river is 1,500 feet wide at this point, and swift-flowing, with many tricky currents. Fed by the heavy rains of January and February, 1945, the river pressed against the two systems of dikes that protected the town from its ravages, flooding the area between them.

The Westphalian plain is flat and has no prominent features in this area except for the heavily wooded Diersfordter Wald, which rises to a height of 150 feet northwest of Wesel. From this forest, artillery could cover the river from Rees to the north to below Wesel, making any crossing of the river a very costly—if not an impossible—undertaking. The gloomy depths of the Diersfordter Wald were destined to be the pivot of the coming battle.

That Field Marshal Montgomery's 21st Army Group would attempt a crossing of the North Rhine between Emmerich and Wesel had long been obvious. In spite of all efforts at camouflage, the slow, steady buildup of men and materiel on the British 2nd Army front had been impossible to disguise. More than a million men (including the attached United States 9th Army, under Lieutenant General William H. Simpson), thousands of cannon, trucks, amphibious vehicles, and supply dumps had been moved in close to the Rhine. If the Germans needed additional proof that the crossing would come here, they had simply to listen to the BBC, which heralded the buildup and proclaimed that "Field Marshal Montgomery's preparations for his next move are being concealed behind a huge smokescreen." Even the sedate London *Times* joined in the publicity campaign to keep Montgomery in the public eye at a time when the American efforts to cross the Rhine in the south had been successful without the overwhelming preparation and buildup that the British required.

On the other side of the Rhine stood the forces of Field Marshal Albert von Kesselring. The morale of the defenders was very low; these German formations had been badly mangled in the fighting on the west bank of the Rhine, which had persisted because of Hitler's insistence on a policy of "no retreat." On March 7 the Ludendorff Bridge at Remagen, to the south, had been seized intact by aggressive units of the United States 1st Army. Three days later Field Marshal Gerd von Rundstedt, commander of the armies on the Western Front, had been ignominiously dismissed by a desperate Führer, who badly needed a scapegoat for the defeats after Holland. Field Marshal Kesselring had been hastily brought in from Italy to assume command.

Kesselring had assigned the defense of the Wesel sector to General Wilhelm Schlemm, who had been given command of the tough professional 1st Parachute Army reinforced with two infantry divisions. Woefully undermanned and short of artillery and other essential materiel, this force was hurriedly moved into the area at the beginning of March to prepare for the Allied attack. At Schlemm's insistence, the XLVII Panzer Corps was also assigned to the defense, being put in reserve about fifty miles north of Wesel.

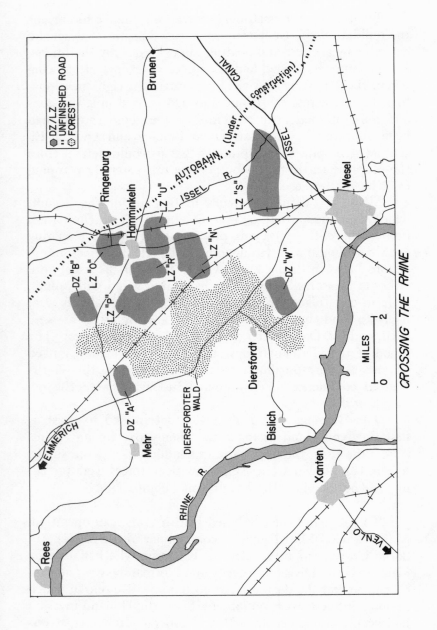

CROSSING THE RHINE

Field Marshal Kesselring, however, was unable to prevent the buildup of the Remagen beachhead, in spite of desperate attempts by artillery and floating mines to destroy the bridge. By the time the bridge had collapsed, nine days after being taken, the 1st Army had already constructed eight new pontoon bridges across the Rhine and had poured nine divisions and most of their artillery across it. This bold gamble had been approved by Generals Omar Bradley and Dwight Eisenhower, despite British protests that it would detract from the set-piece battle that Montgomery was carefully planning to be his masterpiece.

With less than two weeks to prepare for the assault, which they knew would be preceded by an overwhelming airborne attack, the Germans proceeded to dig in, preparing every farmhouse as a strongpoint, with telephone communications between them. There was no time for the usual anti-airborne measures, such as pointed stakes wired with mines, or farm carts placed in the open fields in which gliders were likely to land, but large numbers of antiaircraft guns were sited, and the Diersfordter Wald swarmed with artillery. The mood of the German troops, according to Schlemm, ranged "from suspicion to callous resignation," and even the officers "lacked confidence, and wondered just what were the demands of duty."

The Germans dug in doggedly, determined to resist as best they could and to make the enemy pay for any gains. Across the river, the west bank was hidden in a dense smoke screen, behind which the Anglo-American forces were preparing, and out of which the assault would come.

To command the combined British/American operation, Major-General Matt Ridgway, commander of the XVIII Airborne Corps, had been selected. Ridgway, who had led the 82nd Airborne Division in Sicily and Normandy, was the logical choice, but the decision had been a sensitive one in which national interests were not absent. Since the Holland invasion had been commanded by a British general, Browning, it was the Americans' turn to lead an airborne mission. The British Major-General Richard Gale, who might have hoped for the top post, agreed with the decision and was named deputy-commander.

Ridgway, who had participated in all the planning, requested one major change. Knowing that the fatal error at Arnhem had been the failure of the British XXX Corps to drive through to rescue the airborne division there, he was determined that his command would not be trapped on the east bank if the British river assault were for some reason to be halted. With the agreement of Lieutenant-General Miles Dempsey, commander of the British 2nd Army, it was planned that the Allied assault would begin *before* the airborne attack, and that only several hours after the river barrier had been breached would the paratroopers and the glider infantry come in. In addition, the 2nd Army's artillery was given a role in the flak suppression to be carried out before the airborne landings.

Finally, the planners of 1st Allied Airborne Army had finished their work. Copies of the maps and of the aerial photographs were prepared, field orders were typed up, and officer-couriers left for the troop-carrier wings and the headquarters of the airborne divisions.

Now it was up to the men who would have to do the flying and the fighting.

Dawn on March 24, 1945, came at 5:28 A.M., British Double Summer Time. The combat crews were awakened and the usual generous precombat breakfast (accompanied by the usual remarks of "the condemned men were served a hearty last meal") was served. Then the men were driven to the landing strips. Last-minute checks were made; the glider pilots spoke to the airborne infantrymen who were to be their passengers, instructing them on how to act while in the air and on the necessity of leaving the glider as quickly as possible after they had landed.

Inscriptions were chalked on the sides of the gliders:

"This is a towed target." "Is this trip necessary?" "Stop! Have you paid your insurance?"

One glider pilot wrote upside down on his glider:

IT WAS A HELL OF A LANDING
IF YOU CAN READ THIS

At the British airfields, the chalked graffiti was more threatening:

"We are the Al Capone gang."

"Up the Reds!"

"Up the frauleins' skirts!"

(A humorless German officer who had seen these same inscriptions on British gliders at Arnhem later wrote: "How far this is connected with the political convictions of the troops themselves or whether it is due to Bolshevist or American influences is not known.")

After the last load had been checked, the last instruction given, and the last defiant tag line chalked on a glider, there was nothing to be done except to wait—and waiting was always the hardest part. The C-47s were lined up nose to tail down the center of the runway, with the gliders to the rear, towropes already attached. For the first time in Europe, each plane would pull two Waco gliders in order to get the maximum number of aircraft into the landing zones in the shortest possible time. To avoid midair collisions, one towrope would be slightly shorter than the other, allowing more room for the gliders to oscillate on tow.

The overlap of glider and towplane wings formed a natural canopy against the bright sunlight, and men stood in small groups, exchanging confidences, or wandered up and down the sun-streaked concrete strip to find a friend for a last word. Some sprawled on the ground and pretended to sleep. One glider pilot went behind the tail of his glider and, when no one was watching, vomited quickly on it. This would be his fourth combat glider mission, and he had thrown up on the tail of each of the other gliders he had flown. By now, he had managed to convince himself that it was "for luck."

A number of distinguished visitors had arrived at Field Marshal Montgomery's headquarters at Venlo, Holland, to witness what most of them suspected would be the last airborne operation of the war. The prime minister, Winston Churchill, and the chief of the Imperial General Staff, Field Marshal Alan Brooke, had flown in from England the day before and had been joined by Generals Eisenhower, Brereton, and Ridgway. (Since the linkup between the airborne troopers and the British Second Army was expected to be only a matter of hours, Ridgway had decided not to parachute or glide in, but to cross the river after the airdrop and join his men in the Diersfordter Wald.)

Field Marshal Brooke had been concerned about this trip: ". . . off with P.M. on this visit to see the Rhine crossing. I am not happy about this trip; he will be difficult to manage and has no business to be going. All he will do is endanger his life unnecessarily. However, nothing on earth will stop him!"

After breakfast, the VIPs were driven from Venlo to a hill just south of the town of Xanten, from which ordinarily they might have had an excellent view of the battlefield. "Unfortunately," wrote Brooke, "it was rather hazy, but we could just make out the line of the Rhine from Xanten to Wesel. . . . We are in the middle of the battery positions supporting that portion of the front, and there was a continual roar of guns as they were busy engaging German A.A. guns in anticipation of the arrival of the airborne divisions."

It was now 9:30 A.M., and they had thirty minutes to wait.

At 0600 exactly, the first towplane and Horsa glider combination rolled down the runway at Brize Norton in England. "Operation Varsity" had begun.

The 440 gliders being pulled by Number 38 and Number 46 Groups had started out an hour before the takeoff of the paratroop serial, since the extra time was required to get all the gliders into the air and assembled at the required altitude. The weather was good, with little cloud cover and excellent visibility; yet in spite of this, the tendency of the heavy Horsas and Hamilcars to break loose or to be prematurely released again took its toll. Thirty-five British gliders never left England; two of them went down in the Channel (where the crews were speedily rescued by air/sea rescue launches).

The first paratroop serials were those of the British 6th Airborne Division, being carried by the three American troop-carrier groups from airfields at Chipping Ongar, Boreham, and Wethersfield. As an official history described it: "Emplaning at Boreham was briefly delayed while the British finished their inevitable tea, and there was a flurry of excitement at Chipping Ongar as a buzz bomb passed overhead and exploded near the base." The first of the 242 C-47s took off at 0709, and it required only thirty-one minutes to get them all into the air. They were carrying almost 3,900 British paratroopers and 137 tons of supplies.

The first American paratroop serial took off from Chartres, France, at 0725. In the first plane was Colonel Edson D. Raff, commander of the 507th Parachute Infantry Regiment. Raff had led the paratroops on their first combat jump in North Africa and had witnessed the glider massacre at LZ "W" in Normandy. Today he was leading his men in their last wartime jump.

From three other fields in the vicinity of Paris, six other paratroop serials swept into the air, assembled, and took their positions behind the serial from Chartres. In contrast to the weather conditions in England, although the skies were clear and the visibility was unlimited, there was a strong crosswind of about fifteen miles per hour blowing across the single runway at most of the French airfields. At Achiet, one C-46 lost control on the takeoff and crashed. Two others were prevented by engine trouble from taking off, and one returned to the field after takeoff. Except for three men injured in the crash, all troops in the aborted planes were transferred to substitute aircraft, which took off at the end of the line.

As the paratroop planes assembled over their fields and set off for the rendezvous at Wavre, the gliders began their mission. There were 610 C-47s and 906 Waco CG-4As scheduled to fly across the Rhine, and those who saw the takeoff of the double tows were not likely to forget it. The extra drag created by the two gliders slowed the towplane to the point where it looked as though many of them would never get into the air, even at those airfields in which the runways were over 6,000 feet long. The heavily loaded gliders, airborne long before the towplane had left the ground, wallowed in the crosswind, slipping dangerously close to each other as the glider pilots fought desperately to keep their separation distance and to stay low enough to the runway so that the towplane would have a chance of lowering its tail for takeoff. Twice, the short tow glider in a double tow fouled its mate's rope; two gliders had their wings cut off by the ropes and crashed, and the other two had to be cut loose from the entangled lines.

By 0800, the entire armada was in the air, and moving toward a rendezvous point south of Brussels. It was the largest single-day airborne operation of the war (more planes and gliders were used in Holland, but over a week's time). The entire sky train took more than three hours and twenty minutes to pass a given point, and would deliver over 17,000 paratroopers and glider infantry, plus their equipment, into the small area on the other side of the Rhine.

As the British glider serials approached Wavre, they flew directly over Waterloo. The pilot of one of the Horsas was an RAF flier who had been retrained as a glider pilot and a soldier, to replace the heavy losses the British glider pilot regiment had suffered at Arnhem. According to an apocryphal story, he turned to his sergeant-copilot (a veteran of Normandy and Holland) and said, "My great-great-grandfather fought at Waterloo." The sergeant glanced briefly out the right-hand window at the battlefield, and then, turning back, grumbled with a distinct working-class accent, "So did mine, and it was probably your great-great-grandfather who got my great-great-grandfather killed. Try not to do the same to me today!"

Many of the American gliders also had "virgin" copilots—newly arrived power pilots who had received a minimum amount of glider training. Flight Officer Paul C. Swink, who flew with one of these "throttle jockey" replacements, wrote: "I thought it was great, as I had not had a copilot on the other missions. Immediately after take-off, as we got into formation, my copilot said, 'I'll fly it.' He continued to fly, and this was a long flight. Every so often I would ask if he wanted me to fly awhile, and his answer was always 'no.' When I realized we were getting close to the Rhine, I asked again and got the same answer. I then asked him if he was getting tired. His answer was, 'Hell yes, I'm tired, but I want you rested enough to land this thing!'"

As the time for the arrival of the airborne columns approached, the guns on the west bank of the Rhine fell silent, and all eyes were eagerly turned skyward to detect the first planes. From his hilltop two thousand yards south of Xanten, Winston Churchill was ecstatic. "It was full daylight before the subdued but intense roar and rumbling of swarms of aircraft stole upon us. After that, in the course of half an hour, over two thousand aircraft streamed overhead in their formation. My viewpoint had been well chosen. The light was clear enough to enable one to see where the descent on the enemy took place. The aircraft faded from sight, and then almost immediately afterwards returned towards us at a different level. The parachutists were invisible even in the best field glasses, but now there was a double murmur and roar of reinforcements arriving and of those who had delivered their attacks returning. Soon one saw with a sense of tragedy aircraft in twos and threes coming back askew, asmoke or even in flames."

A British airborne general, Brigadier G. J. Bourne, was alarmed by the view as his plane approached the initial point close to the river. "I could see the Rhine, a silver streak, and beyond it a thick, black haze, for all the world like Manchester or Birmingham as seen from the air. For the moment, I wondered whether the bombing of Wesel, which had preceded the attack upon that town by commando troops, had been mistimed. If this was so, then the whole landing zone would be obscured by the clouds of dust which would be blowing from the rubble created by the attack."

Whether in fact the dense, obscuring layer was smoke from the burning houses in Wesel (which had been blasted not only by an air attack but also by Allied artillery), or whether it was smoke from the generators which had been used to hide the Allied buildup along the west bank of the Rhine, is still not known. In any case, the damage had been done. The drop and landing zones which the paratroopers and gliders were to reach were hidden under a 300-foot-thick layer of smoke that effectively hid all navigation points and obliterated the outlines of the fields. Although the glider pilots looking down could see very little other than a small circle of ground directly beneath them, the Germans, dug into the farmhouses below, had an excellent view of the paratroop and glider train outlined against the sky.

As the first three serials swept over DZ (Drop Zone) "A," on the northwest edge of the Diersfordter Wald, enemy flak was strangely quiet. Almost two thousand men of the British 3rd Parachute Brigade were dropped accurately, although some jumped late and others required a second pass before the proper drop zone was found. At DZ "B," things were rougher. The almost two thousand men of the 5th Parachute Brigade were given an excellent drop, the pilots flying straight and true. But as the formations turned left onto a homeward course, sudden blasts of intense and accurate light flak ripped through them. East of the Rhine, ten planes were shot down in just a few minutes, and seven others staggered to crash landings in Allied territory on the west bank. (It was later determined that these flak units had been too far east to have been reached by artillery fire from the west bank, and had either been missed by the Allied fighter-bombers or else had been brought in at the last minute.)

Even as the paratroopers were landing on their fields, struggling out of their parachutes, and rounding up their equipment, the British gliders began to arrive. The release had been planned for an altitude of 2,500 feet; but because of overrunning by serials farther back in the column, some Horsas and Hamilcars were released as high as 3,500 feet. The long, slow descent from such a high altitude made them doubly vulnerable to the German gunners, who had plenty of time to adjust their aim. Gliders loaded with gasoline were set on fire and plunged like torches into the ground. A Hamilcar crippled by flak broke apart; the small Tetrarch tank it was carrying fell out, followed by passengers and crew. Ten gliders were shot down and almost three hundred damaged, many severely. Most of those that survived the antiaircraft fire were landing casualties because of the smoke and the inexperience of many of the pilots.

Two Horsas collided in midair and, locked together, plunged into a house which later served as a squadron headquarters. "The cockpit of one of the gliders protruded into the ground floor ceiling," Sergeant "Andy" Andrews recalls, "and by standing on a chair I could see that both pilots were dead."

Andrews himself had almost "bought the farm" on landing. Two flak bursts had wounded his copilot and badly damaged the controls, sending the Horsa slipping erratically earthward at high speed. Just missing some high poplars, Andrews touched down in a small field. "In front of us was a crashed glider with the tail sticking up . . . there was a bump on the left, then a lurch forwards followed by a crunching, splintering breaking-up sound as if every piece of plywood was disintegrating into matchwood."

The whole nose and dashboard of the Horsa disappeared, and Andrews was hurled through the air to a sliding landing on his crash helmet. When he looked back, he saw that "the whole front of the Horsa was missing . . . the wings had collapsed and the tail section had broken away and rolled to the middle of the field." He went back slowly to help the wounded and injured; three men who had been sitting in the tail were missing.

Sergeant Harry Antonopoulos, the acknowledged ditching expert of the Regiment, lost his nose wheel on a barbed-wire fence but slithered to a halt without further damage. As he and his passengers started to leave the glider, a machine gun opened fire. "That gun was so fast," Antonopoulos told the author, "that the bullets all come through one clean hole. So we all dived out and hit the ground with the machine gun still raking the rear. I remember thinking, 'We must get out of here,' and then this American voice shouted, 'Over here, buddy.' It was a nice, deep ditch with three or four American glider pilots in it."

The vulnerability of the Allied columns to enemy flak resulted in some bizarre mistakes. About thirty Waco gliders accidentally cut loose from their towplanes while they were still far from their LZs. The lead glider had its towrope severed by ground fire and fluttered down to a safe landing. The other gliders—unaware of the accidental release—came up to the same point and obediently cut loose, following the lead glider in.

At the landing zones, however, the glider pilots were fighting to land safely amid the violent struggle for control of the area. Artillery fire, mortars, machine-gun bursts from strongpoints in the farmhouses, rifle fire—all ripped through the gliders as they descended or came slithering to a halt. Thirty-two gliders were blown up or set on fire before they could be unloaded, and less than one-quarter of those that reached the assault area came through undamaged. The British glider pilots suffered severely: 38 dead, 37 wounded, and 135 missing—a casualty rate of 38 percent. Nevertheless, their contribution to the attack had been considerable, for they had brought in almost 3,400 troopers, 271 jeeps, 66 guns, and 275 trailers, trucks, and bulldozers.

The smoke raised havoc with the American paratroop serials as well. Colonel Raff and most of his men were dropped on the western edge of the Diersfordter Wald, more than two miles from their assigned DZ. This was close to the fortress known as Schloss Diersfordt, which was a major objective that had been assigned to another battalion. The rest of Raff's men landed on the other side of the fortress.

"Instead of attempting a trek to the drop zone," the official history states, "both groups went into action on the spot. Raff's men drove confused and wavering German troops out of good positions in the nearby woods, killing some fifty-five, taking over 300 prisoners, and capturing a battery of 150-mm. howitzers. Then they marched south to attack the castle, where at about 1100 they found the rest of the battalion already engaging the German occupants."

American paratroopers were dropped by mistake on a field intended for the British divisional command post. They quickly cleaned out the flak guns in the immediate area, thus sparing the British an unpleasant surprise when they flew in three minutes later.

Two generals had begged permission from Matt Ridgway to participate in the jump. They went in with a parachute field artillery unit that was to be preceded by a serial of parachutists dropping into the same field. Unfortunately, owing to the confusion caused by the smoke, the parachutists were dropped elsewhere, and Generals Josiah T. Dalbey and Ridgeley M. Gaither found themselves coming down alone on top of a battery of 20-mm. guns reinforced by machine guns and German infantrymen. The field artillery unit (with 75-mm. guns dropped by parachute) was widely dispersed, and slow to get into action. Luckily, shortly after they landed, gliders started to land in the fields around them. Without waiting for other reinforcements, General Dalbey organized an impromptu attack force consisting of the American artillerymen, British and American glider pilots, and any other soldier he could grab in the immediate vicinity. Together they rushed the German emplacement and eliminated the battery plus all other hostile resistance in the vicinity. This successful assault unit Dalbey christened the "Chattahoochee Task Force," after the river that runs past Fort Benning, Georgia.

Larry Rue, the *Chicago Tribune* correspondent, flew in one of the lead planes of the American glider mission. "Miles before we came to the Issel Canal and to the Rhine, we passed over rubble heap after rubble heap, blasted or burnt out towns and buildings . . . here and there, around deserted barnyards, there seemed to be some stray chickens, but there was no sign that any of the civilian population remained in that area at all. There was a slight ground haze as we crossed the Issel and approached the Rhine. Through the window, to the south, I could see that there was still some fighting going on at Wesel. . . . It was immediately after we crossed the Rhine that the flak came up at us. Pilots cannot take evasive action when towing gliders. In the plane, the bursting shells outside —this was small stuff—sounded as if someone were pounding on the bottom of the ship with a heavy hammer . . . the tree-tops over a long distance were covered with parachutes. Flashes from guns and smoke indicated a battle was going on here as well as in Wesel. The flak subsided when we got to the drop zone, but beneath us we could see that some of the preceding gliders had not fared too well. One was burning and another had crashed headfirst, and there were some bodies and equipment scattered around it . . . our gliders unhooked in a good position, and the last I saw of them they were gliding under control, in the center of the drop zone."

Flight Officer Karl F. Harold was flying his first combat mission. "It's hard to adequately describe a glider landing," he later wrote home, "particularly when it is made in the heart of enemy territory, with fighting going on all about. Too much happens too fast. Some lucky gliders made it without a scratch; others became funeral pyres. One glider, ripped through and through with ack-ack, crashed nose first deep into the earth. Not a man came out. In a few seconds, fire started by tracers roared through the fabric. Trying desperately to land before they are destroyed, other gliders smashed through fences, ripped through wires, crashed into ships already on the ground. Men who were unhurt tumbled out of the last ships. Despite the losses, the number of glider troops in the area increases." Harold and his copilot, Flight Officer Bill Waterman, brought their cargo, which consisted of three airborne troopers, a jeep, and a supply of artillery shells, in safely, but they were pinned down by sniper fire for over an hour. After the jeep was unloaded, it was driven over to another glider to pick up the British six-pound gun for which it was the carrier. At that point, the glider pilots started out for their prearranged assembly point.

All over the landing and drop zones, a hundred separate firefights were going on in the midst of the obscuring smoke screen. Germans were being flushed out of farmhouse strongpoints and of nearby gun positions by the paratroopers and glider pilots. German artillery and mortars continued to pound the gliders, making unloading of the cargo impossible. The battle for control of the Diersfordter Wald reached its climax during the late afternoon and early evening, as the paratroopers continued to move in on German fortified positions.

The first American glider crossing the Rhine was flown by Major Hugh J. Nevins; it carried the inscription "Kansas City Kitty—Mary Lou," which he had put on in honor of his hometown and his wife. Nevins remembered that the flight from Chartres to the Rhine had been very choppy and that his airborne passengers had become deathly sick. "Ten minutes out from the initial point on the friendly side of the Rhine . . . I turned the glider over to Lieutenant Bob Burke, my copilot, and went aft to put on my flak suit and helmet with far from steel-nerved hands.

"We turned right at the initial point, and were on 'Last Lap'—the alarming code name given by higher Headquarters to that section of the run-in from the initial point to the Rhine. It was here that Bob and I first saw Marshal Montgomery's unannounced smokescreen at Wesel, billowing northeast to cover the movement of his troops across the river. Unfortunately, the smokescreen was cloud-like, and in penetrating it we encountered horizontal visibilities as low as one-quarter of a mile, all the way to the drop zone. . . . The north-south railroad indicating the release point loomed up ahead . . . the 'light to moderate' flak and small-arms fire increased to 'intense.' A later remark that the fabric-covered glider sounded like 'a paper sack full of popcorn kernels' aptly fitted the situation. Unfortunately, we were above and parallel to the railroad track and embankment, which was infested with Germans and their efficient weapons. While keeping my left eye on my landing zone, I put the nose down and we were doing a whistling 120 miles per hour.

". . . We were doing 100 miles per hour as I turned into the final approach, and had to do an immediate nose-high stall and left side-slip, which dropped us from one hundred miles an hour to fifty miles an hour instantly. Bob rode the controls with me, and we managed to get the left wing up just before contacting the ground some one hundred yards beyond a flaming C-46. The left landing gear sheared off in a ditch, and we groundlooped left and stopped. We were 'safe.' Bob and I jumped out of the glider onto the ground, and were followed by the dull, airsick troops.

"Preoccupied as we had been while flying, it was not immediately apparent that we were receiving fire—accurate fire—from some twelve snipers in a nearby building . . . our posi-

tion was untenable unless we silenced the systematic fire . . .
so I commenced pumping lead from my rifle into the four
nearest windows. Bob reinforced me with his carbine. Fire
also was coming from the Red Cross Hospital steeple, above
us, some one hundred yards away.

"The stunned airborne troops, perhaps from my lurid
demands or from their intensive training, came to life, and by
judicious use of grenades, tommyguns and carbines disposed
of our immediate enemies. We unloaded the glider and
started with three prisoners towards the previously designated assembly area."

American glider pilot Robert "Bob" Wilson, struggling
to land his glider amid the heavy smoke and ground fire, was
barely able to lift his plane above a sixty-foot tree before the
glider started to shake as though it were about to stall out. He
finally managed to put it on the ground safely, and then mo-
tioned for his copilot to leave the aircraft. "He was a nice
guy and I was a nice guy," he said later, "so we unhooked our
belts and I said to him, 'Go ahead.' He said, 'No, you go
ahead,' and all of a sudden, we're both waiting for the other
one to get out of that glider, and we realized that they were
shooting at us! So now we both went at once, and we bumped
helmets right there in the cockpit and knocked each other
back into our seats! Believe me, I got out first after that, and
we both jumped into a little ditch that was there and put our
noses right in the dirt."

The confused fighting in the smoke-covered fields grew
wilder and wilder as the airborne troopers and the glider pilots
groped to find other members of their units. Always there was
another farmhouse to be cleaned out before a field could be
crossed, or the gliders in it unloaded. The Germans resisted
stubbornly and had to be routed out by grenades or point-
blank fire.

In one such action, in a field on the edge of the Diersfordter Wald, an element new to airborne warfare was intro-
duced. Glider pilots who were engaged in a firefight with ten

Germans inside a thick-walled farmhouse were astonished when a "posse" of four paratroopers mounted on farm horses came galloping out of the woods and circled the farmhouse, firing through the windows and letting out Indian war cries at the same time. Even more astonished at this bit of Wild West show were the Germans, who promptly surrendered. The mounted paratroopers (two of whom were wearing top hats) turned the prisoners over to the glider pilots and trotted off in search of more palefaces to scalp.

Wes Hare, who had fought to go on this mission, encountered no ground fire at all while circling for a landing spot. "Everything looked peaceful," he recalled later. Elated, he turned to say to the airborne troops in his glider, "Gee, this is a 'milk run,' there's nothing to this!" Then he realized that the glider was diving straight toward the ground. "There was no chance to do anything, we just *hit*. As soon as I turned around and looked, the ground was there, and we hit. And then the fire started. We were being shot at from three different farmhouses . . . they had us pinned down for two or three hours. Finally the paratroopers and the rest of the airborne troops linked up and went in and cleaned out the houses. One paratrooper had come up over the railroad tracks with a tommy gun and five German prisoners. As he came up the rise in the road at the tracks, some Germans from one of these houses started shooting at him, so he just opened up with his tommy gun and shot the five German prisoners dead and dropped to the ground, staying by the ditch."

As night fell, the confused fighting died down, and both sides dug in to hold their positions. As Lieutenant-Colonel Iain Murray walked along the line of glider pilots, he assured them, "You needn't worry. The Second Army is across the Rhine and we shall leave tomorrow." The answer was a cynical, "That's what you told us at Arnhem!"

Karl Harold later reported, "I met a friend named Larry Waltz from my squadron, and we started to dig holes for the night. We dug in with some airborne troops in the woods.

They had set up a perimeter of defense around the edge of the woods, but moved out about dark. We numbered about twenty glider pilots together at this time, and our captain said we would stay put for the night, right where we were.

"Larry and I dug our foxhole in an L-shape at random near some of our buddies. We crawled out and got a couple of camouflage parachutes to make our little abode more comfortable. We dragged an old pine tree up sort of over the hole, to protect us from any flying splinters, in case of shell bursts in the trees, not thinking of the fact that we were forming a blind side to our hole.

"About midnight I whispered to Larry that I could hear Germans talking, and sure enough here came what we thought was a patrol, but if it was, it was certainly disorganized. Suddenly hell broke loose, burp guns, Mausers, grease guns, Thompsons, carbines, M-1s, grenades—hell's a-poppin'! A glider pilot named Zeke yelled out, 'Hold your fire, men, I've got some prisoners!' In the moonlight I could see Zeke and another glider pilot standing about thirty feet from me with the drop on six Jerries who were reaching for the stars. I ducked back down and told Larry what I had seen, and laid my grease gun on the bottom of the hole.

"As I peeked out again, there in the shadow of some trees not three feet from me are two Krauts, with rifles pointed right at our guts. I might have been able to grab my grease gun and get off a couple of bursts, but from that angle I couldn't have helped dropping some of our guys who were scrambling towards Zeke. Larry and I threw up our hands and the two Krauts jumped right into the hole with us, with their guns in our stomachs. My Kraut said, 'Namen?' I said, 'Karl.' In English, he said, 'Spell it.' I spelled, 'K-A-R-L.' He says, 'That's good. C-A-R-L, I kill you now; K-A-R-L, I let you live a while. I hate British, and you are my American prisoner.' Then he said, 'I've been a soldier for six years. I'm tired. War is hell. How many men you got?' That was my cue to start talking. I said, 'We outnumber you ten to one. These woods are full of our troops. Most of your troops are already our prisoners . . . give me your gun, be my prisoner, and I'll see that you get out of these woods alive.' He thought it over for a while, handed me his rifle, reached down and handed me my grease gun, and told his buddy to do the same. He laughed and said, 'First you my prisoner—now I your prisoner!' "

That night, the Germans sent out patrols to determine the airborne positions. General Ridgway was moving through the dark Diersfordter Wald when he ran into one of these patrols. In the ensuing fight Ridgway received a fragment from a grenade in his shoulder.

There were also more serious counterattacks. At one crossroad which was being held by some forty American glider pilots, several hundred German infantrymen preceded by two tanks attacked the crossroad in the middle of the night. The glider pilots let the tanks approach and then knocked out the first one with a bazooka; the second one turned and ran. This left the German infantry wide open, and in the ensuing fight the glider pilots killed over thirty men and took seventy prisoners. The crossroads were promptly christened "Burp Gun Corner."

The next morning, the British and American infantry which had crossed the river passed through the lines held by the airborne troopers and continued the advance to the Elbe River over the Westphalian plain. Some five hundred glider pilots escorted 2,500 prisoners down to the river. "The march was relatively pleasant," Major Nevins recalled, "since the glider pilots were ordered to present the most healthy prisoners with their equipment, and had only their weapons to burden them. Nothing happened on the route out. The corridor was well-policed and no enemy fire was encountered. General Ridgway came forward through the corridor in his jeep, and we gave him the snappiest salutes we could muster."

The prisoners were turned over to the MPs at the river-bank, and the glider pilots crossed in Navy amphibious vehi-

cles to an encampment on the west bank, where a British sup-
ply battalion had set up a camp with hot food and showers.
At the entry to the camp they had erected a sign saying "The
Rhine Hotel—Glider Pilots a Specialty."

Winston Churchill also crossed the Rhine that day in
an LST (Landing Ship, Tank), but in the opposite direction.
He waited until Eisenhower had left, knowing that Ike would
never have permitted him to endanger his life on the east
bank of the Rhine. Then he suggested to Montgomery that
they cross over, and the field marshal readily agreed. Accompanied by Field Marshal Brooke, they spent some time exam-
ining the German river defenses and the shattered bridge at
Wesel. Wesel was still occupied, and a considerable amount of
sniping was going on inside the town. As the Allies began to
construct a new bridge across the river at that point, German
shells continued to drop in. "We decided it was time to remove the P.M., who was thrilled with the situation and very
reluctant to leave!" Alan Brooke reported. "U.S. General Simpson, on whose front we were, came up to Winston saying,
'Prime minister, there are snipers in front of you; they are
shelling on both sides of the bridge, and now they have
started shelling the road behind you. I cannot accept the responsibility of your being here, and must ask you to go away.'
The look on Winston's face was just like that of a small boy
being called away from his sand castles on the beach by his
nurse! He put both his arms around one of the twisted girders
of the bridge, and looked over his shoulder at Simpson, with
pouting mouth and angry eyes. Thank Heavens he came away
quietly. It was a sad wrench for him; he was enjoying himself
immensely."

It was the afternoon of March 25, 1945—Palm Sunday.
On the west bank of the Rhine, returning glider pilots checked
into the British "Rhine Hotel" for a hearty dinner, hot
showers, and army cots to sleep in. As they dropped off to
sleep, they could hear cannon blasts resounding faintly from
the other side of the river. Their job was completed, but the
fighting between the Allied and German troops continued.

When one group of weary British glider pilots arrived back at Down Ampney airfield, an overly zealous customs official demanded that they fill out entry forms! "He actually wanted to know if we had anything to declare," Andrews recalls. "The glares and the silence quickly drove him away."

After returning from the Rhine mission, the tired glider pilots were allowed a weekend leave from their bases. Flight Officer John Lowden, of the 440th Troop Carrier Group, was assigned by his squadron adjutant to go to Paris and arrange for hotel accommodations for about twelve glider pilots each weekend, since no one could leave the base without the commanding officer's knowing exactly where he could be reached. As Lowden later recalled:

"I started with the hotel *George* V and worked my way down with no luck. Finally I went to the American Express office, where a lovely French girl gave me directions to a small 'hotel.' I went through a small door, and when a bell rang upstairs as I put my foot on the first step I knew where I was. But I figured this 'hotel' was better than nothing, since all my buddies back in Orléans threatened me with slow death if I didn't come up with a place for them to stay. I made the proper arrangements with the madam and cautioned her that there was to be no hanky panky with any of the visiting officers. Of course, she agreed with a great rolling of her eyes!" Lowden gave the name and address of the "hotel" to the squadron adjutant, and the next weekend twelve glider pilots left for Paris. On Monday morning, however, an angry mob came through the barracks door shouting for "that sonofabitch Lowden."

"What it boiled down to was that all the money they had planned to send home had disappeared in the 'hotel,' which they didn't leave once," Lowden said. "But later all agreed that it was the best weekend leave they ever had!"

The madam had asked Lowden and a friend of his who had helped to make the arrangements if they would care to spend an evening free. "We gratefully accepted, and asked for a room with twin beds. She said in French: 'Twin beds in my place? Surely, sir, you jest.' So my buddy and I went to sleep in a double bed, and a couple of hours later two of the biggest American MPs I'd ever seen knocked on the door. We let them in and their eyes really lit up. They had found two officers in bed together in a French whorehouse!" Lowden and his friend showed the policemen their passes with the hotel name and address filled in. The MPs examined their ID cards and the passes minutely, and then handed them back. As they turned to leave the room, Lowden heard one say to the other, "Jesus, these Air Force types think of everything. Maybe they really *are* winning the war!"

Epilogue

By the middle of April, 1945, Berlin was the tantalizing goal of two converging armies.

Sixty-five miles east of the city, the Russians stood poised on the Oder River, massing for the final attack on the besieged Nazi capital. Twice as far away, to the east, the Allied armies were swiftly approaching the banks of the Elbe against crumbling German resistance. There seemed to be nothing to prevent the Anglo-Americans from pushing across the river and taking Berlin—nothing except the political decision made at Yalta that the Allies would stop on the Elbe. To prevent any possibility that the two anti-Nazi armies might fire on each other, Berlin was to be taken by the Soviets.

But in the locked files at Supreme Headquarters, Allied Expeditionary Forces, there was a bulging folder labeled "Operation Eclipse." Prepared as far back as November, 1944, it contained plans for a massive airborne operation to capture Berlin, either as the last stage of the war or in the event of a sudden German collapse.

An assault from the air on a metropolis! The very thought was enough to send shivers through the survivors of the airborne campaigns in Europe. Five airborne divisions and almost three thousand gliders could have been thrown into the shattered city—a ruin defended by 200,000 die-hard Nazis. A battle to be fought among several million demoralized civilians. Every street corner was filled with rubble which would make it a strongpoint for the veteran SS troopers determined to sell their lives at the highest possible cost to their enemies.

Into this fortress, through a maelstrom of flak that would have taken a fearful toll of the troop-carrier planes, the paratroopers would jump to seize the five main airfields. Even as they were fighting for shattered hangars and bunkers, gliders would be weaving their way down through the tracers looking for a clear spot among the craters and the burning hulks of planes—Allied and German. Other gliders would be smashing down among the debris of the Tiergarten park and on the wide boulevards to attack the government ministries that bordered them.

Explosions, the screaming of the wounded, the roar of engines overhead, the splintering sound of gliders disintegrating on impact . . . the din of battle for a dying city. To Hitler in his bunker beneath the Reich Chancellery, it would have sounded Wagnerian, a muted Twilight of the Gods. Perhaps in his last moments, for an instant, he might have remembered General Student and the gliders.

But "Operation Eclipse" never took place. The glider pilots had fought their last battle crossing the Rhine River near Wesel.

A creature of the Second World War, never having been used in combat before and never to be used again, the combat glider now disappeared from history.

The Russians took Berlin—at a cost of 100,000 casualties—and the Germans surrendered. The war in Europe was over.

But the shattered stripped hulks of the gliders remained to rot on rocky slopes, among hedgerows, in vineyards, and on water-crossed fields. The farmers used the wheels for their carts and prized the nylon rope. On a pasture near Arnhem, the fused aluminum from burnt-out Horsas melted into the ground and nothing has grown there since.

The American glider pilots went home or on to occupa-

'T'WAS THE NIGHT BEFORE TAKEOFF
AND ALL BEYOND A DOUBT, OUR
G.R. IS FLYING, SO HE'S
SWEATIN' IT OUT.

F/O Dale Oliver '45

WE'LL LIVE!
WE'RE DOWN —
SAFE - SAFE - SAFE - . . .

— F/O Dale Oliver '45

tion duty in Germany. The British glider pilots were sent to India to prepare for the next Burma campaign; but a storm wrecked their gliders and, before replacements could arrive, Japan surrendered and the Pacific war was over.

Had the price paid in glider pilot casualties been worth it? The answer usually given at veterans' meetings is a shrug. The comradeship of the survivors is too close for this painful question to be answered even after thirty years.

Their attitude is perhaps best expressed by the glider pilot who said, "It was a job. We volunteered for it, we were selected for it, we trained for it, and finally we did it—and lost a lot of good friends. But, in the end, it was just another lousy job that someone had to do."

That is the best epitaph they could write.

Airborne Campaigners

The following ex-Allied glider pilots and other airborne veterans also contributed to this book. They patiently submitted to interviews, filled out long questionnaires, and—by letter, tape, and telephone—answered numerous inquiries on details now over thirty years old. Without their generous help this book could not have been written, and I thank them all:

James W. Agnew, Bennett Y. Allen, Forrest K. Allen, George Allen, James Alspaugh, Gale R. Ammerman, Martin R. Andersen, Elgin D. Andross, S. Antonopoulos (Glider Pilot Regiment), Stratton M. Appleman, Warren G. Austin, Elmer L. Bacorn, Raymond M. Baker, James R. Barley, Allen L. Barnes, Albert S. Barton, Colin R. Beeson, Richard O. Bell, Peter Benziger, Claude A. Berry, Thomas J. Berry, Robert S. Bovey, Andrew J. Boylen, George F. Brennan, William H. Brown, George E. Buckley, Robert M. Burke, William W. Burnett, Harmon Burroughs, Lewis C. Burwell, J. Garth Caldwell, Pershing Y. Carlson, Aldo Carocari, Francis L. Carroll, Howard H. Cloud, Edward B. Cogan, Carl V. Conover, Leo J. Cordier, Charlton W. Corwin, Edward J. Dailey, William B. Dalton, James T. Davies (GPR), Don C. Davis, Lawrence A. Davis, Ronald H. Deck, W. Thurston DeGroff, Ellsworth W. Dewberry, Archie L. Dickson, Charles E. Dixon, Robert D. Dopita, Arnold Dreer, Jack S. Dunn, S. East

(GPR), Charles B. Ellington, Charles K. Emerick, Harry F. Engel, L. G. Erskine, Edward R. Evans, Oliver C. Faris, Samuel Fine, Leo F. Flynn, Richard K. Fort, William B. Foster, Eugene B. Fox, Peter J. Franzak, Arthur C. Furchgott, Frank Gain, Paul T. Gilliatt, Chris E. Gish, Earl Goodwin, Frank Guild, Louis Hagen (GPR), Robert J. Hand, Wesley J. Hare, Karl F. Harold, Vinton Harz, Clark C. Hodges, E. H. Hohmann, Julian B. Hoshal, Paul O. Hower, Parks J. Hunter, Earle F. Hyatt, James G. Janes, William Jew, Harlie B. Johnson, Eugene C. Jordan, Harry P. Jordan, Les Judd, Arthur Kaplan, Jay Kattelman, David S. Kaufman, Jack W. Keiser, Edward L. Keys, Marc Klaw, William D. Knickerbocker, Ernest G. Lamb (GPR), L. Manley Lancaster, John A. Laney, John J. Lang, Charles E. Lawrence, Robert Leginus, Warren W. Lippincott, John L. Lowden, Edward J. McCague, Ennis McCall, Bert J. McCausey, Bernard P. McGaulley, Richard W. Mauger, William K. May, Richard J. Meis, Joseph Mendes, Harold H. Menzel, Grady W. Miller, Richard H. Miller, Robert L. Morehous, Alec Moser (GPR), Virgil S. Neal, Henry H. Nowell, Verne I. Ogden, Dale Oliver, H. H. Osborn, John P. Otte, Peter C. Paicos, Bernard G. Parks, Donald L. Patterson, John L. Patterson, Thomas W. Pearce (GPR), Albert F. Perna, Joseph H. Poindexter, Hammitt E. Porter, L. R. Portman, John D. Potts (GPR), Eric Rafter, Harvey W. Raidy, S. Tipton Randolph, Martin E. Rendelman, William K. Richmond, Bob Ricks, Frank Rossi, Earl H. Rowe, Lee C. Ryser, Theodore V. Sampson, Werner Schultheis, John S. Seawright, Donald G. Secor, Donald E. Seese, Melvin L. Shaffer, Fred G. Shay, John P. Shea, Derrick Shingleton (GPR), Franklin M. Shupp, Charles E. Slocum, Douglas E. Smith, Harry F. Smith, Lawrence A. Spencer, Raymond W. Stevens, James A. Swanson, Charles F. Sweeney, Floyd J. Sweet, Paul C. Swink, Charles A. Trimble, Willard Viall, Victor Wade (GPR), Albert O. Waldon, Earl C. Waller, Edwin C. Walton, William S. Watrous, George Weisfeld, W. J. Wells (GPR), James H. Whitcomb, Norman Wilmeth, John B. Wilson, Robert B. Wilson, C. E. Wysong.

Bibliography

Adleman, Robert H., and Walton, Col. George. *The Champagne Campaign*. Little, Brown, 1969.

Bekker, Cajus (Berenbrok, Hans Dieter). *The Luftwaffe War Diaries*. Doubleday, 1969.

Bradley, Gen. Omar N. *A Soldier's Story*. Holt, 1951.

Brereton, Gen. Lewis H. *The Brereton Diaries*. Morrow, 1946.

Bryant, Arthur. *Triumph in the West*. Doubleday, 1959.

British Air Ministry. *By Air to Battle: the official account of the British airborne divisions*. 1945.

————. *The Second World War—Airborne Forces*. 1951.

Burgett, Donald R. *Currahee!* Houghton Mifflin, 1967.

Butcher, Captain Harry C. *My Three Years with Eisenhower*. Simon and Schuster, 1946.

Carter, Ross S. *Those Devils in Baggy Pants*. Appleton-Century-Crofts, 1951.

Chatterton, George. *The Wings of Pegasus*. Macdonald (London), 1962.

Churchill, Winston S. *The Second World War* (6 vols.), Houghton Mifflin, 1953.

Clark, Alan. *The Fall of Crete*. Morrow, 1962.

Craven, F. C., and Cate, J. L. *The Army Air Forces in World War II*. Vol. 3, University of Chicago, 1951.

Critchell, Laurence. *Four Stars of Hell*. Macmillan, 1947.

Crookenden, Gen. Sir Napier. *Drop Zone Normandy: Airborne Operations*. Ian Allan (London), 1976.

Edwards, Roger. *German Airborne Troops, 1936–45*. Doubleday, 1974.

Eisenhower, Gen. Dwight D. *Crusade in Europe*. Doubleday, 1948.

Ellis, Major L. F. *Victory in the West*. (Two vols.), Her Majesty's Stationery Office (London), 1962, 1968.

Farrar-Hockley, Anthony. *Student*. Ballantine, 1973.

Gale, Gen. Richard Nelson. *With the Sixth Airborne in Normandy*. S. Low, Marston (London), 1948.

————. *Call to Arms*. Hutchinson (London), 1968.

Galvin, John R. *Air Assault: the development of airmobile warfare*. Hawthorn, 1969.

Garland, A. N., and Smyth, H. McG. *Sicily and the Surrender of Italy*. Office of Chief Military History (O.C.M.H., Washington), 1965.

Gavin, Gen. James M. *Airborne Warfare*. Infantry Journal Press, 1947.

Greenfield, Kent Roberts (editor). *Command Decisions*. Harcourt, Brace, 1959.

Gregory, Barry. *British Airborne Troops, 1940–45*. Doubleday, 1974.

Hagen, Louis. *Arnhem Lift*. Hammond (London), 1955.

Harrison, Gordon A. *Cross-Channel Attack*. O.C.M.H. (Washington), 1950.

Heydte, Baron F.-A. von der. *Daedalus Returned: Crete 1941*. Hutchinson (London), 1958.

Huston, James A. *Out of the Blue: U.S. Army Airborne Operations in World War II*. Purdue University, 1972.

Ingersoll, Ralph McAllister. *Top Secret*. Harcourt, Brace, 1946.

Koskimaki, George E. *D Day with the Screaming Eagles*. Vantage, 1970.

Lhoest, Jean-Louis. *Les Paras Allemands au Canal Albert*. Presses de la Cité, 1964.

Liddell Hart, B. H. *The Other Side of the Hill*. Cassell (London), 1951.

————. *History of the Second World War*. Putnam, 1970.

MacDonald, Charles. *Airborne*. Ballantine, 1970.

Marshall, Gen. S. L. A. *Bastogne: The First Eight Days*. O.C.M.H., 1946.

————. *Night Drop*. Little, Brown, 1962.

Merglen, Albert. *Histoire et Avenir des Troupes Aéroportées*. Arthaud (Grenoble), 1968.

Miksche, Maj. Ferdinand Otto. *Paratroops*. Random House, 1943.

Montgomery, Field Marshal Bernard Law. *Memoirs*. Collins (London), 1958.

Morzik, Fritz-Gerhard. *Hummelchen: Die Deutscher Transportflieger in Zweiten Weltkrieg*. Bernard und Graefe (Frankfurt), 1966.

Mrazek, Col. James E. *The Fall of Eben Emael*. Luce (London), 1970.

———. *The Glider War*. St. Martin's Press, 1974.

Otway, T. B. H. *The Second World War—Army (Airborne Forces)*. Her Majesty's Stationery Office, 1951.

Pogue, Forrest C. *The Supreme Command*. O.C.M.H. (Washington), 1954.

Rapport, Leonard, and Northwood, Arthur, Jr. *Rendezvous with Destiny*. Infantry Journal Press, 1948.

Ridgway, Gen. Matthew B. *Soldier: the Memoirs of M. B. R.* Harper, 1956.

Robichon, Jacques. *Second D Day*. Walker (London), 1969.

Ruppenthal, Maj. Roland G. *Utah Beach to Cherbourg*. O.C.M.H. (Washington), 1947.

Rust, Kenn C. *The Ninth Air Force in World War II*. Aero Publishers (California), 1967.

Ryan, Cornelius. *The Longest Day: June 6, 1944*. Simon and Schuster, 1959.

———. *The Last Battle*. Simon and Schuster, 1966.

———. *A Bridge Too Far*. Simon and Schuster, 1974.

Saunders, Hilary St. George. *The Red Beret*. Michael Joseph (London), 1950.

Seth, Ronald. *Lion with Blue Wings: the story of the Glider Pilot Regiment 1942–45*. Gollancz (London), 1955.

Shulman, Milton. *Defeat in the West*. Secker and Warburg (London), 1947.

Stewart, Ian McD. G. *The Struggle for Crete: 20 May–1 June, 1941*. Oxford University Press, 1966.

Student, Gen. Kurt. *Battles of the First Parachute Army on the Albert Canal; Allied Airborne Operations on 17 Sept. 1944*. O.C.M.H. (Washington), n.d.

———. *Kreta*. Steiersche Verlag (Graz), 1942.

Taylor, Gen. Maxwell D. *Swords and Plowshares*. Norton, 1972.

Tugwell, Maurice. *Airborne to Battle.* William Kimber (London), 1971.

―――. *Arnhem, a case study.* Cassell (London), 1958.

United States Air Force Historical Division.

  The Glider Pilot Training Program, 1941-1943; The Army Air Force in the Invasion of Southern France; Airborne Assault on Holland; Tactical Employment of Transport Planes and Gliders; Ninth Troop Carrier Command in World War II; Airborne Operations: A German Appraisal: Development and Procurement of Gliders.

Urquhart, Gen. Robert E. *Arnhem.* Cassell (London), 1958.

Warren, John C. *Airborne Operations in World War II, European Theater.* U.S.A.F. Historical Division, 1956.

―――. *Airborne Missions in the Mediterranean, 1942-45.* U.S.A.F. Historical Division, 1955.

Whitney, Charles. *Hunters From the Sky: the German Parachute Corps.* Stein and Day (London), 1974.

Wilmot, Chester. *The Struggle for Europe.* Harper, 1952.

Wright, Lawrence. *The Wooden Sword.* Elek (London), 1967.

Index